Nuthology Pser 400 Bias Index

And the Secret Capsule of Talents

Mahugu Nuthu

ISBN: 0990852008
ISBN 13: 9780990852001
Library of Congress Control Number: 2014917124
CreateSpace Independent Publishing Platform
North Charleston, South Carolina

PERMISSIONS

Publisher's Note

Dedication

This book is dedicated to the bias conglomerate – the individual facing unique obstacles created when one form of social exclusion combines with others.

Contents

Acknowledgements

This book was made possible by the generous emotional, spiritual and material support of so many people that I can't list them all here. I want to thank you all, you know who you are. Writing the book was a long and difficult journey. I want to thank my family specifically for their enthusiasm and encouragement in spite of all the time it took me away from them.

Introduction

The bus takes two hours, but Tiny Pretty Pencil arrives twenty minutes early. The last dozen interviews in the city turned into comedy shows, at her expense of course. She lives in a stuffy two-room apartment with her four kids; it is a tough life, even for this loud and feisty forty-five-year-old single mother.

Tiny still hopes to secure an office administration job even after nine months of trying, not just as a probation requirement but for the kids also. They desperately need to get out of the "flight-or-fight" neighborhood. Her best friend or her lover, as unfriendly neighbors call her, has suggested that she get a reliable means of transportation and clothes that do not make her look expectant to improve her prospects. Both of these needs are out of the question for now.

Tiny's credit is so horrible banks can smell her application from five blocks away. The four-foot-two disabled veteran weighs almost four hundred pounds. Most people in her city would not call that "tiny" by any standard. She thinks it is her name that makes her appear huge when interviewers meet her for the first time. It doesn't help that her last name is Pencil, another thing that alludes to thinness. Her face is a constellation of spots, but she worries more about her receding hairline and crooked brownish teeth. Not actually pretty by her society's standards the last time she checked.

Deviation from Normal

We live in a world where anyone who deviates in any perceived way from the norm of a population may become subject to various forms of social exclusion. What about multiple deviations? How much does each additional identity exacerbate the experience of exclusion? Let's go back to Miss Tiny Pencil for a moment. How many ways can she be potentially excluded in her quest for food, shelter, clothing, life, liberty, and the pursuit of happiness? None of this is rocket science. I will talk about assumptions later, so please play along. What do we know about this job candidate's concerns so far?

Tiny Pretty Pencil is:

1. Poor—lives in a small apartment with her four kids, no car, and no money for clothes.
2. Single—there have been incidents where businesses have avoided single women.
3. A veteran—there are concerns that businesses are avoiding military veterans.
4. A woman—there have been incidents where gender issues have come up.
5. Disabled—there have been incidents where businesses have avoided disabled people.
6. Four foot two—businesses often prefer taller people in this town.
7. Loud and feisty—there have been incidents where employers avoided extroverts.
8. In need of transportation—there are incidents where, if you don't have a car, then there will be no job for you.
9. Perceived to be expectant—pregnancy discrimination is on the rise in this town.
10. On parole—a criminal record excludes you from many jobs in this city.
11. Concerned about her hairline appearance—hair is considered part of beauty.
12. Forty-five years old—age is not just a number in this city, it is a red flag.
13. Having credit issues—employers and landlords are serious about credit history.

14. A single mother of four—parenthood is an issue that employers use to exclude people.

15. Rumored to be lesbian—most companies in this city are against the gay lifestyle.

16. Going through extended unemployment. It is hard to get a job after a six-month break.

17. Concerned about her flight-or-fight neighborhood.

18. Concerned about weight-related perception.

19. Concerned about appearance of facial spots and crooked brownish teeth.

20. Concerned about her name, Tiny Pretty Pencil, name, name,

I am still making assumptions here for simplicity's sake, so hold on to your horses. I know your mom told you to ignore those who prejudge you. But it is not always easy to ignore them, especially if they are the gatekeepers to food, shelter, clothing, and sometimes your very freedom. Let us look at this from a totally different lens. What can Miss Tiny Pencil see from her intimate vantage point?

1. Poor—Social Class Discrimination
2. Single—Marital Status Discrimination
3. Veteran—Military Discrimination
4. Woman—Gender Discrimination
5. Disabled—Disability Discrimination
6. Four foot two—Height Discrimination
7. Loud and feisty—Personality Trait Discrimination
8. Needs transportation—Transportation Discrimination
9. Looks expectant—Pregnancy Discrimination
10. Probation requirement—Criminal Record Discrimination
11. Receding hairline—Hair Bald Discrimination
12. Forty-five years old—Age Discrimination
13. Horrible credit—Credit Status Discrimination
14. Single mother of four—Parenthood Discrimination
15. "Her lover," as neighbors call her—Sexual Orientation
16. Jobless for an extended period—Unemployment Stigma

17. Weighs almost four hundred pounds—Weight Discrimination
18. Flight-or-fight neighborhood—Place Discrimination
19. Facial spots and crooked brownish teeth—Attractiveness Bias
20. Tiny Pretty Pencil—Name Discrimination

How do you then achieve your career and business goals while mitigating this convergence of bias factors? For a complete answer, you will have to read the rest of the book. But here is a preview of what you will find.

This book is about the player who wakes up to find a field full of obstacles while every player book talks about working hard, living below ones means, and saving for retirement. Are working hard and living below one's means the only keys to success?

First of all, I am all for working hard. I am all for living below your means. To work hard I must find "work." To live below my means there must be some "means." Is it a sin to request that each player have an equal chance to succeed? The "work harder" mantra should not be used as an insult to those seeking equal opportunity. Most people will work hard given equality of opportunity and human rights as endowed by the creator. All they ask is a level playing field.

I am all for positive thinking. While optimism is good, it is imperative to assess the strength of an uneven playing field. We should also not ignore the fact that convergence of factors may also warp a person's outlook and expectations in life and lead to other problems. The "think positive" mantra should not be used as an insult to those seeking equal opportunity.

What Can You Do at the Personal Level?

The greatest risk of this supersized exclusion is that you may start seeing yourself as less deserving and less capable. There is a risk that you will buy into other people's aspersions. You may start setting low goals. You will shrink and play small. You will disappear into yourself. There is a risk that you will remain chained to a certain past or tethered to a certain factor of exclusion you identified with as a child. You will stand in your own way. You will put traffic cones and yellow tape on your own path. On your own path you will erect giant boulders and great walls.

Self-exclusion, the disengagement that results from negative experiences or discouragement, is a major problem among people who come across bias-related obstacles. Being realistic drives you to take steps to improve your life. Initially this might sound counterintuitive and a bit mercenary. In the long run, however, it works better than forcing yourself to stay positive by suppressing genuine concerns. That makes more sense than sitting in the doldrums. How else do you navigate through this inter-bias convergence zone, anyway?

Someone once said that the first step in solving any problem is recognizing that there is one or twenty. I totally agree that it is not fair. It is grossly unfair that you—the one on the receiving end of injustice—have to do something about it. I have a whole chapter explaining why. This book is all about self-talk, reflection, and strategizing. You are only talking to yourself here. Nobody else needs to know.

Potential Social Exclusion Factor or Risk, PSER

For our discussion in this book, a social exclusion factor is a characteristic or a status of a person that can be used by a gatekeeper to exclude an individual from an opportunity or a right. It can be protected or unprotected. It can be mutable or immutable. It can be real or based on stereotypes, negative group attribution, or prevailing public sentiment. It can be legal or illegal. It is a structural-barrier risk to personal mobility. Whether real or fabricated or based on some stereotype, the impact is the same, at least financially.

Social exclusion conglomeration is a situation in which multiple potential social exclusion statuses converge on an individual. In this multidimensional phenomenon, an individual faces more than one factor of social exclusion. That means increased risk of being blocked from rights, opportunities, and resources. Tiny is facing twenty such converging factors.

The Problem

In our society, each excluded group is often focused on only a single exclusion class that is nearest to its heart. In reality we know that individuals are seldom affected by only one form of exclusion. Even when you identify within a larger class, there will be issues to consider that are not being addressed by that group.

Understandably, it is not easy to conceptualize this multidimensional phenomenon at the societal level. If you add the fact that we are all endowed with different talents and capabilities, you will quickly realize that society can help the affected individual only up to a certain point.

Solution

If you had twenty stigmatized identities, addressing only one factor while disregarding the others would not get you far. A woman of color with special needs, for example, may still be a minority when it comes to disability, even when race and gender issues are fully addressed. Nothing stops the same woman from having other, simultaneous concerns like age, weight, colorism, credit, and height, or any combination on the side. The potential turbulence in reality or psychologically can only be seen from inside. On top of societal efforts, one must develop a holistic financial approach.

Since everyone will have his or her own combination or conglomeration, it is hard for others to relate, conceptualize, or design an effective solution that fits all. The whole experience of conglomerating and interlocking identities can only be viewed through a very personal lens. This is not your daddy's personal finance. This book is about that mind-blowing complexity.

I don't want to sound too academic, but I have to mention about the "multiplier effect" created by additional factors. There is a significant synergistic effect for every additional social exclusion factor, in a negative way. The effect of the combined factors is qualitatively different than merely adding two or more statuses together. I like to think of the additional status as an accelerator on an already existing disfranchisement, both in terms of severity and reach.

While there is no attempt in this book to calculate the "multiplier effect", it doesn't take an abstract statistical study to conclude that a disabled woman, potentially facing gender and disability discrimination simultaneously, will have more challenges than just combining the two factors. This synergistic nature of multiple classes makes it harder to frame public policy and makes subtle discrimination more difficult to monitor.

This conglomeration of multiple exclusion factors in one individual is by far the biggest obstacle facing the fight against inequality worldwide.

The Conglomerate

In this book, an exclusion conglomerate, or simply a conglomerate, is the individual who is a member of more than one subjective group simultaneously. You want an example? A gay, disabled, minority single mother who lives in a poor neighborhood may have seven concerns simultaneously: sexual orientation, disability, race, parenthood, place, marital status, and social class. This conglomerate is subject to a tsunami of converging bias factors in the person's social and financial life. This is not a permanent status as we shall see later. Any one of us can be the conglomerate at some point.

Nuthology Strategy

Nuthology is a user driven risk management strategy for coping and mitigating intersectional social exclusion factors in a free market system. The Nuthology concept deals with how to identify and efficiently use meaningful patterns in data not only to survive, but to thrive and prosper at the individual level in a bias environment.

The goal of this mitigation strategy is to reduce the negative impact to your financial security and future self-reliance. The foundation of this strategy is individual uniqueness. Underneath this heap of conglomerated social exclusion factors lies your leverage. Every one of us is divinely endowed with a unique capsule of talents. The strategy deals with how to unlock and unleash the enormous potential in your unique capsule.

I know I started with bad news, but we will be talking about unique challenges alongside opportunities and limitless probabilities. You just cannot have a singular sunny view when dealing with risk management. The premise of this strategy is that you can accomplish anything you want. You will have to compensate a little and be a little more creative. Your take-off speed will have to be adjusted because of the uneven and short runway, but you will land among the stars. You and the stars are from one creator.

We shall see how to stop chasing other people's talents but emulate their work ethics and approaches. Would you rather be the first version of yourself or a cheap replica of somebody else?

It is not lost to me that life is a very unpredictable affair; we can learn from history, but it is not a predictor of future. Our obligation is to do our best. How can you at least avoid actions that aggravate or exacerbate the current situation? I believe any mitigation effort must involve reducing bias factors where possible, assessing competition, and increasing your chances.

Observations stipulated here are intended to illustrate some of the ways to absorb the impact of the various biases, making them inconsequential, at least financially. I will teach you how to approach career planning as a lifelong business venture. I will teach you how to approach a business venture as lifelong career planning.

Thanks to technological advancements, financial literacy information has never been easier to obtain. It is not for the shortage of financial information that I wrote this book. I should also point out that I define financial literacy somewhat loosely to also include closely related aspects of marketing, economics, and business in general. For those looking for dry numbers, like toxic credit swap derivatives and quantitative easing tragedies, I beg to disappoint. Who can resist those mind-splitting advance bond valuation theories?

In all seriousness though, I use a non-academic approach in this book. Consequently, most of the financial aspects discussed in this book may seem "number light" and nontraditional. I am just trying to make financial education more palatable.

I have constructed some fictionalized case studies that are based on the exclusion factors to spice things up. Here is the good old fine print. The characters and actions in the case studies are purely fictitious. Any resemblance to real persons, living or dead, is purely coincidental.

Money is not everything. I would totally agree. But social exclusion is manifested mostly through material deprivation. Money represents food, clothing, shelter power, love, self-worth, and connection for today's hunter. It is the center piece of equality discussion.

While most of the attention in the world is focused, understandably, on aggression-driven exclusion, most of exclusion in a free market system is driven by in-group favoritism and negative group attribution stereotypes. These factors can be strong barriers of entry in careers and business if not mitigated.

The benefit of this theory goes beyond material success. I hope the lessons that are included here will be priceless and timeless.

First things first. How do we translate the relatively abstract and sometimes unobservable concept of social exclusion into something that we can measure and visualize? Is the presence of prejudice cardinally measurable? Probably for the first time ever, we have done just that. I know that is why you are here. Drum roll please. Presenting Nuthology Bias Index!

1

What is the Nuthology Index?

The Nuthology Potential Social Exclusion Risk 400 Index is a personal risk visualization construct of plausible bias statuses converging in an individual. There are forty risk classes admitted in the Nuthology Bias Index.

The index is based on the assumption that we can attach specific numerical value to each status. Each admitted exclusion factor is simply assigned ten points, which makes the total score 400. Why ten points? The ten point scale can be used to produce a more defined rank if needed in a mitigation situation. For now, let us keep it simple.

Are There Only Forty Exclusion Factors Out There?

Absolutely not. New stereotypes, ignorance, and other "incubators" will ensure that we have a good supply of exclusion factors for years to come. This is a flexible and personal index. There is no earthly reason why you should not admit your own classes. Most of the data will be based on personal observations and mental calculations. While this is not necessarily considered scientific data, this is how you perceive your environment organically anyway.

Are These Factors Equal?

We are not equating any factor to another. Equating them would trivialize factors with dark legacies. The points indicate real or perceived existence, not density. Each admitted status means something to the human being on the receiving end. I am sure you feel strongly about the ones that directly affect you or your loved one.

Since this is a self-talk strategy, all we are saying is all these factors are economically consequential in their own way to an individual conglomerate. Suppose I was denied a job opportunity because my star is Virgo. Am I economically better because racism was not used in the decision? I still did not get the $50,000 per year job, right?

Admission Criteria

Since the idea is to measure ways businesses and individuals may attempt to exclude you based on appearance, prevailing public sentiment, in-group favoritism, negative group attribution, antagonistic stereotypes, and outright aggression, the index list in not limited to immutable characteristics or legally protected classes in your country. It includes anything from genuine business concerns, people preferences, and tastes to other tools of exclusion like body art, taboo, etiquette, character, likability, language, fashion, and grooming. There is a chapter reserved for each of the forty factors in this book explaining how each factor may manifest itself.

The Nuthology PSER 400 score is dynamic in nature because it is dependent on factor relevancy and the prevailing backdrop, which are themselves moving parts. Think of the index as your personal potential social exclusion scanner in a particular backdrop. It attempts to answer questions like: How many ways can you be potentially discriminated against simultaneously? How large is the gap between the current you and how gatekeepers perceive you to be?

The exclusion backdrop can be a situation in employment, housing, health care, civic engagement, democratic participation, law enforcement, due process, or a social relationship. **Chapter 2 covers calculations** and will go deeper into backdrop, factor relevancy, rules, and assumptions.

Uses of the Nuthology PSER 400 Bias Index

The index can be a priceless tool for career planning, self-branding, and other life decisions that require an individualized holistic approach to mitigating social exclusion. Addressing the multidimensionality of social exclusion is a big step toward financial independence.

How Do You Know They Are Real?

You don't, and I will explain this later in the book. As a matter of fact these are risks that may never materialize. I really hope they never do in your case. But they are concerns that you may internalize unconsciously.

Let us assume a certain social exclusion factor does not exist and it is just an unfounded concern. Is that concern unimportant? You still have to overcome the self-doubt forces in your head. We should address all concerns real or imagined. As a user of the index you will be able to account for these as risk factors in your planning. This is what this common sense induced all-encompassing financial strategy is about. Chapter 3 covers in detail the uses of the index while chapter 4 delves further into why this can only work as a personal approach. Now, how does the index become yours?

Nuthology Unique Bias Conglomeration (NUBC)

Every individual has a Nuthology Unique Bias Conglomeration based on the index at a given time and backdrop. It allows you to get to the root cause of your problem by asking yourself questions that will bring you clarity. As we shall see later, NUBC is very contextual and will vary with your changing backdrop. For now let's view NUBC as simple way of visualizing the bias convergence.

Let us consider a poor disabled single mother who is rumored to be HIV positive and has perceived gang body art is looking for a job she is qualified for. Her NUBC, assuming that these factors are a concern from her vantage point, may look like this:

Gender bias
Disability bias
Parenthood bias
Marital status bias
Disease stigma

Affiliation bias
Social class bias
Body Art

What if this chain smoking middle aged lady is also concerned by the fact the she may be considered aesthetically, vertically and horizontally challenged on top her age and aloof demeanor? We can add six more bias factors based on:

Age
Personality traits
Height
Weight
Attractiveness
Lifestyle

Note that the conglomeration will include real and perceived exclusion points. Note that shyness is perceived as being introverted. Rumored health status is also counted. The main take here is that bias conglomeration is very unique and dynamic and not necessarily permanent. It has a lot of moving parts. Doesn't all of life?

I know what you are thinking. This isn't fair. This is immoral. This is unethical. This is illegal. We are less concerned about value judgments at this point. It is not how things should be but how they are right now. If things were the way they should be, we wouldn't even be talking about it, right? Remember, you are still talking to yourself.

The NUBC is a personal objective assessment of exclusion risks at a certain backdrop and time; it is not an excuse to be perpetually alarmed. It is not about who is to blame either. Most bias discussions at the societal level end up in blame territory. Tons of books have been written about who is to blame. This book is about seeking solutions at the personal level. The discussion in this book is centered on how to develop your own coping and mitigation strategies. Since discrimination still drives most of the barriers discussed here, let us talk about it a little bit.

Isn't Discrimination Illegal?

Discrimination in all of its forms is a violation of human rights. It is one of the few practices that encapsulate all the seven deadly sins. Unquestionably, there is only one thing that is more dehumanizing, inherently insulting, and profoundly wrong than discrimination: the convergence of multiple "discriminations" on one solitary soul.

Around the globe there are numerous efforts by various justice departments and advocacy groups to curb bias through legislation for some "protected classes." Depending on your country, state, or jurisdiction, some discrimination may be illegal. Most of these are concerned with tolerance. Tolerance is not the same as acceptance or approval.

This is not a legal advice book by any means imaginable. Additionally, the book takes a global perspective while most laws are tied to locational and timing jurisdictions. The Nuthology Index is not just about discrimination classes alone anyway. The index includes some exclusion factors that get very little attention but still can cause issues at personal level. Astrology, alma mater, character, etiquette, protocol, body art, taboos, and other classes that are not traditionally discrimination are therefore part of this ground breaking index.

The terminology as used in this book is also street level. Though the terms bias, prejudice, partiality, favoritism, and discrimination have their own specific formal definitions, they are used interchangeably in society. The book reflects society's contextual and liberal use of these terms.

Although this book dwells mostly with the subtle forms of discrimination, explicit bias still exists. We all agree that there is need for more effective and equitable enforcement of criminal law to protect the vulnerable classes. Remember that even with great laws, businesses and government institutions unofficially perpetuate exclusion when their employees reflect their prejudices through their positions.

There are also many laws still in books that encourage exclusion. Some actions can be legal and unethical at the same time. Laws are self-preserving in nature and usually hard to amend because they are made by a dominant group. History is full of examples on state-sanctioned exclusion. It was at one time legal for people to own other people as property. Some people could not participate in public policy because of their gender. People with no property could not vote. It is still legal to do these things in some countries today. We approach this topic from a humanitarian point of view.

Nuthology is not conformity. I should remind you that you are still talking to yourself. Nobody needs to know that you are using this strategy. In this way you are not encouraging discrimination. Do not misinterpret the purpose of this approach. Nuthology is not meant to excuse or explain away discrimination at any level. It is about how you can realize and release your talents. I would be the first one to admit that there is a risk in conformity. You must never conform or encourage bias, but you must try to arrive at a sense of equanimity about it from a risk management point of view.

Sometimes the laws are not evenly enforced, which works against a subjective group. Let us also not forget that laws can also be counterproductive. Legislation of every bias conceivable will not only paralyze judicial systems but also negatively affect economic growth.

We have to get back to human rights to get a definition of what is fair. It will take an informed and committed global citizen to protect humanity not written laws alone. It is not a coincidence then that the guiding light for Nuthology strategy is human rights.

Since laws can be morally and ethically questionable, human rights should be the litmus test by which we measure fairness. Somebody once said that cultural changes occur one conversation at a time. Well, let's talk. By actively involving the self-empowerment approach, this tool enhances societal efforts. It is all about you.

Nuthology Index Credits

Nuthology PSER 400 Credits is another unique and interesting feature of this strategy. These are factors that permanently or temporarily absorb the impact of the various biases, making them inconsequential, at least financially. You might be a high-score conglomerate, but if you have high-value connections, money, power, fame, extraordinary talent, or a combination of these, the financial impact is somehow neutralized. Personal structural economic safety nets like a rich uncle with twenty pizzerias or having the queen as your friend can be such credits.

Look at any celebrity who has overcome some adversity. For one brief and shining moment it appears like social exclusion is over. He has triumphed over his past. Successful racial-minority members have their exclusion factors so significantly diluted by these Nuthology PSER 400 Credits that they seem to have overcome social exclusion, albeit temporarily.

There is a "mist factor" that hovers over celebrities, sports figures, entertainers, and those in power. Have you ever wondered why the famous are always beautiful and smart? Their crooked teeth become fashion statements. And yes the seventy-year-old most eligible bachelor is never the poor man on the street. It's material success that masks all the intolerance these figures face in their daily lives. We are brought up thinking about exclusion in terms of material success.

In this context, Nuthology theory holds that the more value you are perceived to hold, the more you are likely to be tolerated. The density and the resulting impact of NUBC will depend on the components of the conglomeration and the available offsetting credits. It should be noted that these credits do not heal the psychological damage caused by bias. We have not designed a way of calculating these offsetting credits. Allow me to introduce some terms that you will see thrown around in this text.

Who Is a Bias Gatekeeper?

This is the member of the dominant group who is potentially biased. Using the privilege of being part of a dominating group is an age-old way of maintaining control over others. This is the decision maker, the offending character who consciously or unconsciously takes unfair preference depending on the backdrop.

In a workplace backdrop, for example, employers receive tons of qualified applications. They will have criteria to pare down the selection and exclude the least desirable applicants. Least desirable applicant does not necessarily mean least qualified. Nuthology Index contains forty ways they can do this. Bias gatekeepers have perfected the art of plausible deniability. They have learned to be subtle enough so that they don't get in trouble. Later I will show you how the bias gatekeeper is you. You didn't see that coming did you?

What Is the Dominant Group?

Dominancy is a temporary condition caused by superior resources or sheer numbers. This is whoever has the upper hand. A dominant member in workplace backdrop has a greater chance of bonding with his in-group colleagues and superiors over some shared interests than an out-group member. This in-group favoritism creates more inequality than hostility driven social exclusion.

A dominant member can get away with actions that a subjective member could be crucified for.

Realistically, if those members happen to be the gatekeepers evaluating your situation, you may be judged solely based on that factor even when it does not affect your ability to perform.

You will also be surprised by how many ways you are in the dominant group. It is not hard to tell. Every time you laugh or look down upon a person who appears different, you are in the dominant group. This time you are the dreaded bias gatekeeper. Your group asserts its superiority over others and seeks to establish or maintain dominance over them.

I want to note that sometimes the dominant group is also blamed for a member's wrongs. The dominant group is perceived as benefiting from the gatekeeper's actions. The argument is that they are aware of malfeasance in their community and yet they remain silent. The dominancy as defined here is not permanent.

What Is the Subjective Group?

This is the opposite of the dominant group. This is the underdog in terms to resources or sheer numbers. Members of the subjective group are often judged by the acts of other members. Group attribution error is high and very consequential. While a criminal act by a dominant member, for instance, is described as an individual failure, it is stigmatized as a group failure if committed by a subjective member.

Everyone makes a mistake, right? For a subjective group member, the imbalance lies in how many strikes you get before you're out. Since the subjective member was viewed as a risk to begin with, any mistake is augmented. At a certain point the subjective member loses confidence in his own ability.

While the primary idea of Nuthology is to take stock of the various ways that others may attempt to block a subjective group member's financial pipeline, we will also ask two uncomfortable questions. What is the subject's contribution to his predicament? And, even more interesting, what is his role as a member of a dominant group in another context?

Why Do You Need the Nuthology Approach?

The discovery of these structural obstacles should not be a basis for reinforcing inherent self-doubt. On the contrary, they should make you stronger. What about if you recognize these risks beforehand? The chances that you will catch yourself are very high. You will have designed escape routes in the form of some spiritual practice. You will have developed an emotional GPS that is unique to you and your purpose. That is why you need this unique custom approach. You are just mitigating the risks. In chapter 5 I will introduce Nuthology SCHOOL of Mitigation.

What do we have right now out there? The feel-good stuff: motivation. Most advisers and some motivational speakers will only tell you to close your eyes and go for it. They will tell you to ignore the structural barriers. One thing I hate to admit is that bad ideas are sometimes fascinatingly seductive. Since when did emotional intensity replace evidence-based assessment?

Ironically, I should say sadly, these same motivational and positive thinking coaches are themselves very pragmatic. I bet you a shiny dollar that they spend sleepless nights planning. Look at the way the speaker is dressed, that bulletproof lesson plan, the delivery flow, and choreographed PowerPoint slides. Do you think it all just happened accidentally? If you say yes, I need what you are smoking.

The motivation experts already know that reality is infinitely complex. No amount of plausible deniability, contrived ignorance, or syrupy positive affirmations will make your issue disappear by itself.

It will be there when you wake up from the high of the motivational trance. It is far much better to be forthright about these sensitive issues rather than hope they will disappear by themselves. The least you can do is to talk to yourself and think pragmatically.

The Nuthology Index marks a starting point to a journey of the pragmatic and conscious approach to problem solving. Since the critical first step in mitigating any risk is measuring it, the Nuthology Index helps you to identify and acknowledge existing bias-related challenges you may face. It therefore becomes a tool for risk analysis and problem visualization. Even if it is from only an efficiency point of view, it is still a big plus. Now we are starting somewhere and not waiting for society to deliver.

Does This Approach Promote Pessimism and Paranoia?

The Nuthology strategy is about optimization of your talents in a challenging backdrop by analyzing risks. The NUBC review is designed to be used in tandem with your strengths analysis as part of a comprehensive personal approach. This self-reflection does not have to end up with you wallowing in self-pity. Drowning in feelings of hopelessness will only cloud your judgment.

Anticipating the barriers allows you to pivot smoothly when you hit them. You buy insurance to get a better night's sleep. You don't buy insurance or a warranty because you are paranoid. The act of buying insurance does not encourage the event. Similarly, these factors are risks that may never materialize.

Think of the risk of disproportionate exposure to discrimination in a specific backdrop. There is also the risk that you may misinterpret temporary setbacks as a permanent indication that a certain stereotype is true. What about the risk that you or your kids may set low goals and fulfill a negative stereotype prophecy? Since we are prone to do this organically, this approach keeps us conscious.

Motivation is always stronger than the friction. Motivation is seductive and sometimes deceiving. I have to apologize first because this book has a lot of friction. We are talking about an emotional and usually controversial issue.

There are tons financial of literacy sources out there that offer great advice: how to increase, revenue cut costs, and protect the net worth. Basically, work hard, live below your means, buy insurance wisely, and reduce taxes. Many of these sources conveniently avoid the "equality of opportunity and human rights" part of financial independence.

2

Nuthology PSER 400 Index

How Does the Nuthology Potential Social Exclusion Risk 400 Index work?

There are forty bias classes admitted in this index. Each admitted exclusion factor is simply assigned ten points, which makes the total 400. You must follow the rules of factor relevancy and backdrop described in this chapter.

Step One

Simply develop a candid bias conglomeration self-profile using the table based on the backdrop in question. Is there a possibility that you will be treated unfairly based on any of the forty admitted grounds of exclusion below? Choose all that apply. That will give you your Nuthology Unique Bias Conglomeration (NUBC).

Step Two

Assign each factor ten points. That will give you your Nuthology PSER 400 score.

What Are the Effects of a High Nuthology PSER 400 Score?

A high score means you have more concerns to consider. It doesn't suggest severity. The potency of NUBC lies in the factor combination. It is the quality not the quantity that matters most when it comes to conglomeration. The impact of the NUBC is also diluted by existence of Nuthology PSER 400 Index Credits as explained later in this chapter.

Future Self NUBC

You can also create a hypothetical future self-profile; for example, factoring in the effect of future changes in appearance, weight gain, hair loss, credit score, criminal record, family situation, kids, or aging. Now that is planning. This is the main reason I created this index.

Nuthology PSER 400 Index Example

A quiet, heavily tattooed fifty-five-year-old homeless war veteran has finally decided to look for a job, a car, and a place to stay in an upscale area despite his well-documented criminal record, shoddy credit, and disease rumors. Stonie Riot, the short, fat, balding, single, and openly gay man has definitely seen better days.

Stonie may identify eighteen social exclusion risks based on his unusual name, height, weight, hair, marital status, sexual orientation, body art, age, criminal history, credit, unemployment, shelter, veteran, disease stigma, transportation, place, social class, and personality traits. **Total score 180.**

Nuthology PSER 400 Index Admitted Classes	Point
Affiliation	10
Age	10
Alma Mater, Credentials	10
Astrology	10
Attractiveness, Lookism, Grooming	10
Body Art	10
Character, Taboo, Weird	10
Class, Caste, Descent	10
Colorism	10
Credit History	10
Criminal Record	10
Disability	10
Disease, Genetic, Blood	10
Ethnicity	10
Etiquette, Protocol	10
Gender	10
Hair, Baldness	10
Height	10
Language, Accent	10
Lifestyle	10
Marital Status	10
Military, Veteran	10
Name	10
National Origin	10
Occupational, Professional	10
Parenthood, Childless, Caregiving	10
Personality Trait	10
Place	10
Pregnancy, Childbearing	10
Race	10
Religion, Sect, Spiritual	10
Retaliatory	10
Sexual Orientation	10
Shelter Stigma	10
Social Class, Rank	10
Speech, Sound, Tone	10
Transportation	10
Tribe, Clan, Family	10
Unemployment Stigma	10
Weight, Size	10
Total	**400**

Nuthology PSER 400 Index Rules

The Nuthology Index Is Not a Self-Valuation Tool

This is not a measure of your worth or value as a human being. Again, do not misinterpret the message: It is not about fairness, morality, or legality but whether the factor exists or may exist. The question is if you should recognize it as a legitimate risk or concern in your planning. You were created perfect. You must not use the index for self-valuation. These are ways gatekeepers may attempt to clog your financial pipeline from a personal point of view.

The Nuthology Index Is Strictly for Self-Evaluation

These fears and anxieties and experiences of exclusion that come with being a conglomerate are personal. This is strictly self-evaluation. It should be a matter of individual judgment. You don't have to share the information. Use it as a planning tool. The conglomeration and the score will change with individuals and the situation in question. The Nuthology Index is not a tool for evaluating others.

Don't attempt to do somebody else's NUBC without consent. The Nuthology Index is not a tool for the valuation of others. This is a personal environment scanner. It is not meant for comparing two people's scores or conglomerations.

Factor Relevancy Rule

A factor has to be potentially relevant, consequential, and applicable in a given backdrop. For a factor to be relevant, the subject must be qualified to perform. The conglomeration and the score will change with relevancy.

A factor must visible, known, or perceived to be at play. The gatekeeper must be aware of the factor by observation, stereotypes, records, or other means to be potentially consequential to you. If it is a future profile, then the factor must be expected to come up in that time period.

Factor Backdrop Rule

Backdrop is the environment, circumstance, or situation where the subject is affected by the gatekeeper's decision. This will also depend on time period changes: spirit of the age or spirit of the time. A factor backdrop will vary depending on the geopolitical and the corresponding sociopolitical contexts of the time.

A scene might be any situation: workplace, educational settings, health care, criminal justice system, dating, and even in one's own family. A workplace situation, for instance, can then be broken down to any aspect or condition of employment, including hiring, firing, pay, job assignments, promotion assessment, performance review, layoffs, training, and benefits. The conglomeration and the score changes with the change in backdrop.

No Double Counting

Do not double count where factors seem to overlap. For example, you may not count sexual orientation under lifestyle if it is already counted under "sexual orientation" class.

Only Count Where You Are Subjective

You could be dominant in one area and subjective in another. Only count where you are part of a subjective group. Only count instances where you are concerned with people's acceptance and expectations, not because of the appearance, per se, but because of the norms. For example, your size may not matter in some instance, but it does in others. Being a minority member or belonging to a protected class does not automatically make a factor relevant. You just count when it matters and needs a mitigation strategy.

The potential existence of factor risk must not necessarily be beyond a reasonable doubt. Note that even an imagined bias is an obstacle that needs to be addressed somehow when doing personal strategic planning. It is a concern. I want to repeat: these risks may never materialize.

No Equating the Factors

The ten points indicate the existence of a concern and not quality. Every ground for discrimination has its legacy, severity, impact, and density. Every class carries its own set of experiences and history. Race and gender are not equal to say height and thinning hair. The factors are not the same in different people because of their unique mitigating circumstances. The Nuthology Index is a quantitative measurement not a qualitative one. In the book, factors are organized in alphabetical order to avoid ranking.

Non-expert Definitions

Definitions used here might be different from what experts in professional fields might use. Non experts might see you as an introvert. You don't have to be clinically an introvert. You just need to be perceived as so. You could be just shy or have language barriers that make you seem like a person of few words. You might be perceived as a witch or a devil worshipper for some reason. Perception does not make it a reality. But that means you face the same social exclusion accorded to those groups and therefore should count it as a risk.

Equal Opportunity Analysis

Because the index is looking at things from the individual view, the index does not recognize the difference between discriminating to deny equal opportunities and discriminating to impose them.

Most public data may show that there is a disproportionate number of racial minorities at risk of social exclusion. But for this index to work you don't have to be a legal racial minority to count race as a factor. If the government's effort to ameliorate the past exclusion damage puts a member of the dominant group at a disadvantage, then that member will count race as a factor.

Suppose males are the dominant group in a certain environment, but companies are in a rush to hire females to be in line with diversity expectations. If you are a male in such a backdrop, the index will show gender as a risk to you.

The Index and the Strategy Must Be Part of a Comprehensive Analysis

The matter-of-fact analysis of the bias can seem pessimistic if all you see are obstacles. It must be part of a 360 degree view where you can see your skills, potential, and God-given talents. Conglomerating all the factors and developing a single strategy, as we shall see later, will reduce the obstacles into one and immensely increase your view of your power.

Social exclusion is not the only set of obstacles that one faces in life. There are many things that will also affect the trajectory of your future from aptitude, attitude, and work ethic to just being at the right place at the right time.

The index and the strategy should be used as a part of a comprehensive analysis under challenges, threats, and weaknesses.

You Must Factor in the Effect of Nuthology PSER 400 Index Credits

As described in the introduction, Nuthology Credits are offsetting factors that temporarily mask existing society biases, giving an illusion of diversity. A high-score conglomerate who has quality connections, money, power, fame, extraordinary talent, or a combination may appear to have overcome the social exclusion. Other things in your environment like good neighborhoods, emotional support, mental support, financial support, and family ties are examples of credits that may dilute the acidity of your NUBC.

Consider a racial-minority celebrity who has enough credits that he seems to have overcome. You will notice that the credits will help only when people can recognize that person. For a moment, the impact of the exclusion appears to be neutralized by counterbalancing powers.

Their Nuthology PSER 400 Credits allow them to get away with some actions, body art, and dress while these same things can be a major barrier for you. This explains why copying celebrities may not work for you. These credits do not work all the time. We have not designed a way of calculating these offsetting credits.

Nuthology PSER 400 Index Assumptions

Assumption of Risk Existence

Nuthology assumes that there is a risk based on patterns of data. Note that due to mitigation, Nuthology Index Credits, and other interference, a risk may never materialize as an exclusion. You may also discover that your anxiety and fears about the factors were initially exaggerated. This is not necessarily a bad thing. You initially count it because it is a concern in your backdrop. Nobody should tell you it is not a concern even if it turns out later to be unfounded.

Assumption That Masses Are Not Always Logical and Reasonable

There is a tendency to put people into pigeon holes. We listen to talking heads that reaffirm our conceptions. We use selective polls or studies whose only purpose is to confirm what we believe of other people. We get the high that comes with having our prejudices validated. We are the masses. Masses are not always logical and reasonable.

Assumption of Suspended Blame

There is enough trading of blame at the societal level. It is a blame market out there. This is a rare opportunity to talk to the person in the mirror without all that noise. It is not lost on anybody that sometimes correlation can be confused with causation. Some factors have correlation or causation in relation to others. We can argue about this until the cows come home. For a moment, let's not go there and stay here by the mirror. Put the sword back in its place.

For a few minutes, forget about the past circumstances that allegedly or actually created the social exclusion. I am making an assumption that you are logical, reasonable, and realistic. You don't have to be 100 percent logical, just enough not to lie to yourself in broad daylight. "To thine own self be true," Shakespeare.

Microcosm Assumption

Bias gatekeepers are a microcosm of the population not a separate species. Employers, for instance, are a miniature representation of your society. Chances are some of the uneducated, insecure bullies from your high school days also made their way to positions in law enforcement, justice departments, recruitment desks, corporate corner offices, and other gates.

In a law enforcement scenario where your group is caricatured as the face of crime based on some group attribute, then members risk being profiled. If your group is perceived as lazy free loaders, you stand a chance to be viewed as such.

I am not saying you have to be distrustful of human sincerity or integrity. You will have to do some research depending on your backdrop. What stereotypes exist in the backdrop? There is a risk that whatever stereotypes and generalizations that are in the society will be reflected in the gatekeepers' decisions.

Free Market Economy Assumption

Nuthology theory may only work in a free market enterprise system but can be customized to suit other economic systems. There is an element of the free market system in most modern economies. There is no country with a pure free market economy anyway.

You must also understand that equality of outcome is not the objective of a free market enterprise system. This book is about equality of opportunity and not necessarily equality of outcome. In a capitalistic free market society, the employer will still choose who the likeable person is. The customer will decide what to buy. These decisions may not be necessarily based on bias.

While the Nuthology Index will still be applicable, Nuthology mitigation strategy greatly depends on the forces of scarcity, demand, and supply. That means it will be least effective in situations where markets are not allowed to prosper. Nuthology mitigation strategy will not work if there is a risk that your safety may be compromised. This could be in fragile states, bad neighborhoods, or any situation where personal security is a concern.

How Do You Know Social Exclusion Risk Exists in Your Backdrop?
Most of the existence of social exclusion risk may be identified through observations, experience, and research. Are there records where individuals or the state have attempted to deny human beings their humanity based on the factor in question?

Are There Bias Incidents in Your Backdrop Related to One of the Forty Factors?
A bias incident is a prejudice-motivated conduct in the form of speech, expression, or any other action. We are talking patterns of discrimination, stigmatization, prejudice, bullying, humiliation, ostracism, exclusion, shunning, partiality, favoritism, and other variations of bias-driven rejection in your backdrop. If a factor is a concern, count it.

Are There Patterns of Aggressive Teasing?
Teasing is a hedged passive-aggressive form of veiled bullying. Look for teasing that is incessant and cruel against members of an exclusion factor. Targets of teasing are often also targets of some stigma. It is usually a choreographed power play. A negative point is thrown first, followed by a thin mask for the negative criticism: "I was just kidding." Lastly, it can be topped with an accusation of oversensitivity "Lighten up. I'm just joking," or, "You are too thin skinned."

Teasing across factor lines is a slippery slope. What passes for humor in one country or culture, for instance, can be misinterpreted quite differently in others. Regardless of the motive of the teaser, the result is humiliation and emotional abuse. If it is a concern, count it.

Are There Patterns of Passive-Aggressive Shunning?
Shunning can be the act of social or mental rejection. Groups might socially exclude someone as a display of control or power. A person or group deliberately avoids association with, and habitually keeps

away from an individual. Shunning is difficult to spot because it is bullying by omission where one is treated as if they don't exist. In a school setting it can be accompanied by whispering, gossiping, and mocking micro-aggression campaigns. This passive bullying at work or school can be very damaging. The errors of commission are often easy to spot; it is the errors of omission that constantly bedevil us. If it is a concern, count it.

Are There Patterns of Unwelcome Lines of Questioning?
Look for patterns of unwelcome lines of questioning that may indicate you have deviated from some society norm or that contain veiled contempt undercurrents.

> Why aren't you married yet?
> Why are you always so quiet?
> Why don't you have kids yet?
> Where are you from?
> Is it true that your people eat rocks?
> Since you don't have a family, why do you need the same pay as the guy who does have a family?
> Where do you get your confidence given the fact that you are a "fill the blanks"?
> Of course not all questions are a signs of aggression; this will depend on the context.
> If it is a concern, count it.

Are There Patterns of Negative Humor?
Exclusion factor based humor can act as an indicator or releaser of prejudice. This can happen subconsciously. If there are a lot of jokes about one gender being bad drivers, you can bet that the chances of that gender being hired as drivers will decrease. Jokes about hair color and intelligence correlation affects the subjected group's earning power. I am beginning to sound like a midnight infomercial: if it is a concern, count it.

Patterns of Discriminatory and Dehumanizing Language

Patterns of discriminatory and dehumanizing language toward an exclusion factor are reflective of a culture that supports negative practices toward a group.

Keep an eye on language workarounds, phrases, and coded offensive terms. These do not have to be slurs, derogatory terms, or forbidden terms. "Welfare queen", "diversity hire", "grievance industry", "these people", "man up", and other PC-laundered words are examples of phrases that are used for aggression.

Some of these are coded, "dog whistle," communications that are supposed to be inaudible to human ear or they are loaded with tons of plausible deniability. Beating the xenophobic drum is a popular tactic for ineffective leaders. Are there politicians or polemists peddling twisted information and bizarre conspiratorial statements about a certain excluded class? Repeat after me: if it is a concern, count it.

What about Patterns in Published Data?

Patterns of data in public and private statistics allow you to look for facts not faces. This data can include:

High school graduation data
Reading and math proficiency
Education levels
Employments prospects
Neighborhood property levels
Family incomes
Teen birth rates
Levels of domestic violence
Levels of drug use
Well, if it is a concern, count it.

Patterns in Media and Cinema Portrayals

How is your group portrayed in movies and mainstream media? Is your class always the bad guy? What about a lazy, freeloading, or untrustworthy piece of—this is a family book. But you get the idea. There is a risk that you cannot be trusted because of these portrayals. If it is a concern count it.

Look for Patterns of Data Related to Representation

Underrepresentation in policy-making bodies.

Underrepresentation in good living wage paying jobs and opportunities.

Underrepresentation in small business start-ups.

Underrepresentation in governments, parliaments, and in private-sector managerial positions.

Overrepresentation in low paying jobs, homelessness, refugee camps, and prisons.

If it is a concern, count it.

Ask Family and Friends

Some objective family and friends might be able to tell you how you present yourself. There is a risk that you will get a sugar-coated answer. There is also a risk you will get a wet blanket. "Do I come across as a Fortune 500 CEO?" If they say you come across as a serial killer then that could be your deviation from normal. Count it.

If it is a concern, count it. You are counting your concerns as part of your planning after all. You are putting all your ducks in a row. Keep counting.

Are There Patterns of Negative Group Attribution Profiling and Stereotypes?

Most of the factors are driven by stereotypes, negative group attribution, and public sentiment. If you live in a society where members of a group can be singled out as suspected shoplifters, are unfairly profiled, and disproportionately investigated, all based on negative group attribution, that is a red flag. Is there a risk that the members will be denied jobs or other revenue opportunities based on the group attribution error? Is there a risk that the members will face social exclusion in other facets of their lives? Count it.

Public sentiment at a particular location and time period is a major driver of this index. Nothing is more volatile than public opinion. Notice the role of perception from the opening story: "Her lover, as neighbors call her" means they think Tiny is a lesbian. She might be treated the way lesbians are treated by those who recognize the factor. She "looks expectant" so she might face pregnancy discrimination. We shall see in later chapters how each factor manifests in the exclusion index.

Mean-spirited stereotypes and group attribution errors drive much of the public opinion. If a group is sold as lazy and freeloading, the members may be seen as such and excluded. If negative-stereotype confirmation kicks in, it is not hard to find members confirming by naturally living out the stereotypes.

Mob judgments are based on the sentiment of the day and are no indication of your intrinsic worth, so never sell yourself short.

What Is the Risk That You Will Be Considered a Risk?

Nuthology is about managing the risk that you may be considered a risk based on the factors of exclusion. Nuthology PSER 400 Bias Index loosely utilizes in reverse form the predictive models used by institutional gatekeepers to evaluate a candidate. Fair or not, how many ways can you be considered a risk? How do institutional gatekeepers evaluate candidates for risk?

Risk and uncertainty have always been a part human activity. The notion of making predictions and mitigating risk is widely accepted today as a business best practice. Insurance industry actuaries use sophisticated statistics and programs to gauge the cost of future events and develop policies to minimize their own risk. They evaluate the financial risks a prospective customer represents. They even have the customer's death date estimated.

Banks, employers, landlords, and numerous other entities have gatekeepers who collect tons of information to evaluate the creditworthiness of their applicants. For the institutions, denying some customers loans, jobs, shelter, and insurance coverage is part of risk management.

For obvious reasons, most military and other uniformed services have strict physical ability and appearance guidelines that include restrictions on body art, hairstyles, height, weight, age, general health, and mental capacity. Your 101-year-old, black belt grandma may not qualify for SWAT. Age would be an exclusion factor here.

Some countries have bona fide occupation qualifications or some sort of defendable exclusion. An example would be the gender of the attendant for a woman's bathroom. The index will still count this as exclusion since it is part of your planning. If you are a male, you may not choose a "female bathroom attendant" major. Bad example, but you get my point. I should also point out that even genuine legal policies can be exclusions from your point of view. Suppose you don't qualify for an opportunity because you are not a citizen or a minority? That's a barrier that you should factor in your planning. It is a risk that should be mitigated in some way.

At street level, prejudice is another way we consider others as risks on the spot. Based on appearance and stereotype alone, we prejudge others before gathering specific facts about them, either consciously or unconsciously. It is human nature to make assumptions about strangers when you meet them for the first time.

People's preferences can be a business or personal risk. Some people's preferences will exclude you at some point. Your preference will exclude some people at some point. To the extent that preferences affect your goals, you should count them. You count them as part of your planning not because it is an aggression against you. It is a business decision. That is the main reason, as mentioned above, the bias ecosystem cataloged in this index includes a cocktail of genuine business concerns and people's preferences and tastes.

I should also note that a company's culture and how you fit in may play a big part in workplace decisions. The interviewer will come with that in mind. That is something to remember when you show up for an interview in pajamas holding an old toothbrush. So, what is the risk that you will be considered a risk? Count it.

3

Uses of Nuthology

1. Career Planning

There is a growing canon of books offering advice on how to choose a career that is best for you. The assumption that career paths are typically orderly, sequential, and continuous is very theoretical if not deceiving.

The index provides a personal conceptual framework where you can play with several variations and contexts beyond the GPA. I know there are basics of career choice and that is understandable. They say talk to your parents, guardians, and counselors and take aptitude tests. What are your natural talents? How do you deal with stress? Would you rather work alone or do you like working with others? What are your expectations for money? Nothing is inherently wrong with all that.

But there is a little one-ton elephant in the corner. Everybody knows it is there. Everybody wishes it was not there. Parents, guardians, counselors, and aptitude tests will tend to stay away from the exclusion question. They might not realize the impact or what it means to you. They might not want to discourage you or scare you. Most importantly, they don't have the answers.

While a career coach may help you identify your academic strengths and weaknesses, he or she may not talk about land mine–filled issues like race, gender, weight, religion exclusions, or other sensitive factors.

Most career sources will tell you that any individual, if he works hard enough, will be able to realize her or his occupational dreams. And that is generally true. Should we ignore all of those multilayer glass ceilings and crumbling floors that remain omnipresent? Should we ignore the fact that many talented employees never reach their goals even after working their tails off for decades? And that some people never even get a chance to try a job.

The mere impact of negative-stereotype confirmation alone on individual achievement does not allow you to entirely ignore structural obstacles. Add some toxic group attribution errors and you got yourself in a corner. These may be subtle, but they are very real and consequential. As painful as it is, we have to speak to ourselves and speak up at the societal level.

Nuthology strategy goes beyond academic grades to the deeper realities of life. Are there entry barriers to career and business beyond mere qualifications? How do you mitigate these structural barriers? How do you maintain your optimism? We are asking the big questions. In what ways do other human beings exclude you from the career of your choice? What can you do about it?

Nuthology strategy will have you find a solitary spot and talk to yourself. This sounds crazy. Figure out what your purpose, interests, and talents are. Take a pencil and a piece of paper. A napkin will do. No fancy electronics required. Now, figure out what obstacles will need to be factored in using the Nuthology Index.

From there you make a general direction decision. People change careers several times in their working lives, so do not be worried if your target field is not as defined as you want. As you create networks and experience real-life job situations, your capsule of talents will open up.

Create a Preemptive Approach.

The index is not creating new classes; it is just helping you avoid surprises that might affect revenue generation down the line. The index deals mostly with predictable risks. This is not brain surgery or rocket science quantum mechanics. These are worries that you may have organically already. The index will help you catalog the areas that may expose you to exclusion and help you plan defensively. The few examples below illustrate the point, but I could give a million scenarios.

In a conventional-beauty-driven industry like entertainment, a candidate's beauty shelf life is shorter than that of some vegetables. A person in an appearance-sensitive industry should not pretend to be unaware of what is coming. No, it is not fair, but your NUBC will change.

It is the duty of the individual to plan for that future. The fact is that in the not so distant future there is the risk that she may be considered old, fat, and unattractive. The ugly averse gatekeepers will never tell her that outright. This is an exclusion that should not come as a surprise. I know that sounds brutal, but it is self-talk. You work a few years then retire or you are forced out somehow. Your retirement planning might need to be more aggressive. Now we are talking finance. Better yet, you plan for your next move.

Longer careers are also affected. Chances are if you live long enough you will collect museum-grade wrinkles, some pounds, cellulite, dull hair, bad knees, and back pain. You will lose some hair, balance, bones, and teeth. Will they still let you in front of the camera or at the front desk? If it is appearance that worked in your favor originally, is it possible that there will be younger people to be compared with over the years?

It does not have to be age related. Childbearing may generate factors of its own. You start with pregnancy discrimination. You might gain some weight, a normal thing for most women. All of a sudden weight and attractiveness become exclusion factors depending on the backdrop. The kids and their schedules may become a business concern. Parenthood discrimination is an open secret in some industries. It is even worse if you are a single parent. You should see this coming. Circumstances may change unexpectedly; you have to adjust to the new reality. Listen to your inner NUBC GPS and recalculate.

The job of a career counselor is to guide you, not to tell you what to do. They cannot make your career choice or tell you what decision is the right one. Use Nuthology strategy as a guide to personalize your career choice and achieve self-actualization in a biased environment.

Negative-Stereotype Confirmation to Your Career
In-group favoritism and negative group attributed stereotypes subtly create barriers to mobility. You must be aware of how you react to stereotypes lest they become self-fulfilling prophecies like I mentioned earlier. When internalized they can make you underperform or set low career goals.

My group is not good in math or science, so I will just take dinosaur dancing.
My group cannot jump.
My group does not love money.
My group doesn't produce leaders.
We are not good at marathons.

The stereotypes prevent you from performing at peak level. Income gaps and other inequalities can be maintained partially by this line of reasoning if you have one group being complacent based on baseless generalizations.

2. Personal Branding

Congratulations, you are now your own chief campaigner, chief of staff, and chief PR representative. You are the chief of your own capsule of talents. You are your own chief anything. This position is not limited to your life campaign, but it is one that lasts a lifetime. I cannot think of a better person for this office. That is the good news.

Now, get ready to hear the potentially bad news. The buck stops here. Not just today or the next four years. Forever. Now my friend, you will make decisions. Decisions have consequences. What damage will today's decisions do to your future? How large is the gap between the current you and the person you want others to perceive you to be? You are the keeper of this brand. The "you" brand.

That means you have to constantly review your tangible and intangible characteristics, including attire, hair, and body art. To these let's add your verbal and nonverbal communication skills. Does the total image give a hardcore thug vibe? Why then, for heaven's sake, should a stranger see you as Mother Teresa? You look like you just swallowed a gallon of pure lemon and twelve innocent puppies. Am I being judgmental?

In a free world you may have all the rights to express yourself. You have both the right of self-expression and an obligation to deal with the consequences. Does a stranger have the right to deny you the babysitting gig if you look that mean? The index gives a visualization of how you may be perceived.

Even social media posts should stay within your brand, and I would add it should be representative of how you want others to perceive you. Most factors in the Nuthology Index are based on appearance not reality. How are you perceived?

How Do You Handle Fashion Statements?

Always use good judgment in projecting a professional appearance. When should you be making extreme fashion statements either in dress, hair, or body art? We are not talking about immutable characteristics that you cannot control like age, skin color, or gender.

I want to give you a simple example. You may like clothing with stains, wrinkles, or holes, tight-fitting clothes, revealing clothes, loose pants, and items with insignias or slogans. These may not be an issue in certain backdrops. But there are backdrops where the index will show them placing you in multiple bias classes. Some places forbid house or shower flip flops, jeans, sweats, or cargo pants while others don't. Some mode of dressing can indicate affiliations you don't even belong to or care about and cost you opportunities. You may never even know. Your favorite T-shirt may be a gang flag.

Handling Voluntary Information

This company doesn't like tattoos, so you keep your tattoo is covered. But there is a small problem. It is on your online profile. How are the factors known by the gatekeeper you ask?

Obviously, most factors are known by observation of visual characteristics, such as color, mode of dressing, body language, body art, hairstyles, protocol, and etiquette. People can easily tell one's affiliation by one's walk or swagger and other nonverbal communication. Voluntary information provided before, during, and after the interview gives the interviewer something to work with. People notice things when you work together. Observations by coworkers and management during work hours counts a lot when it's time for promotions, assessments, or layoffs. That online picture of you smoking a quadruple joint is not actually classified information. I hate, puff, to break it to you.

As we shall see later in the application level, if a company is interested it will get your information. Digital footprint, news, published works, resume, public records, consumer reports, bumpers stickers, flags, decals, and even means of transportation can give you away. Recall that the ultimate purpose for this index is identifying what damage today's decisions will cause your future.

Depending on jurisdiction, the laws might prevent employers from asking some questions. What about that informal chat before, during, and even after the interview? Being honest does not mean voluntarily disclosing information that is not required. If you bring up a topic such as your cat Joseph, your religion, military discharge, your children, your loser ex-spouse, or your sexual orientation, does the guy behind the desk have the right to ask further questions? He is not a rock; he will be swayed one way or the other. Don't ask, don't tell.

If you ask if bus number seventeen stops at that site, the interviewer will know that you don't have ride. You can also fall into a trap. He might compliment you for something or talk about his family. If that pushes you into verbal diarrhea, some factors might come up that might raise red flags. They call it TMI for a reason. Too much information!

As I mentioned earlier, there is no shortage of information if the company is interested. I should add yard signs, logos on clothing, body art, wedding ring, the proverbial little bird, rumors, and, yes, that noisy rebel bike to the public information data.

Something might be innocent or even funny but still convey your decision-making ability, line of thinking, or emotional intelligence.

In a court of public opinion, you are what you like, what you look like, and who you hang out with.

How do you handle information in a work environment? Some personal information can make the interviewer uncomfortable. He may develop concerns about how you will handle confidential company information if you can't handle your own information.

How Do You Handle Digital Information?

The percentage of corporations that are using online profiles to make hiring decisions is increasing every single day. You are actually giving the employer information that would not be available otherwise.

Your online footprint is a major source of information. How are you sabotaging your future chance of getting the job? Those not so flattering spring break pictures posted ten years ago can be used against you for eternity. God forbid you became rich and famous someday. The images or written content can follow you to the gates of heaven.

Your tweet is a permanent record that may work against you ten years from now. Without body language to go by, written communication is easy to misinterpret, especially when taken out of context. With no tone, laughter, wink or smile to accompany it, the little joke will turn you into a puppy-killing monster in a minute.

Censor Yourself on Social Media.

Can your post be misconstrued as racist, sexist, or otherwise bigoted? Is it okay to criticize, make fun of, or make harassing comments about coworkers? There are posts that may reveal company trade secrets, confidential information, or other things the company would rather not make public.

Online data is not limited to content. It can also show that you update your status every twenty minutes. When do you actually work? An employee who doesn't display professionalism online may, one way or another, influence an employer's judgment.

Imagine your post five years ago: "My boss is off today. I am doing the minimum. I will sneak out two hours early." What does it say about your work ethic? It is a permanent record. It might show up in a future job interview or when running for public office.

Candidates would not necessarily know their social media profiles have been snooped. Clean up your social media profile. Character is one exclusion factor on the index that you can control. Be the king of your brand.

3. Develop Efficiencies

A conglomerate with twenty-five bias factors may spend a whole lifetime chasing solutions for each one of them. How much time do you spend with deniers and range riders?

Aggregating your exclusion factors allows you to leverage your uniqueness and manage expectations. A lot of motivational speakers promote blind optimism based on faulty logic. This index encourages you to factor in the expected speed bumps on the road to success.

Self-development, while important for everyone, is crucial for bias conglomerates. Develop a holistic financial approach that takes all of these factors into consideration. The act of collecting the factors is just putting your ducks in a row.

The Claim

Use the index to size up your options and develop efficiencies. The index helps assess the landscape and to figure out where the diamonds are. We can then excavate the diamonds in the most cost effective way and make the best jewelry. A high score may mean your claim has more dirt before you reach the course gravel. It is not an excuse to give up or get discouraged. If anything it is more wind behind your back. You are breathing the same air as your competition. He has the same twenty-four that you have.

We all know the first scarce resource is time. Don't waste your own and others time looking to prove a point. How much time should you waste feeling sorry for yourself? How much time should you spend complaining about factors that are generally or, should I say, genetically beyond your control? Maximizing personal effectiveness means looking for ways to use your talents, not for punitive purposes, but for competitive advantage.

It is okay to learn from our history and past experiences. But how much energy should you spend dwelling on the past wrongs? Should you spend an inordinate amount of time quibbling over minor semantic points? Even for important points it is still inefficient if you are dealing with mean-spirited, cruel, and uncaring people. You will run out of steam. Don't burn more fuel than you should. Measure your own successes based on your goals.

4. Identifying Friendly Fire

Improving personal habits will reduce the character- and lifestyle-related factors. The index list includes some elements that can be avoided. Early understanding of the index can prevent you from accumulating these self-inflicted wounds in the first place. If you get a facial tattoo during a spring break drinking excursion, you may have to switch your major if your industry does not allow such displays. Some parents open lines of credit and damage their children's credit history. Other parents choose creative names that later turn out to be sources of ridicule and bullying. A football field–size rap sheet and stinky attitude all fall in this category.

Your exclusion concerns at the **beginning:**

Social class	10
Gender	10

Your concern after "friendly fire":

Social class	10
Gender	10
Body Art	10
Credit history	10

Criminal record	10
Name	10
Character	10

Talk about hoisting by your own petard as Shakespeare would say. Later I will talk about how reaction to bias can create more bias classes. This includes rebellious responses. "I will not lose weight because bullies will win," or, "I will procrastinate because I am being pressured to finish this project. This will show them." I understand you were wronged. But who wins with this reaction?

5. Contribution to the World-Hate Kitty

This is where this book contributes to world peace. Most bias in the world is cultivated and based on stereotypical assumptions and implemented via in group favoritism. At the end of the day, there is a pooling of hate and stereotypical assumptions reminiscent of a mega-depository bank. Today you are depositing; tomorrow you are on the receiving end.

Consider a situation where one is a member of dominant group in one context and subordinate in another. As a member of the dominant group, you spend days clogging other people's financial pipelines. As a member of a subjective group, you may spend nights complaining how others are clogging your pipeline.

Look at how discrimination discussion plays out in your country today. Each subgroup defines "bias" in its own way. Each subgroup may attempt to paint itself as the most discriminated against. Each subgroup has a list of negative group attribution stereotypes against another group. Groups may tend to focus on their differences rather than their commonalities. The world-hate pool stays well replenished thanks to contributions from the conglomerates themselves.

Now you know that a gatekeeper could be the man in the mirror. Every time you look down upon or unfairly deny an opportunity to a person who appears different, you are the bias gatekeeper. The index helps you catalog how many ways you potentially discriminate others. We are all evolving on this issue. Nobody is perfect. I wish I didn't have to say this. But it's your turn on the prie-dieu. How big is your hate print? Calculate.

6. Pedagogical Application

Since our conglomeration and talents are different, we can teach our kids how to avoid exacerbating their current exclusion status. The index can be used, for instance, to demonstrate numerically the effect of reducing negative interactions with the criminal justice system and staying in school.

Consider a potentially hirable kid who had initial exclusion concerns based on:

Race	10
Social class	10
Place1	0

He drops out of school, joins a bad crowd in his environment, gets bad credit, and has a kid of his own. Fast forward eighteen months. There is a huge likelihood that his risk exclusion now includes:

Race	10
Social class	10
Place	10
Crimina	110
Affiliation	10
Body art	10
Credit history	10
Character	10
Etiquette	10
Parenthood	10
Total NUBC	**100**

Is he more or less hirable? Wow! We have not even factored in the lack of education and skills. You do the math. It is no wonder some youth have never considered the possibility of positive outcomes.

Let's picture another scenario where the kid completes college. The same kid may have had a chance to join the middle class. There was a good chance he would have moved out of "that place." The two are not necessarily immutable characteristics. Only the race risk concern would have remained. Total you ask? 10 points

7. Manage Workplace Bullying and School Bullying

Most workplace bullying today involves being ignored. Workplace ostracism is more common than active aggression but just as devastating if not more so. An employee may be excluded from cliques that form naturally due to shared interests or culture. Promotion usually comes within those cliques while layoffs come from outside. Excluded people are more likely to quit due to the "out of place" feeling.

All subtle forms of bias demand a swift response from individuals and society. Paying attention to your unique conglomeration will enable you to set ground rules way before things get out of hand. Suppose you are extra tall and bald. If you have identified these as exclusion factors in your society, you cannot let people make a caricature of you for a year and then try to stop it.

School yard bullying is an area that parents and educators can utilize risk assessment techniques. Can the leaders develop some version of Nuthology Bullying Risk Index? What factors in your backdrop increase the risk of a kid being bullied? Some parents can organically sense when their child has some factors that can cause bullying. They just know it.

If a kid has an exclusion factor or a combination related to known bullying issues, shouldn't the concerned grown-ups engage experts before things escalate? An example would be an introverted, obese kid who is rumored to be gay just because he has issues socializing. As factors accumulate and, consequently, the potency of the combination, the likelihood of abuse becomes greater. Should we wait for kids like this to file a formal complain? He might always be quiet, but the storm might be brewing.

In most cases it is the mental issues that come back to affect the subject's ability to be financially independent later in life. Poor academics, depression, and low self-esteem will lead to poor revenue generation down the line.

Educators can develop steps for responding to bias incidents. They can find a platform to denounce hateful acts and address fears without pointing out the subjects. The educators may involve community and thought leaders in finding solutions. The community might organize assertiveness, speak up, reach out, and respect campaigns before incidents occur. The subjective group will at the very least get the signal that they have empathetic leaders.

Based on the factors and patterns of data, leaders may have to create rules and teach kids to refuse to join in bullying by laughing, cheering, or staring. Cyberbullying is on the rise. Bullying that happen online might go unnoticed for a long time. Kids should know not to engage in forwarding hurtful messages or spreading rumors. As a parent you may have to teach your kids ways to safely speak up and put a stop to the hurtful behavior even without vivid evidence that this is happening.

8. Expose Multidimensionality of Social Exclusion

Multidimensionality of social exclusion makes it difficult for most societal programs that address access to resources, opportunities, and rights to work. No one structural factor is a unitary concept. No subgroup is purely homogeneous. Society finds it naturally efficient to fight these issues as independent factors.

Every major factor has its own activists. Civil rights advocates prefer a one item approach most of the time. A gender issue is taken as separate from a race issue, as are disability, poverty, and place issues, among others. But can you have a poor, disabled, racial-minority single mother living in a marginalized neighborhood and desperately in need of a car to get out of long-term unemployment? We can now demonstrate this using the Nuthology Index as a visual.

Race 10
Social class 10
Gender 10
Disability 10
Marital status 10
Parenthood 10
Place 10
Transportation 10
Unemployment stigma 10

Concentrating on gender as a unitary concept may have little impact on the mobility effort. Every additional factor here is an accelerator of an already existing disfranchisement. While some of these concerns may not be insurmountable obstacles as stand-alone factors, they hold a substantial punch when conglomerated. I hate to repeat this fact. If the only thing that this book does is to expose the bias convergence, I will have achieved a great goal. I sincerely believe this convergence is the biggest obstacle facing the fight against inequality worldwide.

4

Capsule of Talents: Why the Personal Approach?

Nuthology strategy is about confronting the risks of stereotype effects, group attribution errors, groupthink, and in-group favoritism without conformity. How will other people exclude you? How do you exclude yourself? How do you exclude others? Here are a few reasons why this can only be done effectively at the personal level.

1. Unique Capsule of Talents

For any mitigation to work you must first start believing in yourself, your value, and your worth. You are divinely endowed with a unique capsule of talents. You and the capsule are one. The world did not get an advanced copy of you before you were born. You came as a gift to this world with no envelop. You had no return address or pin number. The world has no right to re-gift you. This was your intended destination. Nobody, including your own parents, received a user manual when you came. That means nobody should use or misuse you. As an individual you have that great competitive advantage.

This uniqueness is what gives you a hell of considerable leverage. You are not only one in seven billion; you are one in the billions that have ever called this rotating rock a home. That means nobody knows you like you except the creator of you. What you have to offer to this world in your brief stopover is as important as what anybody else has to offer. You have every bit as much value to offer as the next person. We believe nobody knows better than you about your qualities and capabilities. Nobody should be expected to be a better advocate of you than you.

We waste a lot of time trying to be cheap copies of other people. Sometimes we even seem to succeed. The happiness we derive from copying is almost always very short-lived: it was just a copy. A copy is a copy is a copy. The worst version of you will always be better than the best copy of somebody else. You are the original version, and I dare say, warts and all. I call it version "warts point all." Version 1.0.

You have to use what you have been given. Follow your purpose. Once you discover the contents of the capsule and follow your strengths, the possibilities are limitless. You are as unstoppable and mysterious as the powers that created you. You are just that powerful.

If you have to copy anything, emulate the tactics, discipline, and work ethics of your heroes. You will need both will power and skill power to open this capsule. The capsule is not unlike a precious gold claim; there will be work to be done. There will be some digging, some smelting, some carving, some cutting, some polishing, and some setting. There be will internal and external resistance. The Nuthology Index consists of forty such points of resistance.

You are the only one who can fight the internal resistance to handle things that need to be done. There are things society cannot do for you even if they wanted to. There are things that will remain at the personal level. We all have the ability to grow and to learn, to master our lives, our choices, and our behavior. Most of the solutions will demand that you must have a sense of self-discipline. You have to wake up and go study, go to the gym, make the cold calls, or any other uncomfortable activity. This is something society cannot do for you, bias or no bias.

Realizing the contents of your capsule calls for a special strategy. You have come to the right place. What do you do with this priceless uniqueness?

2. Unique Bias Conglomeration

In our discussion here, external resistance involves ways other people may try to make sure you don't harvest your unique talents based on one or more of the forty factors of exclusion. As a person belonging to multiple disadvantaged groups simultaneously you have two options. One is to stick your head in the Pollyanna-ish sand and pretend the factors do not exist. The other is to conglomerate the structural barriers and design a plan to take them head on.

The talk about a capsule of talents was the offensive side of this strategy. No game plan is complete without a sound defensive strategy. There are structural barriers that are unique to you only. It is because of this individual uniqueness—I hate to break it to you—that there will never be a cookie-cutter solution.

What Nuthology provides is a platform, a sort of operating system. With this system you can craft a solution as unique as your DNA. The strategy ensures that you don't waste your precious time trying to fit a square peg in a round hole.

Learning how these forty factors can be used to exclude you should be a part of your financial strategy. Society handles these factors one at a time and in a general sense. There is always a risk of misclassifying people who experience discrimination based on one class or another. An overweight, disabled, minority single mother who lives in a bad neighborhood may only get help on race issues. But she may have concerns regarding:

Gender
Race
Weight
Disability
Single parenthood
Place
Social class

Transportation

These are barriers that are handled one at time at activism level. The risk of multiple disadvantaged statuses is too complex for society to conceptualize, let alone design a meaningful policy for. Some factors are even ignored. Since every person in a subgroup has a different conglomeration, it only makes sense to have a personal approach on top of whatever effort is being done at the societal level.

3. Unique Nuthology PSER 400 Index Credits

Imagine two kids of the same race who decides to drop out of high school or college. One lives in a good neighborhood. He has adequate emotional, mental and financial support, as well as good family ties. His family has quality connections. The other one goes home to a crumbling neighborhood and no structural safety net. While both made bad decisions, their risks are very different.

As introduced earlier, credits are things or people around you that may help directly or indirectly to neutralize social exclusion. It can be as little as a street address where you grew up or the aunt that drags you to church every Sunday. Your dad's coworker's cousin has a roommate who knows the granddaughter of the guy who got you the job. The take here is that your credits will never be like somebody else's. If that is true, why should you take a risk just because somebody else did it? People like quoting famous people who quit school and succeeded wildly as their own excuse to do the same. What they don't see is the combination of talents, social exclusions, and naturally occurring credits. Your success will depend on how you manage your capsule of talents, exclusion factors, and credits.

4. Unique Personal Level Efficiencies

Time and Energy Efficiency

Nuthology is a holistic and efficiency-driven approach by the very design. Jumping from one factor to another often leads to exhaustion and frustration. By putting all these pieces together you are getting your ducks in a row. You can then craft a holistic plan that factors talents, skills, and exclusion classes. That will save you tons of time and energy.

Societal Dilemma Efficiency

Society struggles to differentiate in-group favoritism with out-group derogation when looking for the best solutions for bias. What we have today in the developed world is mostly in-group favoritism. At the personal level, as far as the Nuthology Index is concerned, you just need to know that the exclusion exists. And let us be real, whether you were excluded because you did not belong to the group or due to prejudice does not change your economic situation.

Social exclusion is a touchy subject in the community. We talk and scream about it when there is a tragic incident. Most financial literacy sources, counselors, motivational speakers, and even parents understandably avoid this subject.

Sitting at a confluence of multiple exclusion factors is a multiplication of that touchiness. But you have the best view of this elephant in the room. At the personal level, you have the ability to seek mitigating strategies without making anybody feel uncomfortable. You don't need permission.

Since Nuthology is individual driven it does not overlook your rights, feelings, and complexities or underplay your unique abilities. You have a right to be useful, respected, accepted, and an equal member of society.

Personal Empowerment Efficiency

Most social exclusions are stereotypically, unfairly, and, sometimes, unconsciously propagated. Negative stereotypes affect both the way others view you and the way you view yourself. Either way they are risks to your individual mobility. You will join the society to fight how others view you. How you view yourself through the lens of these stereotypes is something only you can deal with.

You are not taking personal responsibility because you caused these exclusion risks, but because you have a purpose. What would you do if you were your own cheerleader, chief of staff, chief campaigner, and marketing analyst? Well, do it now because you are. A drowning man cannot learn to swim. You have to immerse yourself into these issues proactively.

With this in mind, it is very important that you start by giving yourself the permission to accept the past as it is. You can develop a psychology of resilience. Biography is not destiny. Give yourself the permission to fail. It all starts with an inherent desire to change one inch at a time. This is something society cannot do for you.

The exclusion conglomeration concept is abstract; others cannot touch, feel, or see the synergistic effect of added social exclusion factors. But the individual feels the weight and sees the results.

Climb the ladder of success rung by rung. Just make sure it is leaning on the right wall. You are able to develop a killer work ethics, tenacity, and resilience in a way that you cannot when following groupthink.

Temperament Efficiency

Society has a rigid temperament when it comes to controversial issues. That is why it takes a strong leader to lead a revolution. A lot of activism today is based on an approach that paints a whole dominant group as an enemy. Demonizing a whole group of people is almost always counterproductive.

At the personal level you are flexible enough to engage in pragmatic networking that goes beyond your driveway. You are able to consciously monitor your attitude, mood, or behavior in a way that benefits your purpose. Nuthology encourages working with members of a perceived dominant group.

Appealing to shared values can be a way to begin discussions among different groups. At the personal level this immensely increases the surface area of your networks.

"We build too many walls and not enough bridges." Isaac Newton

Imagine a feminism forum that includes men and boys. Imagine a racial forum that has all races represented or that social class gap discussion that includes the poor and the rich. The thought leaders in society might not see this. They are caught up in the web of perpetual warrior mode. At the individual level, you can do it.

Friendly Fire Efficiency

How much are you contributing to your own entropy? The Nuthology Index calls for a degree of reflective self-examination that only you can engage in. It is a mystery to everybody else. How are you sabotaging your chances for success, happiness, and freedom? How are you sabotaging your kids' chances for success, happiness, and freedom? I gave an example of the misuse of a child's identity and credit history. Another example in this book is giving kids unique but parent-centered names. Character, protocol, etiquette, and other controllable exclusions may fall in this category.

"Most of the shadows of this life are caused by standing in one's own sunshine." Ralph Waldo Emerson

Expectations Efficiency

For the most part, recruiters are required to consider a candidate's skill set when hiring. Using this index, a candidate will attempt to foresee areas in which he or she may be perceived as deviating from normal even with all the qualifications met. There are tons of unwritten qualities that are not on the employer's job qualification description. You will be surprised to find an industry never hires "your type." This is something to factor in your planning but not necessarily a deal killer. It could even be an advantage. You might be the first person to do this.

Use the index conglomeration to perform extensive research. Match your challenges, skills, and talents to the market demand. Look for unwritten rules in market expectations. It will be mean for others to tell you what you can accomplish. No one knows like you do.

Reduced Groupthink Dependence Efficiency

The desire for inclusion and solidarity may temp you to follow groups. Recognizing your unique conglomeration will make you establish new thought paradigms. Regardless of your biography, you must always be in your zone where you can call the shorts. Conglomerates run the risk that they will be hesitant to think for themselves, because they may have been programmed to believe that there is one right answer. While we are all created equal as human beings, we are endowed with different capsules of talents.

Career and Financial Planning Efficiency

Like long-term weather, predicting social exclusion is not easy. But understanding how it affects your bottom line is priceless. The index is not a perfect crystal ball; it was not designed to provide all your future financial answers. The factors that end up drastically affecting our finances are not that unforeseeable. You know there is a good chance that you will retire someday, be a parent, have gray hair, and develop weak bones.

The Nuthology Bias Index is a pragmatic-oriented, evidence-based assessment that can be crafted into a priceless planning tool. Yes, the future is unpredictable in reality. You can prepare by setting up your financial life in a way that you can easily adapt to what the future holds. Develop the best array of transferrable skills you can. Seek knowledge and financial intelligence. It is the agility to adapt and the flexibility to change that will give you the greatest competitive advantage.

Why should you pick that oversubscribed "underwater basket weaving" major knowing all too well that your demographic has a higher unemployment rate? Feel-good courses might not feel good on graduation day. Marginalized people have a right to complain of a lack of education opportunities but given a chance you've got to take the right courses that will better your situation.

Hate Print Contribution Efficiency

At the personal level you are able to see instances where you unconsciously send a monthly check to a world hate kitty. If each of us reduces our own hate by half, the world will hold half as much hatred as it currently holds. That translates to double the world food supply and half the weaponry requirement. I see more weddings and fewer funerals. It all starts with you as a player in society. What a concept, naïve as it is.

Happiness Efficiency

When you define what success means to you, there is less pressure to compare yourself with others. You can visualize your path in a way that nobody else can. Contentment is an attitude toward a situation that is very personal. Society cannot feel that for you. This contentment becomes the central piece of your spiritual practice that will save you time and energy and earn you some sanity brownie points. Is it just me, or do you see reduced debt, medical bills, therapy visits, and dependency on escapism products?

Innovation Efficiency

Sometimes transformative ideas are so esoteric and crazy that only the owner can believe in them. When you initially birth an idea, you have to nurse the craziness. Sometimes you will need to do this alone. Everyone else will try to book you into the nearest mental institution. It is not until you turn the idea into a product that people start coming around. Most of the greatest innovators in history were regarded as a little crazy by their peers. This is a point where groupthink becomes a liability. It can only hold you back. It is this innovation that can transcend most social exclusion.

5. Public Policy and Personal Responsibility (3PR)

The most efficient way to approach exclusion in a free market system is to engage both public policy and personal responsibility. Nuthology strategy is rooted in PPPR. I call it 3PR. At the individual level you are at a good vantage point to engage both. As a bias conglomerate you are trying to build a house but somebody is trying to stop you. Time is a limited factor. You cannot spend all your time defending your site lest all you will end up with is a vacant building site. You will not succeed if you spend all your time building when somebody is taking away some blocks. Your have to use both hands. You must fight with one hand and build with the other. Albeit figuratively, you have two hands for this reason.

Public Policy

I hope the index contributes to the understanding of how several factors can work in concert and inspire creation of more rounded policies. What is your vision of a just society? This is where you use whatever resources you have to influence policy for your generation and the future ones. With modern technology you have more power than any generation in history. Social media, for instance, has been very beneficial to advocacy. At this level you express your views and concerns. You don't have to talk only when the friction involves one of your classes. Whenever things go wrong in your society always remember that you are a snowflake in that avalanche. You are the penny that completes a million dollars. Promote good ideas that influence public policy and resource allocation decisions. Point out the wrongs whenever necessary. But don't make this your only occupation.

Personal Responsibility

What is your obligation to yourself? What is your obligation to occupy the space that has been created for you by freedom fighters and humanitarian moral luminaries who preceded you? The space may not be as big as you want, but it will shrink if it is not occupied. There is also the risk that you will buy into stereotypes. The greatest danger of any exclusion is when you start seeing yourself as less deserving and less capable. That's when you transfer the divine power. Keeping this power alive will therefore depend on how you manage both the capsule of talents and your unique exclusion factors. The Nuthology Index helps in gathering information and collection data. From there you can develop a strategy that can help you achieve your goals, which includes generating enough revenue in this challenging environment.

5

Nuthology SCHOOL of Mitigation

After extensive research that included hundreds of biographies of people who have overcome various forms of exclusions, I have discovered some unique patterns of data. All of those people had unparalleled levels of pragmatism and adaptability, which enhanced their talents immensely. The combination of the ability to change, acquire knowledge, and network beyond one's group created a force of its own that became a major source of their competitive advantage.

I have condensed all of my findings in one word: SCHOOL. This is not your grandfather's regular stone and mortar learning institution around the corner. Many people facing various forms of social exclusion have never considered the possibility of positive outcomes. Nuthology SCHOOL of Mitigation is a philosophy based on a theory that it is possible to create viable and sustainable financial independence strategies in a bias market ecosystem.

The Acronym **SCHOOL** stands for:
Seek the ships
Conglomerate
Human needs and wants
Obligations
Opportunities
Law of C attributes

The order of these mitigation strategies does not matter. The strategies work best when used concurrently. They work in concert in reducing self-inflicted bias factors, reducing competition, and increasing competitive advantage. Of course, your interests and needs will evolve over your lifetime.

Seek the Ships

You have to always actively seek what I like to call the pantheon of "great ships." These ships will take you beyond your dreams. There is an old Irish blessing that begins with the words "May the wind be always at your back." So, what are these ten big ships? Relationships, memberships, mentorships, internships, apprenticeships, scholarships, sponsorships, craftsmanship, entrepreneurship, and self-stewardship.

Craftsmanship

Allow me to channel Shakespeare for a moment. The civil society bemoans the cost and irrationality of a college education but acknowledges the alternative might still be worse. As an individual you find yourself in a dilemma. To be a college student or not to be a college student, that is the question.

One common argument is that not every student is meant for college. The first problem is that as an individual you are not "every student." How would anyone know that you were not meant for college given that you never been to college? I have some good news for you about another mystery of the capsule of talents. Nobody actually knows your real intellectual horsepower. Let us start from there.

One of the assumptions of the index is that you are qualified to perform a certain craft. One of the cornerstones of this Nuthology mitigating strategy is that you become the best in that craft. That ensures you are not competing with millions of people for a few jobs with your high point NUBC. Whatever develops that craft in terms of credentials, skills, and experience should dictate what route you will take. Your purpose becomes the tie breaker; again it's not some analyst's opinion.

If your purpose is curing world diseases, your craft might be medicine. If your craft is ensuring justice and fairness, your craft might be law. Making cabinets, plumbing, cutting hair, wielding, accounting, selling, public service, preaching, singing, entertaining, and teaching are just examples. You will discover that every craft will require skills and talents to a certain degree.

Let me repeat, nobody actually knows your real intellectual horsepower. It is hard for society to estimate your potential, which, coming from the creator of the universe, can be mind-blowing. A college education or trade school will allow you to develop your craft.

I like to view education as this survivor train that people jump out off. Some people have safety nets to absorb their impact. Those who jump without safety nets end up on rocks and thorns, and they may end up in steel cages. Some people are forced off by lack of resources. Those who stay longer increase their odds of landing on good probabilities.

Many conglomerates do not have safety nets so the probability of ending up in rocks, thorns, and steel cages is high. I don't know anything in this world that changes the trajectory of a marginalized child more than a good education. Thank heavens that, at least in most of the world, you don't have to dodge acid sprays to go to school. Forget handouts and other stopgap measures. For the marginalized kids, education is often the only way out of place-related social exclusion.

"Education is the most powerful weapon which you can use to change the world." Nelson Mandela

One of the most effective methods of social exclusion in the past and in the present is to keep people ignorant. In the dark and middle ages, ignorance was used to control people's minds. The greatest enemy of any tyranny is the truth that is found in the knowledge of how things work. Today most dictators and oppressive non-state actors use ignorance to control sections of the population. When you drop out of school for no apparent reason or refuse to seek knowledge you are walking away from the best equality tool ever. Ever!

The function of education is to help you discover the contents of your capsule of talents and hone your craft. Some talents require some formal education to manifest. You may need some education to develop most science-related products and cures and to access most well-paying jobs.

Nobody is saying for a minute that the power of certificates will replace street smarts, but for minorities, staying in school or having middle-class aspirations should not be sold as a negative. Formal education and street smarts are not mutually exclusive. Who says you can't have both smarts?

For a young person with no experience that's the only thing you can show. My argument here is not whether education is good or bad. If most employers prefer a Rhodes Scholar to a road scholar, that's exclusion risk that needs to be mitigated early in your life.

Family challenges at home, the poor state of many schools, and potential social exclusion should be reasons to stay in school, not to drop out. There is a reason children walk miles in other parts of the world to get to a school. There are reasons children risk acid sprays and other bodily injury to get to a classroom that is under a tree in extreme weather conditions. There is a reason education has been denied to marginalized groups. It is the invisible gold. It is almost a given that you will need that post high school diploma one way or another in your life. I can guarantee you that. This is for you, your family, and your society.

Education is one thing that has helped many to get off of the multi-generational poverty hamster wheel. They may not necessarily be millionaires but they have broken off the dearth orbit. They may have to pass through middle-class air space, but they are experiencing decreased gravitational pool from poverty planets. That's a great start. The next generations can build from there.

Your weaponry warship has just docked. Let us look at this triple-mast destroyer: **academic knowledge, professional literacy and financial literacy**.

Academic Education

One major assumption of the index is that you are a qualified candidate before you claim bias in a certain backdrop. In a world where credentials are needed, street swagger alone may not work. A college degree remains the best investment that a young person can make. A college degree continues to be viewed as necessary for successful employment.

College education increases your chances of earning a higher wage. For a conglomerate, good education is a not a just a path to economic self-sufficiency and a way out of a toxic neighborhood but also a way to become part of the system. Being part of the system will enable you to address the bias-related issues in society.

It is your duty to constantly look at your craft enhancers. The war chest has to be updated aggressively. Based on your NUBC you might have to work harder than the potential competition. Your take-off speed requirement will be relatively higher because of the NUBC weight. You cannot slack on personal development.

Conglomerates who stay in school should avoid feel-good majors, like synchronized under-water quilting. College gives you a runway to test that intellectual horsepower; crank it up to the max. Get a major that give you a reasonable chance of getting a job. Avoid degrees with low return on investment. Avoid degree programs that are oversubscribed. The index can help you perform predictive risk analysis before making life-altering decisions. There is no way a one-size-fits-all approach will apply. Take that to the bank.

What about the fact that some people are forced off the education train by lack of resources as indicated above? For a conglomerate, this calls for a shrewd scotched-earth policy. In most of the developed world, if you want some education you will get it. Work three jobs if you have to. Work some nights. Use the community college route. In this section we see how you can utilize scholarships, sponsorships, mentorships, apprenticeships, internships, partnerships, memberships, and other relationships to cultivate your craftsmanship. Get creative with meal plans, housing strategies, transportation, entertainment, and other personal expenses. Borrow some of the textbooks and school supplies instead of buying them. This is not the time to buy whatever tickles one's fancy.

You can also take out student loans wisely. Student loans can haunt you for life, but without a degree, you may not get far. Talk to yourself. Look at the risks and rewards. Approach this as a business decision. There are people who manage the loans well. There are people who obtain worthwhile degrees with average student loan debt. It is a balancing act. The loans are not necessarily always the problem. Blindly taking out loans and misusing the funds is clearly a financial move that ends up exacerbating the problem.

Professional

For anybody, future financial success relies on the ability to continually improve, innovate, and change. You can bet for a conglomerate that may mean doing this better that anybody else. Be an expert in something marketable. Learn a marketable skill that will give you a competitive advantage.

Be adaptable, not rigid. There are vocational schools and job-training programs that can help you discover and polish the contents of your capsule of talents. Seek transferable and independent life skills needed for long-term success. You might end up working in a totally different industry than the one you start in.

A lot of people take an illogical career route to get where they end up. You will find a boxer who became the president, a PhD who started at a community college, and a doctor who became a news anchor. You will find a teacher who later became pope and a paper boy who became a billionaire. Understand your own strengths and weaknesses. Architecting your beliefs requires approaching problems preemptively, even for those not facing exclusion.

Basic Financial Literacy

For anybody, financial literacy should be a basic requirement like reading, writing, and arithmetic. It is not just for those who major in finance or are going to be entrepreneurs. Everybody should be financially literate. It is something everybody should acquire at an early age.

For a conglomerate, basic financial literacy is not an option. It is a must. The fact that you are starting your life probably in a materially excluded situation only makes this more urgent. You may need to be shrewder than a competitor who does not have your conglomeration. Without basic financial intelligence it becomes hard to earn money and even harder to keep it.

Few things can break your spirit and leave you with a sense of hopelessness than a bad financial situation. It is your duty to seek financial literacy aggressively. This helps you recognize the importance of managing cash, credit, and customers. The customers include the potential employer who will buy your services.

There are tons of books and free information on these issues. Technology is a wonderful thing. Today I want to encourage you to develop curiosity about this subject, regardless of your career path. You will never regret financial literacy. It is priceless. In a later section I will talk more about personal finance as related to conglomerates.

Understanding your own situation is critical, even when you work with qualified and trustworthy financial experts. To get optimal service you need to communicate your goals. Without a basic understanding of financial matters your funds are likely to be mismanaged. There is no excuse in today's world to not take advantage of having so much knowledge at your fingertips.

Relationships

"Give me a lever long enough and a place to stand, and I can move the Earth." Archimedes

You will be working smart if you use as many "levers" and places to "stand on" as you can get. This brings me to leveraging networks. Despite all the hype, success isn't just a matter of hard work, talent, and a fat GPA—it also depends on your networks. More often than not jobs come from knowing people. Networking is one of the most important career and business skills. In today's world, personal recommendation from friends and colleagues is invaluable.

Networking is creating meaningful relationships long before you need them. Your end goal is connections and knowledge but it starts early and stealthily. Start a conversation in such a way that it appears you are just looking for a valued opinion. Ask how you can improve you resume, career strategies, or industry.

Look for events for young professionals in your city. Form a support group in a related field. Attend a local career fair. Work via referrals. Stay in touch with your college friends and professors.

Use social networks, blogs, and search engines to locate other professionals that share your interests. Use the online networks wisely. Approach this as a business decision rather than accumulating twenty thousand friends who cannot help you move your couch. Think about the impact of customer referrals and employee referral programs. These are essentially network dependent business moves.

If you are young and starting out, you should never feel entitled to a job based on academic qualifications. Stem, flowers, leaves, or roots, there is no one major that guarantees a job. The real world doesn't work on guarantees. You have to get out there and sell your qualifications.

Seek the right people and businesses. Networking can give you that pivot that you need. Those people who attempt to enter into entertainment know that sometimes you need an agent even to get an agent.

Even when employed you will still need to do some networking inside your organization so that the decision makers know who you are, know of your interests, and develop an appreciation for your skills and abilities, and your achievements to date.

Networking is not treating your friend's kitchen like a free all-you-can-eat buffet or a food bank. Networking is not begging. Begging is always a real turn off.

Meaningful Partnerships

There is a man in your church that is good in advanced calculus but needs a lot of help with the new-age technology. You are very good in the computer space. You can even make your laptop make you a sandwich. But calculus is another animal.

In exchange for your computer training, the man will teach you calculus at a pace that you can understand. A partnership is created by individual parties believing they can better achieve their goals by working together. The mutual mentoring you just created is a partnership.

In a business formation context, partners work together to start and grow a business in a way a single person cannot do. That million-dollar idea you have been nursing for the last seven years may never come to fruition if you don't get a partner. It requires seasoned programming skills and you don't have money to hire people, but you know some good technologists.

The partner may provide feedback, opinions, skills, funding, or a combination of these. There are situations when you may require a partner to take the next step in achieving your specific goals.

Expand Your Networks

Expanding your network beyond your subgroup helps your course and creates peace on earth. Who knew? There is a chance that your primary subjective group generally demonizes everyone in the dominant group including tomorrow's newborns. Inside that perceived "evil crowd" there are angels that will put the "human" in the word humanity. These diamonds in the rough are not as identifiable as you would like, but they are there. These people may not come off as neighbors, priests, and Levites at first sight. There are a lot of unsung dominant group well-wishers that can enhance your networks. Ironically you may face resistance from your own subgroup.

"Am I not destroying my enemies when I make friends of them?" Abraham Lincoln

Do your own independent research. This is about you, what you want, what you are good at, and what your possible structural barriers are. In the battle of burning bridges, the person with fewer resources on their island loses.

Learning to work across group barriers is a skill that demolishes some of these barriers. This can seem a Sisyphean task given the toxic relationships at the societal level. This is what our transformative forefathers did. They made efforts to make relationships. They did not simply wait for them to happen. Leaders are proactive, followers are reactive. Be the chief officer of your goals. Transcend beyond the societal level's perpetual alarmism and warrior mode.

Reduce Dependency on Vertical Relationships

Bad things happen to good people. You may have to depend on help at one time or another. Work to wean yourself out of any social programs and anti-social programs, like mooching. No handout-driven intervention has ever worked in the long run. Show me one place on earth where handouts to nations or individuals have worked in the last six decades. Handouts to individuals or nations create vertical relationships. These relationships always run top down, in a master-servant angle. Solidarity refers to relationships that are horizontal in nature. That is the good foundation for mutual respect. Nations and individuals who rely on vertical relationships always find respect a scarce import. Every moocher ends up losing his dignity in his friends' couch cracks. Every handout-dependent nation ends up losing its sovereignty in the donor nation's pouch hems.

Memberships

Seek organizations that promote personal growth, leadership, and community service. Some of them look very good on your resume and college applications. Seek memberships in associations and professional organizations that put you in a positive light. The fact that you are keeping up-to-date with your profession or that you are developing useful industry contacts may earn you an interview.

Stay miles away from affiliations that portray you as a credibility risk. I talk about this in detail in the affiliation and character sections.

Mentorships

The wise leader has been mastering his craft for the last three hundred years. Now you want in. To learn how to make the best mousetrap you have decided that you must be his mentee. As mean as he looks, this is your golden chance to make the best mouse trap mankind has ever seen. That's not the only motivation. There is a slight chance he might eventually delegate a portion of his job responsibilities.

There are different mentoring relationships. Some are formal, and others are just casual arrangements. The impact of a meaningful mentorship can be very rewarding. Think of it in terms of transfer knowledge, wisdom, and experience that cannot happen in a classroom setting. As the protégé or mentee you stand to get instant recommendations, feedback, and encouragement in a real-life situation. You get to ask questions that cannot be answered with a simple online search. Find yourself a huge giant in the industry you are interested in.

Modern Role-Modeling Mentorship

If you are like me, you probably want your mentor to be Abraham Lincoln just because he is one of the greatest examples of persistence ever. Thanks to technology, now he can be! Well, sort of.

With modern technology you are able to use a mentor without developing a direct relationship. You can develop a mentorship relationship without the mentor knowing or being alive. Just follow his work online. As a bonus, you get to skip the bad personal baggage a mentor may have. This gives you a chance to emulate your mentor without necessarily imitating him. This DIY self-help mentor doesn't even take bathroom breaks.

Since the aim is to grow professionally, you can model your goals and follow your mentor's decision making step by step. You look for people who have done certain tasks. You look at situations where they applied certain principles. Reorganize these principles to fit your situation. What would Abraham Lincoln do in this case? Quit?

Internships

How can an internship position help you? There are some ins and outs that an industry only experience can provide. You will gain exposure to real-world problems and issues. You get to meet the burned-out zombies who have been working in the company before soil was invented. You can learn the attrition patterns of the industry. Is it a glamourized career where people leave after a few months of reality dosage?

What about the chance to kick those tires? Evaluate the industry; "try before you buy." It is also a decision-making exercise: now you have some data about what you like or what works for you. What works and what sucks.

Then there is always a catch-22 where you need experience to get a job, but you actually need a job to get that experience. How do you get experience if no one will give you a job? With an internship you ease the transition from school to work. Problem solved.

An internship will put you ahead of the many faceless applicants piling into e-mail queues and the recruiter's trash can. It's an excellent way to obtain professional references and increase marketability. They know you by name.

An internship program increases advancement opportunities in cases where you get hired by the host company. This is because the internship experience adds to your work years.

I can name many other benefits of this program, like helping to fund your education, earning school credits, developing new skills, and increasing self-confidence.

Watch out for internships where you are given pointless tasks that do not enhance your career. There are companies where you are taken on as an assistant rather than an employee, making coffee, cleaning, or printing some unneeded reports.

Apprenticeships

Ladies and journeymen, this is another valuable program that not only puts you in front of the faceless applicants but delivers you from the cruel recruiter's trash can. A lot of candidates at trade-certified organizations continue to work at the same place after the apprenticeship ends.

Like internships, an apprenticeship program has a lot of benefits. Apart from insider connections, you develop new skills and increase self-confidence. That hands-on exposure to equipment and technology is priceless in most fields. The ease of the transition from home to work ensures that you are not caught up in the experience dilemma.

If the arrangement involves training in exchange for your labor, then this saves you a lot of money. This can work well in cases where money for training is a big concern. For many conglomerates, money is a huge concern.

Scholarships

A server in a restaurant may recommend specials but may not make the best choices. A career counselor for the most part will recommend loans and majors based on the institution's need. Colleges are quick to talk students into loans. They may not mention scholarships, studentships, and other sources of funds that contribute less to their bottom line. It is your duty to do some legwork.

Don't limit your search. There are non-tuition awards that can save you tons of money, but you have to look for them. We are talking about free transportation, free college textbooks, free supplies, rent-free housing, meal plans, or other assistance

Nobody is saying for a second that scholarships are easy to get. You will have to be shrewd and proactive about obtaining them. It is your duty to aggressively seek various forms of scholarship grants. Your parents' employers or church may offer scholarships, but you won't know if you didn't ask. Colleges also offer their own scholarships, so I'm not saying that you ignore them entirely. As a matter of fact, that is where you start looking for information. Seek, seek, and seek.

Look for ways to differentiate your candidacy. Scholarship evaluators are often looking for students who stand out. Seek constructive criticism on your essay from teachers, mentors, or other students. Start as early as possible.

Sponsorships

As a way of financing education, sponsorships are common in many countries. In this arrangement, a third party provides money to help pay for a student's education. In this context it means financial support received from the sponsor. You go about finding a sponsor the same way you would find a scholarship. Crowdfunding is one way that students are using to have strangers pay for their education.

In a business context, sponsorships mean support for an event, activity, person, or organization. This can be done financially or by provision of products or services. In this context, sponsorship is done with the expectation of some commercial return. A return could be the sponsor displaying his name on your property or website for branding to increase awareness and sales. Depending on your goals, you might find yourself seeking a sponsor aggressively.

Entrepreneurship

Entrepreneurship is the process of starting a business or organization according to most sources. Entrepreneurship and freedom are very close cousins. While people are looking for a boss to hire them, you want to hire those bosses. The only way to make serious income is by starting a business. For conglomerates it might be the only possible way of earning a living.

With the technological developments available today, the only person preventing you from starting a business is you. Here are some reasons why:

New Capital Age

Social exclusion involves denial of resources and access, which translates to barriers to market entry. The age when you were supposed to have access to big chunks of capital is over. With the new technology, we are moving from resources to resourcefulness. Starting a business has become increasingly accessible to the small investor. Thanks to technical innovations, the Internet, and social media there is visible entry-barrier erosion and reduction of access costs.

We have moved from selling products in high-cost shops with small customer bases and tons of overhead to selling online to the whole world with little start-up and barely there overhead.

Before this age, individuals were not allowed to present their equity funding offerings publicly. Today through crowdfunding, besides having a global audience, as potential investors you are able to publicly solicit equity offerings. In the countries where this is allowed, it is like having an IPO in your garage. Your backers receive unlisted shares of your company before it starts.

Free Marketing and Networking Tools

This is the most equipped generation in the history of civilizations. It is a time when you can reach billions of people with a single click of a button. Think of today's possibilities that were not there a few years ago:

- Peer-to-peer initiatives
- Strong distribution channels
- Internet-driven lending and borrowing avenues
- Improved payments and settlement methods

We live in a world where a person can get an internship by tweeting and people can fund your idea by donations. Just a few years ago book authors grew old waiting for agents and publishers to give them a green light. Today you can write a book and publish it within hours. Print on demand is common and economical, no warehouses required!

Free Training and Information

They are tons of good resources out there on behaviors that will get you money and help you keep it. You can get training for skills that other generations would never have dreamed off. Financial literacy is the ability to understand how money works in the world: how someone manages to earn or make it, how that person manages it, how that person invests it, and how that person donates it to help others. The information is out there in the open. There is no excuse not to take advantage of it.

Taking the Plunge

We must dare to take risks and to fail as many times as it takes. I get it: It is harder for those of us who lack social safety nets. We have already faced enough rejection, so we don't want to hear the word "no" again. It is a dirty two-letter word. We don't take rejection well.

As I write this little book, I am not aware that one day you will read it. Who am I to write a business book anyway? Aren't there thousands of gurus out there? I am hoping that by the time you finish this book you will realize that we all have many more degrees of freedom than we give ourselves credit for. Give yourself permission to fail. Don't be afraid to fail a million times. The more you fail, the more you learn that the seeds of opportunity can disguise themselves as challenges and obstacles.

Focus on the Upside

Most financial instruments are mostly overvalued. They have little upside. It is hard to catch a bargain on stocks, bonds, commodities, or real estate. Your talents have the most upside. This upside is divinely hidden from other people. Ask any parents whose child ended up becoming a world-level transformative figure. They may try to justify their children's success, but the truth is that they did not see it coming. It is your obligation to release this upside.

Efficiency

It is easier to create additional streams of income. Think of online brokerage accounts where one can trade securities and participate in online auctions and shops. What about self-publishing of music and books plus airing an online broadcast channel from your basement. Computers have opened up a new world. There are affiliate programs, classes, and tutorials. It is like doing four jobs in the same time period. You can do this without leaving your primary job. That home-based business will allow you to crawl before you walk.

Start Somewhere

You will have to start somewhere; otherwise you'll always be waiting for that perfect time. Somebody once said, "Shoot for the moon. If you miss, you will still land among the stars." It is okay to examine opportunities realistically. You don't want to take uncalculated gambles. That's not a sustainable business strategy. But it is also important to realize that there are always going to be some uncertainties in life whether there is bias or not. You will be vulnerable to changing conditions and new realities. Learn how to examine an opportunity and analyze the risk. More importantly, learn to make decisions without a 100 percent guarantee.

Self-Stewardship

You have the right to select a spiritual practice to deal with the bumps and bruises in life. You have the right to a worship and wellness program to deal with the banal aspects of daily life. If you cannot afford a way to recharge and keep your spirits up in a healthy way, one will be automatically selected for you even if you don't wish for that to happen. If you decide not to channel your energy and pick healthy rituals food abuse, substance abuse, or any other harmful escapism may be selected by default for you.

Knowing and understanding your rights of emotional, physical, and financial health as I have explained them to you, are you willing take time alone to reflect on your life? This would be a funny Miranda-rights version if this was not such a serious subject.

I am both intrigued and enlightened by many of the findings that I stumbled upon when researching this topic. Like many of you I am not an expert in this subject, but I consider myself a good student. At the very least I believe in research-driven efforts to improve oneself.

I selected this as a major "ship" because it a can be a big source of your problems. It can sink and wreck all the other ships. It can also tow them to safety. It can be that light tower deep in the horizon. Most financial goals are not achievable without emotional and physical goals. For that reason, I have to say I found this to be a very enriching topic.

As non-experts we can agree on some observable patterns of data. We know mental and physical health issues can lead to financial issues. We know financial issues can lead to mental and physical health issues. Let's follow that trail further. Who has more financial issues per capita than people who have been materially marginalized? Consequently, it won't be a stretch to say that the risk of mental and physical health issues is considerably higher for this group. Stay with me here. You can now agree with me that for a bias conglomerate it doesn't take much to slip into some harmful escapism. This is not an excuse, but a risk assessment on your backdrop. Now we're cooking with gas.

People have different approaches to how they keep their spirits up in a healthy way. Who doesn't want to be happy, healthy, and wealthy? I am not recommending anything in particular here. Healthy rituals are not carved in stone. Do whatever floats your boat. Here are a few findings.

Meditation, Yoga

Both yoga and meditation are used as ways to decrease stress. The popularity of yoga and meditation is immense; I cannot even start to cover it. The origins of yoga dates back to 400 BC or earlier. The ultimate goal of yoga practice is a state of permanent peace.

Forgiveness

Forgiveness is a self-gift to the forgiver. Holding a grudge backfires and consumes you from inside. Those sour grapes turn into bad whine that gets worse with rage. Do you have a tendency to pull the running tab that contains the wrongs against you and your people for the last 800 years? This may not help your sanity and bottom line.

Letting past issues go is freeing. Ruminating over issues that are considered "settled" makes current arguments unfair. It creates a no-win situation for descendants of those you accuse of doing wrong. It also limits your network as we saw in the relationship section. Are you able to practice forgiveness and compassion in life? That's a financial strategy.

One of the uses of the Nuthology Index is efficiency. It is your obligation to decide how much time you will spend on past grievances at the expense of today's spirit of innovation.

Getting Enough Sleep

Most professionals recommend sleep as a stress buster. While you are preparing for bed you can use meditation or some quiet prayer to focus and re-center yourself.

Making Sports and Exercise Routine

We all know that exercise is good for us. This also includes relaxation exercises. Exercise has been credited for improved mood changes by a lot of research. Sports keep young people out of trouble.

Reading

Reading provides an ability to escape to a world of your own. A book is a magical and personal thing for most people. They get to be transported to another place, into another time in history, or into some fantasy without ever leaving their favorite spot on the couch.

Sometimes all you need is the only free thing in today's world: sunlight. You can be in the jungle or on the beach. I have to admit that this is something I have used for a long time. Read stories of triumph, creativity and find ways of coping. Find yourself mentors from the bowels of history. Read about world transforming heroes and how they overcame adversity.

Music and Dancing

These are stress relievers that need no introduction. Music and dancing has been used as therapy since time immemorial. We all know dancing will give you a "runners high" if nothing else.

Non-medical Social Isolation

This one got me thinking. There is one thing that almost all our mythological and spiritual figures engaged in: they disappeared from the public for some time. Some people take pleasure in some version of solitude. For the record, I am not suggesting you pick up a blanket and head for the hills leaving unpaid bills.

Positive Affirmations

Some people swear that self-affirmation exercises and eternal optimism can lead to happiness.

Take on a Hobby

I found drawing, painting, and other hobbies are popular ways that people ground themselves.

Volunteering and Mentoring

Who knew that the lawyer who teaches art to kids for free or a doctor who teaches piano lessons for free is helping himself in the process? It helps to go out there and teach people a skill that you are good at. Coaching empowers you. Mentoring is a very rewarding exercise.

Giving

Who would have thought giving is a selfish thing? Doing-good turns out to be a therapy of sorts. Do you show care for the welfare of others and the environment? If so, you are on the right path.

Gratitude

Did you have something to eat today? There are millions out there far less fortunate than you in every measurable aspect. Replace some of those complaints with compliments. Focus on appreciation and gratefulness.

Worship and Prayers

For most of us believers, seeking divine intervention comes naturally. This is where you turn to a power that is bigger than you, not only to reduce stress but find joy and happiness. Believers also engage in other wellness practices.

Simplify Your Life

Automate your savings and bills. Go paperless. Create routines and schedules without being compulsive about it. Now, this sounds like something you read in a personal finance book.

Stop Collecting Expensive Toys

Stop buying unnecessary stuff, especially by borrowing. And stop chasing the next shiny thing on the market. This is another personal finance maneuver.

Stop Comparing

Would you rather be the first version of yourself or the second version of somebody else? Stop looking for validation or matching accomplishments. Nothing is more stressful than trying to keep up with the Joneses. The Joneses will always appear to walk faster because they are the Joneses and you are you.

We are all unique. You will burn out real quick. There will always that person who runs the 1000K marathon, writes a better best seller, or wins a Nobel Prize for something. Live in this moment and in your zone. That is where you are always the winner.

Suspend or Give up Unrealistic Dreams

Do you still have dreams of playing in the NBA when you are 500 pounds, three feet tall and forty-three years old? So what if your mom told you can do anything thirty-seven light years ago. Sometimes circumstances change. In real life you have to adapt. If you have twenty goals, you may have to suspend some. You don't owe anybody an explanation. It is your health and wealth.

Unplug

I found that people who are keen on this practice unplug at least several times a month. Step away from that electronic device slowly and nobody gets hurt. Your ten thousand friends will still be there when you come back.

De-clutter Friends

Hold an annual "bad affiliation" spring cleaning. Cut loose toxic and high-need personalities. Turn yourself into an emotional-pest slayer. It is a sound financial strategy. Playing a people-pleaser, especially when dealing with shameless moochers, consumes your energy, your money, your time and, ultimately, your happiness.

Nuthology Intelligence

There are thousands of pseudo-scientific theories that are based on the "correlation to causation" game that are usually sold to vulnerable people who are desperate to try anything. The people who sell them talk about some vibrations and some expanding snake oil energy that is meant to cleanse your soul. I can attest to one thing about these: they cleanse your wallet for sure. That is one scientific fact that never disappoints. You have the right to find ways to ground yourself, but that does not mean opening yourself up for exploitation.

You don't have to choose one method. You can pray and still get busy outdoors, meditate, exercise, or share your concerns with experts or friends.

Conglomerate

Positive self-talk, affirmations, and bright false smiles are one thing. Now, let's go back to the drawing board and smell the coffee. We know for the most part that society handles each factor on its own. To an extent this is understandable. Earlier I gave an example of a disabled single mother who is a racial minority. At the societal level, you will have race, gender, disability, and single parenthood as single concepts, each with its own activists. I am not diminishing those who fight for equality at the societal level. At the individual level, all these bias factors are in one person. Society can only help you to a point because of this uniqueness. It is your duty to put your ducks in a row. You will also be exhausted if you try to chase each factor at a time.

The conglomeration of exclusion factors can be confusing if you attempt to deal with each factor as a unitary concept. Bias conglomeration has an extraordinary impact on personal finance, career planning and almost all facets of your life. I like to think of Nuthology as a philosophy because it affects everything in personal improvement. This concept attempts to help you design a repeatable approach that directly addresses the common problems associated with bias conglomeration.

This is something that you will not find in books because it is unique to you. It requires that you develop an effective non-utopian vision and mission by consciously examining your talents and analyzing the risks. Set realistic expectations and goals.

At first this will appear pessimistic and counterintuitive. What is wrong with trying to figure out what your strengths are, what your true talents are, and your structural bias risks? Are we supposed to disregard the effects of external conditions in our backdrops?

My hope is that you will be surprised that, due to the uniqueness of your challenges and talents, this will end up being your greatest competitive advantage. By not being tied to one bias at a time, you will save sanity, energy and time. I can't think of better efficiency.

As Benjamin Franklin once said: "All mankind is divided into three classes: Those that are immovable, those that are movable, and those that move." Which one do you want to be? Despite your bias conglomeration status, I really hope you choose to move.

Human Needs and Wants

Bias conglomerates who have experienced exclusion earlier in their lives may be tempted to seek validation. "Look at me and my big car, giant pool, humongous mansion, motorcade, and expensive jewelry". You may reason out that you grew up poor and that you deserve those things. You desire validation, but people cannot see your fat savings account or a super clean credit report. You want people to love you for once, so you keep buying the attention with the credit card.

Give yourself a generous dose of honesty. A debtor-spender is a truth bender who uses a lender's plastic to self-endear. In this process the pretender-spender makes the creditor the master. Debt supported "shopping therapy" is a form of self-entitlement. It is a gate that opens multiple doors to other therapies in the near future. As a conglomerate you probably have been fighting unearned privilege all your life. A debt that you know you may never be able to repay is a form of unearned privilege.

Is it a human need that your "Mars rover" pickup truck must have forty-seven-inch wheels that you know are beyond your budget? We are often tempted by the next shiny thing. There will be a new shiny thing every day. Don't blame the shiny thing for your problems.

"Wealth consists not in having great possessions, but in having few wants." Epictetus

Happiness can't be bought in a store. You will be bombarded by ads for products with catchy slogans like, "You deserve this," and "This is your time." They make sure you get sucked into spending your money on something dumb. The fact is that just because a product is 70 percent off or the store is promoting the deal of a lifetime does not change the definition of a "want" to a "need".

"Having the fewest wants, I am nearest to the gods." Socrates

Delay of gratification is an essential part of financial acumen. The problem therefore may not necessarily be the lack of money per se but that of saving and investing. Somebody once said that when you constantly need more, it is impossible to fully enjoy the abundance of now.

It is not necessarily about being cheap; it is about setting financial priorities. We are talking about avoiding money pits and feeling that you deserve nice things. It is ironic that the rich stay rich by saving and investing while the poor stay poor by spending and borrowing.

As a conglomerate or a formerly materially marginalized person, it is very crucial that you recognize that your validation appetite might be higher than normal. I like to think that financial planning is as simple as developing a killer work ethic, living below one's means, saving money, and investing it. Living below one's means and saving money are tied to recognizing the difference between needs and wants.

Obligation

As you might have discovered already, the Index has a very intuitive design. Nuthology mitigation strategy, on the other side, is counterintuitive. The strategy suggests that you, the person who is on the receiving end of social exclusion, should do something about it. How unfair. You are not the bad guy here. Why should you be expected to do something about it? This doesn't make rational sense at all.

The convergence of exclusion factors can easily push you into learned helplessness, making you surrender all your obligations, and, with them, your unique capsule of talents.

What are your obligations to yourself, society, and the people who fought to create the "not-enough" spaces that are available today? Does the lack of equality at present justify letting yourself drift away and let the tide bounce you around? You cannot abdicate your responsibility because of the existence of structural barriers.

"I am only one, but I am one. I cannot do everything, but I can do something. And because I cannot do everything, I will not refuse to do the something that I can do. What I can do, I should do. And what I should do, by the grace of God, I will do." Edward Everett Hale

Obligation to Thy Self

Nobody out there gives initiative the last time I checked. You have to wake up, seek it, and take it. You owe yourself the very basic. At the very least I believe you should go to the end of the world to make a modest income, meet your expenses, and live well. Your dignity starts there. Deeper in the book I will discuss how you can use the index to reduce lifestyle-related factors like body art, criminal record, questionable affiliations, creative names, and other controllable threats to your personal brand.

Obligation to Thy Society

Social exclusion involves rejection, which can be very demoralizing. If one gives up on looking for a job, for example, it is not only a terrible waste of human resources for society, but leads to dependency and poverty. It is a double blow to society. We are missing both your $100 expected contribution, and your $100 unexpected distribution. We are off $200 in one hit. That's how empires fall.

Paying for rent, utilities, and groceries is what adults do. While most parents don't mind supporting kids while in college, there are great worries behind those loving, fast wrinkling faces. Be a good mind reader. Stay in college and work part time wherever possible. Go to the end of the world. Start by paying for your car insurance and catch yourself segueing into similar expenses without being egged on.

Learn to cut through family members' double-talk. "Sure you can live in the basement as long as you want. I don't mind at all." The faster you find yourself the better. They are called loved ones for a reason:

they are able to bend all the truth to make you happy. They may tell you what you want to hear for now; it might be the calm before the storm.

Be realistic about how much time, money, or effort your family and friends will be able to provide given their daily work demands and priorities. Listen for hesitation and doubt in people's voices, especially if there are other needs and siblings. You want them to sell the only family car just because you sing well in the shower and want your own label?

It is one thing to get help after a rough patch. Expecting others to perpetually compensate for your laziness or lack of responsibility is a very unfair practice. As a conglomerate, you should understand unfairness enough not to subject your family, friends or that sweating taxpayer to it.

Close Relationships

When assessing your talents and skills, perform independent research without putting people close to you on the spot. Friends and family may tell you whatever you want to hear to spare your feelings or prevent a cold war.

Imagine you are writing a book like this and you ask family for reviews. Most of them will just praise your book. "It is a page turner," your mom might say. She probably turned from page one to two and quit. She may not have the courage to tell you that your book looks like prehistoric hieroglyphics. Look at it this way: if everyone sugarcoats all of the concerns, you may never improve.

Close relatives and those who are providing you with financial support can hurt you in two ways. They may sugar-coat their advice or pressure you in making decisions. Whenever possible seek independent constructive criticism for your work.

Do You Have to Completely Love the Job?

Yes, it is important to love what you do. But how do you define job love? Even the most glamorized jobs have a burnout element. If you are still living in your parent's basement at forty-eight and thinking of a job in terms of fuzzy kumbayah, corporate jets, and client conferences in some Caribbean resort, you may need help. If you think there is a job out there tinged with gold and scented with roses, I have a bridge to sell you. Forget the roses, wake up and smell the burning coffee in the common room.

Jobs come with stress and sometimes long thankless hours. Even for those that are self-employed constant pressure is not uncommon. It is better to love the relief that comes with providing for your family and giving to the needy. If you have to love something, love your purpose. We live in a world where the media tends to glamorize certain careers and disparage others. There is dignity in holding any job

Remember when you were younger and everybody wanted to know what they would to be when they grew up? You wanted to be a turnip farmer. I get it. It is time to align education, expertise, skills, experience, and networks realistically with the opportunities that are out there. In the corporate world it is not uncommon to have three consecutive meetings about the upcoming April meeting that will discuss December meetings. It is not always entertaining.

Nobody wants to talk of situations where the career chooses you. Circumstances or choices arise with such a force that you find yourself in a career that you would not have dreamed of. That's more realistic than what you read in many books. There are more compromises than we would like to admit. Your financial freedom, life balance, and self-actualization needs also keep evolving constantly as circumstances change. Nothing is carved in stone. The take-away here is simple. There are definitely bigger factors than coolness to consider when choosing a job.

Should You Drop School and Follow Your Passion?

I know some people whose passion is hanging out and drinking beer. I know people who follow and live off other people to pursue passions that they have no skills or talents for. Passion with no vision is fruitless. Vision with no passion is fruitless. I am all for passion, but it is often overrated or used as an excuse.

Passion does not pay bills. That fire-in-the-belly and ride-without-a-helmet strategy may work sometimes. What about the 99 percent of the time that the dish-the-parachute strategy doesn't work? For a person with complicated NUBC, that could be a devastating blow. Somehow you have to marry your passion to your purpose, capsule talents, and skills.

There is always some temptation in high school to quit and hustle some dollars here and there. Almost always these passions are just not sustainable business models. What is passion anyway? There are a lot of people who get caught up with what is being celebrated out there at the moment. It is usually some sport or entertainment occupation. It is usually not being a pharmacist. Most of the time it turns out to be another person's passion. For a marginalized kid without good safety nets to fall back on, this may mean a cycle of endless dependence. This often leads to a life under a highway bridge or in a tax-funded cage.

Don't be fooled by the popular "billionaire dropouts storyline" that everyone throws around. Most of these billionaires are avid learners outside of the four walls of the classroom. They have a different capsule of talents and environmental credits. They have a different exclusion conglomeration. They have different backdrops. School might be your one chance to leave the orbit of multi-generational poverty.

Obligation to Freedom and Human Rights Defenders

I like to think that the obligation to freedom and human rights defenders can be paid in two ways. First, to occupy the space that has been created by these heroes and second, to continue their work in every small way. This is the best way to pay homage to these moral luminaries without whom the world would be very different today.

Every inch of freedom created must be occupied, otherwise some other form of tyranny will occupy that space. Blood-bought freedoms and civil rights require constant attendance. Occupying that space that has been created and advancing it is part of your obligation.

No civil rights movement in history was ever an overnight success; it is a course that is passed on for generations. You may be tempted to think of your efforts as inconsequential. Who knows what is in your capsule of talents? You may be the straw that breaks the camel's back; yes, you may be that drop that made the cup overflow. Become an advocate for policies that are consistent with human rights. You must rise to the defense of human dignity, rights, and freedom of people everywhere. When can you start? Today. Where do you start?

"Start by doing what's necessary; then do what's possible; and suddenly you are doing the impossible." Francis of Assisi

Opportunity

"He stole my idea." How many times have you kicked yourself when a new idea is presented in the market? You have probably done it more than one time, and you are not alone in this department. Opportunities are always around us in the form of problems. It is your duty to find ways to provide relevant and compelling solutions that customers can only get from you.

You don't have to reinvent the wheel. It doesn't have to be rocket science. Become an authority in something. Be the expert to go to. The best barber in your city is always overbooked. The best plumber in your city is always unavailable because of the volume of incoming calls.

At some point professional persistence drowns away the discrimination noise. If you are the only reliable brain surgeon in your city, people may not care if you are green, fat, and old and have thinning hair. Think of it this way, water possesses a value far lower than diamonds even though water is far more vital to a human being. It is about uniqueness and scarcity. Keep your pipeline full of transferable skills, good networks, products, and innovations and you will have enough people to buy.

Your First Person Voice

This is another angle to look at opportunity. The age of "breaking news" is over. People have been telling your story for ages. They have been turning your character into caricature. The new media places you in the anchor's chair. You can tell your story. This is something that was impossible a few decades ago.

Ride the Wave

Public and private organizations are aware of the need for workplace diversity. There is a visible momentum to recruit and maintain a dynamic, diverse workforce. Many corporations and institutions have established diversity policies. They have recognized that diversity brings fresh ideas and perspectives. The new generation is more open and accommodating. It is your obligation to ride this wave all the way to the bank. When the history of your zeitgeist is written, it will be about the wave that you helped create today.

Law of C attributes

In this section I want to talk about some essential attributes that I have observed in those who have overcome diversity. I believe these concepts are very critical to everyone's financial intelligence. I am calling them the law of C-attributes. First of all, they prevent you from getting the C syndrome. C syndrome in personal finance is a condition where you suffer from a deficiency of credibility, cash, credit, and customers. Customers here include employers. In its acute form this syndrome can attract another C-word, crime.

Let's turn to these fundamental qualities of success that also start with C. These are qualities that you can easily cultivate but nobody can do it for you. I will list them and then briefly introduce them. Feel free to do more research on these qualities.

Curiosity
Character
Creativity
Courage
Consciousness

Confidence
Competency
Common sense
Commitment
Clarity

Curiosity

Nothing drives success more than the thirst for knowledge. The appetite for knowledge and change is a very personal thing. It is pangs of hunger on steroids. Society cannot create this appetite in you. You must create that demand. Don't get me wrong, I am talking about thirst for knowledge not the scandalous, idle, or indiscreet kind of curiosity.

Nothing frustrates a parent more than observable lack of curiosity in a child. It is associated with attention, learning, and motivation. I am sure you have dealt with people who have no desire to improve or learn simple skills, not because they are unable to but because of a lack of motivation. I dare you to find any intellectual giant who was not a curious person. It makes life a never-ending adventure for those who have it. You are never bored. There is always something to discover, a skill to learn, a book to read, or a concept to absorb. You can develop this trait. We are born with tons of it. If you spend a day with a three-year-old you will agree with me. "What does this button do?" It is a gift of nature. Most people have learned financial concepts by curiosity. Personal education is about growth and exploration. It is part of curiosity.

Character

We all know somebody who screams bloody bias all the time but his own mom won't hire him to save her life. He has managed to repackage his stupidity, lack of manners, and rudeness into some popular social exclusion. They say character is ethics in action. People of good character are guided by ethical principles. In good character you will find trustworthiness, respect, responsibility, caring, credibility, and fairness to others.

How come your friend always forgets his wallet at home every time you go to a restaurant? Established reliability is very important, even at home. Can your word be trusted? Integrity and trustworthiness are crucial in business and workplaces. It is also tied to expertise. We all quote sources that we believe are credible.

Use of profanity, for instance, might look cool in the short run. You might even get some laughs. Depending on the backdrop, you may lose credibility in the long run. Freedom of speech does not mean free from repercussions and consequences for what you say.

Capitalism needs to be guided by compassionate and ethical decisions. Most corporate walls are full of colorful policies. There are lists of impeccable company values. But where the rubber meets the road, these values are often missing in action. Good character lets you set an example of the world you want to live in.

Creativity

I like to think of creativity as the ability to come up with solutions. The ability to make new things or think of new ideas. Life is filled with countless moments when you have to think on your feet as opposed to pushing buttons. You will be called to improvise. I read somewhere that necessity is the mother of invention and ingenuity is the father.

Creativity is a close relative of innovation. We are all gifted in some version. In this context I am talking about creating something of value. Think of a service or a good that people can pay you to provide. Leverage your creative talents to do something completely unique.

In marketing school we are taught to do surveys and ask customers what they want. This line of thinking can be very restrictive to your creativity. For the most part, customers can only suggest improvement of an already existing product. Most innovators of today create stuff they think customers will like. I am reminded of a quote by Henry Ford, "If I had asked people what they wanted, they would have said faster horses."

Who could have thought of the gadgets we have today? Only the creators who had it in their minds. Although we didn't know we needed them before they were invented, we can't live without them now. That's the beauty of it.

Cough it out. We are talking about a solution to a problem, an idea, a painting, a musical composition, a book, an invention, or a joke. Anything, if you get my drift. Tap into your intuition; you know you have it.

We shouldn't think of creativity and talent in a narrow way. You can be an innovator in any field. We know sports figures who changed the way the game was played and writers who changed the language forever.

I hope that you focus on utilizing your strengths to achieve your best self. Come up with an idea, formulate a plan to market that idea, and find people who will back that idea. My hope is that this book will spark your imagination and get your business creativity juices going. All you need is some courage.

Courage

I like to think of courage as the ability to make decisions without 100 percent of the information. When you give yourself permission to fail as many times as it takes to succeed, you begin to see the definition of courage.

When you start up a business or a project, you often have nothing to go by but courage. There are no guarantees. Can you pivot if you hit a wall? This is a decision that only you can make, and your decision won't align with all the other conglomerates you know.

It is okay to have concerns about risks that go with venturing into uncharted waters. This is not limited to people facing exclusion. It takes courage to execute a plan. We are not talking about lack of fear here. Courage is not recklessness.

In the business world there is no such thing as a future fact. Facts are always yesterday's animals. Your obligation is to look at patterns of data as analytically and creatively as you can then make that decision. You push that button to strike gold or a brick wall. Ouch. It takes courage to believe that tomorrow will be brighter than today and that the best has yet to come. That's the beauty right there.

Consciousness

This is the state of self-awareness. Without going deeper into philosophical definitions, I like to think of consciousness as being here now and being in control. At the personal level it means profound self- reflection and the inclination to do the right thing without following some groupthink. We can also think of consciousness in terms of emotional stability. Can you think independently? You are the manager. You are the boss of your life every minute.

You don't have to make decisions under the influence of a harmful substance. You don't let a magazine define your beauty. This reminds me of a Mahatma Gandhi quote:

"I will not let anyone walk through my mind with their dirty feet."

Consciousness is a close cousin to mindfulness. Most sources define mindfulness as a state of active, open attention to the present. Have you ever driven to work, but you can't recall how you got there? You finished your food but don't remember eating it? Your mind was miles away. Instead of letting your life pass you by, consciousness means living in the moment.

Nuthology strategy encourages looking at bias at the personal level and deciding how best to achieve your goals without resulting to conformity or encouraging the exclusion. Let's look at how consciousness can be applied in dealing with social exclusion.

Reacting to Bias Decisively

People react differently to prejudice, bullying, humiliation, ostracism, shunning, partiality, favoritism, and other variations of bias-driven rejection. This can range from one extreme to another. We have seen people harm themselves or others. We have seen people attempt to get respect by force and start a vendetta chain that lasts generations. Others go into a bias-shaming rampage.

Is avoiding conflict a weakness? I believe whenever possible any reaction to subtle bias should be based on the "non-maleficence" principle. Do no harm to your purpose and goals. You will still react but on your terms. You will also cause less damage to your credibility and career.

If you are a conglomerate, chances are you will be provoked. You know the hurt feelings will trigger some emotion, be it sadness, loneliness, or anger. In the heat of the moment there is a risk of a disproportionate reaction to a provocation, real or perceived. We are talking about reactions that lead to financial or legal consequences.

This is something that can only be mitigated by thinking about it before it actually happens. This is probably the best time to decide when to use honey and when to use vinegar. You don't buy insurance out of paranoia. You buy it, take defensive driving classes, and pray the accident never happens.

When do you fight or argue? When do you just walk away? Is your reaction just a symbolic act that is punitive in nature and does not advance your situation? Will your reaction aggravate your situation further by feeding into an existing stereotype and myths? Will you get violent, lose your job, and probably collect a criminal record in the process only to realize later it was a false start?

In a fit of pique, you have broken office furniture and caused unnecessary drama. You end up creating several extra bias classes, including extended unemployment, bad credit, and even a criminal record.

Don't let anybody take way your rights and nights. At the same time, don't take away your own rights. You have the ability to control your response, so do not give away that power. Learning how to control your emotions and reactions might give you time to craft your response in a way that you will come off as the adult. When the moment arrives you will make a rational decision that reflects positively on you. That is better than rushing out.

Some people prepare sound bite ripostes that they can regurgitate in their sleep. You should always carry an arsenal of snappy comebacks. These may even help you buy time to collect enough evidence in case you pursue legal action later. A knee-jerk reaction may create a scenario where you lose all credibility to legally pursue a case even when you deserved one originally.

The most harmful reaction occurs when conglomerates abstain from bias situations entirely. They may decide not to look for jobs and depend on help indefinitely.

Catch Yourself Not Catastrophizing

Watch out folks, the sky is falling. You have been thrown under the bus so many times that you have tread marks on your back. As a conglomerate, you will be tempted to interpret every setback in life as a sign of exclusion. You will find yourself making the proverbial mountains out of molehills. Your antennas may always be up because of past experiences. Knowing that is a good start.

Even in the pure absence of prejudice, life is not always fair. Don't construe equal opportunity with equal outcomes. There will be more setbacks from real-life happenings than from other people's aggression. Equal opportunity setbacks and wins are part of a genuine capitalistic system. If you are in business, the risk of bad times is always there. Bias or no bias.

In today's business world you will have to compete. Many times you will lose as part of the game. Dust off and start again. There is no space or time to turn those sour grapes into a never-ending whine. There will be many occasions when you are not picked as the best singer, best player, most talented, or the most qualified that have nothing to do with bias.

I want you to think about this approach every time you want to elevate a small matter into a five alarm fire. The plan is to get to a point where you don't have to reflexively see bias but react to it in a way that promotes your goals. Catastrophizing and being oversensitive may work against you in the long run.

Since bias is just a fraction of life's challenges. We must transcend provocation, and spend less time cursing the darkness and more of it looking for the light. Nuthology encourages you to foresee these risks and avoid the derailing surprise factor. Things are almost always more overwhelming when less planning is involved.

Learn how to accept constructive criticism. Criticism can be healthy. Not all criticism is discrimination.

"To avoid criticism say nothing, do nothing, be nothing." Aristotle

Not every difference between us is a sign of oppression. The anxiety created by catastrophizing can paralyze you and make you mentally exhausted. Life is full of banter and disagreements that are not related to exclusion. Be fully prepared for any eventualities and always take the time to understand the messages you are sending when you choose an action or inaction. It is economically important that you maintain your integrity. Avoid making every minor issue into a category five hurricane. The fact that your boss forgot your birthday should not be a Sarajevo incident.

Yes, there will be those trying to snap your wings so that you can't fly. Do not walk around looking like you just swallowed a gallon of stale lemon juice. Just because a member of a dominant group did something wrong does not mean you should alienate everybody in that group. That is the same group attribution error you have been fighting against. This reduces the scope of your networks. Identify people who understand your concern in the community and work with them. This may include legal, medical, or spiritual advisers.

Catch Yourself Not Anchoring

There is a risk that you will focus on one factor as the cause of all your problems even when you know the facts do not support it. This is the exclusion factor that you tend to blame or identify with most of the time when you hit a roadblock. This anchoring may explain why some people may think one discrimination class is holding them down while it might be an entirely unrelated factor. You might be inefficiently barking up the wrong tree.

Think of it as a personal tethering. Flawed understanding of any problem can be more harmful than the problem itself. What would Abraham Maslow say?

"If all you have is a hammer, everything looks like a nail."

Conglomerates are often tempted to tether themselves around one issue and blame it for all the obstacles they face. While you may not be able to control all the variables in your life, you can control your own perspective. It is only by having a 360 degree perspective that you can see the open doors, stairs, and highways behind you. When mindfulness leads to self-discovery it becomes a major contributor to your progress.

Confidence

Sometimes potential exclusion makes people lose confidence in themselves, which hinders progress within. Recognizing that fact alone can dramatically change your attitude. This strategy is part of a broader program of planning that includes personal talents. It ensures you can focus on the things only you can do. Working on self-confidence is one of them.

Do you disappear in yourself when your idea is challenged? Do you "over-hedge" your ideas in a way that raises doubt in them? Let's look at patterns of data. The group with more confidence dominates the corporate culture and politics and makes more money. I am not suggesting that confidence is essentially the only reason for wage-gap disparity. But having confidence that you are equally valuable and your ideas matter is part of the fight.

People with more confidence on average make more money than those with less confidence. The salesman with more confidence makes more money. I can go on until you stop saying it is a coincidence.

Do not get me wrong here, I am not talking about arrogance or ego-induced hubris. In a sense, the confidence I am describing here is related to faith and trust that you will succeed. This is especially true if you have done your best and you have given it all your all.

Self-confidence in particular has been linked to high levels of success. Even a display of confidence can work in your favor. It is a self-fulfilling prophecy. Think of it this way: If you don't believe you will succeed, why should others believe in you?

You should feel confident and empowered when you manage your financial future. For the most part, business is an informed gamble. Honing your skills increases your confidence tremendously. This brings us to the competency question.

Competency

As a conglomerate you often find yourself in a situation where you do not have two more strikes. It is one strike and you are out. You can't afford mediocrity. Competency is basically the ability to do a job properly. This is closely related to having the knowledge, skills, and abilities required to complete a specific task. How are you on spreadsheets? Novice, expert, knowledgeable, confidence, competent, or just capable?

There is theory and there is actual practice. It is your duty to work on being the best on your craft. It is also your duty to make sure people know that you are the best. It is part of your personal development. It takes practice, perseverance, and raw, dirty grit.

"We are what we repeatedly do. Excellence, then, is not an act, but a habit." Aristotle

Common Sense

This is the ability to think and behave in a reasonable way and to make good decisions according to your reliable sources. In this life you will be called upon to make responsible decisions without all the facts.

You will need a dose of street smarts. Sometimes it will come down to how much research you have done about a situation. In an interview situation for instance lack of common sense can be detected in the questions you ask. They say there are no stupid questions. Sometimes I wonder if the jury is still out on that.

You may not ask questions that defy laws of gravity. Imagine a candidate in an interview who is given a chance to ask the interviewer questions. He opens his mouth and asks a bunch of questions about the company that he could have researched beforehand. What does this company do? How many warnings do you get before you are fired? Do you do background checks?

You must be prepared. You must research the company, its competitors, its products, its industry, and its goals and successes. This is a part that is within your control. Common sense is currently in extremely short supply. How do you dress? How do you respond to bias in a way that you end up on top?

Commitment

A wise old man once said that the best doctor is an amateur who refused to quit. The best professional you know today is an amateur who refused to quit some time back. It is through hard work and perseverance that you inch your way to your goal. Commitment, they say, is the quality of being dedicated to a cause.

I like to think of commitment in terms of dedication, devotion, and allegiance to a particular goal. Giving it your entire all. You must have a strong commitment to work on your purpose. No school will teach you grit. Studies have been done. Throughout history, people who were deemed more successful and influential than their contemporary counterparts typically possessed tons of grit. Grit is defined as perseverance and passion for long-term goals.

Who needs more mental capital to stay the course amid challenges and setbacks than a bias conglomerate? The zeal and persistence of motive must come from within. Imagine a world without a light bulb. If Thomas Edison and his cohort had given up, we could still be living in darkness.

"Many of life's failures are people who did not realize how close they were to success when they gave up." Thomas Edison

Whenever you are starting a business, it is sometimes hard to get funding for your project; but if you attract a few thousand customers, the investor community starts taking you seriously. Luck favors the diligent. You must stay committed to your strategy and have the confidence you need to successfully execute your plan. What is your plan anyway? You must have a clear plan.

Clarity

We can all agree that no dream is too big and no vision is too bold. But you have to have some goals. You cannot afford to be a headless chicken or a rudderless vessel. Your vision stands tall like a light tower, even when you are feeling bogged down by life's ups and downs. You can see the tip of it even when you are way down.

So long as you can see the light tower you are going in the right direction.

How tall is your light tower? You will need to challenge yourself by setting high goals such that every achievement becomes another step on the staircase toward your greatest, happiest self. And yes, you will need a divine sprinkle of luck. Who doesn't?

You will need to define your own satisfaction and happiness separate from the material measures of success. Money's sugar high will only take you to a certain worldly point, and then you will crash.

You must set personal goals and develop a plan to achieve them. Plan your work and work your plan. If you have trouble defining your goals, start by defining your success. Then move backward toward the start.

What is my definition of success and failure you ask?

Success is that upward-trending "moving average" of life's peaks and inevitable valleys recording the change you have made on your life and that of others. Failure is measured by how long you lie down after you fall. It is the duration of the personal pity party. That attempt to turn sour grapes and spilt milk into aged whine. There you have it.

Nuthology strategy is very introspective in nature. It pushes you to take inventory of your innate strengths and weaknesses, even when the latter involves structural barriers created by others. You then develop killer skills to accentuate your unique capsule of talents.

Life without a personal strategy is like a rudderless ship; it has no clear direction and drifts about bumping into others without reaching a destination. Work ethic as is crucial, but it is just one piece of the puzzle. If you row with all your might without watching what is turning your rudder in the wrong direction, you will either succeed toward that wrong direction or succumb to exhaustion. Working smart is as important as working hard. Execution of the idea is as important as the creation of that idea.

Once you develop your own goals and definition of success, there will be less pressure to be perpetually alarmed. Positive affirmations usually do not work unless they are part of a comprehensive program of self-growth. Soldiers in the trenches depend on planning and strategies, not positive affirmations alone.

Social exclusion is a complex problem. It is naïve to think that just happy thoughts will mitigate the issue. No amount of pseudo-psychological cheerleading from those feel-good "millionaire makers" will do you any good if all you are seeking is passion but no goals. Ask those who have been doing it for years. You must have some plan, written or otherwise.

When Will You Consider Yourself a Success?

Nuthology is about setting up a bottom-up operation as opposed to the usual top-down expectations. The only way you can live deliberately, boldly, and consciously is to design the definition of your own success.

Develop goals with measurable benchmarks of success and tangible timelines. The exhilaration of achievement of short term goals acts like a pit stop: it spurs more thrust toward the main goal. These short goal mile markers will boost your happiness tremendously as you cross them on your way to the long-term vision. When would you consider yourself a short-time success? Is it some wealth accumulation? Having lifestyle options? Increased free time? Creating social impact? Making connections with friends and family? Traveling around the clock, around this rock? Whatever creeks fill your well will make you feel well. At this point what matters is that you own the definition of your success.

6

Affiliation

The Oblivious Members

Frank, a resident neurologist at the State Research Hospital, had dearly missed his three high school buddies. Two of them were actually his first cousins. He was happy to spend some few hours with them shooting some pool. When they asked for a ride to the nearby gas station to grab some smokes, it was not a big deal. He did what any friend would do in this neighborhood. He didn't even think twice.

Frank has been out of the loop for most of the last seven years. Medical school was more involving than he had originally anticipated. But it was worth every minute. The whole community was proud to call him doctor.

The two cousins got in the back and a friend of theirs in the front seat. Frank would later swore he didn't see the guns when the three got in. He started the car and his lifelong nightmare as the fourth bandit.

How would he have known their little robbery plans? He also had no idea that the two cousins had outstanding warrants. Why would he risk such a promising career to be a getaway driver for some thugs? They stole twenty-eight dollars and two cents, for heaven's sake! But theft was the least of his problems.

The team also mortally wounded an innocent customer. That was the biggest issue in the courtroom and for the perpetually salivating news media. The hardworking father of three was just grabbing a gallon of milk when his life was cut short by a bullet. It later turned out to be a mistaken identity situation, a fact that made even the suspects tear up in court. His only crime was his choice of a simple T-shirt. An innocent man was dead just because he was inadvertently wearing a shirt a with popular local rival gang's colors. It beats any shred of common sense. This is what Frank when to school to get away from.

The state law was very clear. If a person is wounded or killed in the commission of a robbery, it didn't matter who pulled the trigger. Dr. Frank was part of the gang of four as far as the prosecution was concerned. The cameras placed him in the driver's seat. "Lock the doors and throw away the keys!" the prosecutor screamed. Will the twelve members of the jury buy the doctors defense?

Fictional Case Studies

If you are looking for a smoking gun, legal gibberish, and the splitting of hairs, I hate to disappoint you. The above story is not true, so don't get lost in the legal mumbo jumbo. I will be using such cases throughout this book for your entertainment. Don't forget that this is a book about money, not a novel. Like I said in the introduction, the characters and actions in the case studies are purely fictitious.

These stories do not show anything that doesn't happen every day. In the above case, for instance, I wanted to show how both Dr. Frank and the innocent customer were sucked into this unfortunate situation from different affiliation angles. So stay with me at the "not a legal expert" level.

Manifestation of Affiliation-Based Social Exclusion

There is no doubt that you are who you are when no one is looking. What about when someone is looking? What about when the person looking is a gatekeeper of some sorts? In the context of career and business planning, we will take a wider view when it comes to the definition of affiliation.

Gatekeepers, for instance, might view some social networks and professional clubs as affiliation positives. Gangs and cartels, real or alleged, may be viewed as negatives. Unions, political, religious, and activist affiliations may go either way depending on the backdrop in question.

Like any other street-level judgments, affiliation does not have to be real. Perceptions play a big role. Perceived membership or non-membership in a certain group category can cost you financially.

Social exclusion on the basis of affiliation and can take many routes:

- Unfair hiring, firing, promotion, and demotions
- Partial and targeted enforcement of company policies, standards, and production expectations
- Denial of business opportunities

Although most of my examples in this book are business or workplace related, this can happen in any situation: housing, law enforcement, justice system, social services.

Discrimination based on political affiliation is well documented. History is full of cases where intellectual freethinkers and dissidents whose ideas and views ran against those of the mainstream were accused of belonging to an organized group.

In academic circles where a candidate has been involved in politics or has opinions that are widely published, political affiliation will come into play when he or she is applying for a job in a rival party's territory. A known conservative may face hell working in a liberal ecosystem if he is lucky enough to get a position. The opposite is also true. Even your former employer's ideology may be viewed as yours. Faculty members have been denied tenure because of their politics.

For practical or political reasons, many employers avoid hiring people who have declared any political affiliation or activism on their resumes or in public profiles unless the company directly deals with politics. The law of public opinion states that personnel is policy. As a public relations and marketing strategy a political party may avoid hiring outspoken members of a rival party. Who will say corporate employers may not follow the same law?

We have seen government agencies targeting political groups with audits and denial of services. It is not uncommon to hear stories of elected leaders denying people in certain neighborhoods services just because they voted for a rival.

There are areas where unions, cohorts, sororities, fraternities, crime syndicates, cartels, and other non-state actors have great influence over who gets a job or a contract. We have seen companies that won't hire union workers. Those who work in contract dependent jobs know that procurement of tenders, contracts, and small business deals may depend on some affiliation whether legal or illegal. This exclusion is alive.

Conglomeration of Exclusion Factors NUBC

Like fine wine, this factor works well with other social exclusion factors to deliver a devastating blow to a conglomerate's dream. Consider a long-term unemployed job candidate who dresses in a certain way that makes him appear to be associated with criminal elements even when that is just a stereotype. The racial-minority youth lives in a bad neighborhood with a distant aunt and needs transportation but has a bad credit history. A hiring gatekeeper might see:

Affiliation
Age
Race
Place
Social class
Unemployment
Credit history
Shelter

These elements might work in concert to propel the poverty orbit with unimaginable gravitational force.

Nuthology Strategy

At the personal level, the first thing is to seek a comprehensive solution for all factors, not each separately like most of society approaches it. This strategy is about optimization of your talents in a challenging backdrop. The NUBC review is designed to be used in tandem with your strengths analysis as part of a comprehensive personal approach. Your success will therefore depend on how you manage both the capsule of talents and your unique exclusion factors. Learning how affiliation can be used to exclude you should be a part of your financial strategy.

Index Calculations

You will have to answer a few questions in order to count this as a social exclusion factor. Are you qualified to perform? Is this factor potentially relevant, consequential, and applicable in your given situation?

Feel free to include any bias that is related to actual or perceived affiliation in this category if it is not covered under another admitted class. Matriculation and personal association bias also fall in this category.

There Is No One Silver Panacea

These perceptions may not be fair, legal, or moral but affiliation bias was admitted in the index because it exists. Even the recognition that this happens in and of itself can keep you out of harm's way. Pretending they don't exist when you a looking for a job, promotion, or dealing with a gatekeeper is not a wise decision. Since this is a personal index, it doesn't affect everybody all the time.

Addressing Gatekeepers' Concerns and Dilemmas

In a workplace backdrop, the distance between your values and those of the gatekeepers will determine the cultural fit. The gatekeeper must be able to see his company in you. Personal branding, when used effectively, will help mitigate this exclusion. It is your duty to anticipate the gatekeeper's real and imagined concerns that might affect your goals. If you do not belong to a certain bad group, for example, do not dress, talk, walk or give indications that you belong to them just to fit in a certain environment. Do you wear a game face that makes you look like you just swallowed seventeen toxic lemons? No big deal, you just want to project a bad boy image to achieve coveted street credibility. If you walk and dress like a member of a certain group, you are a de facto member of that group. The gatekeepers will not distinguish between the pretenders and the real ones. They see how you present yourself as your brand.

There may be nothing wrong with being a hipster by choice, but let us say you are not a hipster. Your hairstyle, dressing, facial hair, body art, and number of baths per year can place you in that group in an instant. You don't want to be seen as representing some anti-establishment cultural phenomenon inadvertently. Some hiring managers may view you as a potential risk.

You Are Who You Caucus With

I read somewhere recently that if you are always accompanied by four losers, the public always sees five losers. I found that "street wisdom" somewhat insulting but, amazingly, rather interesting.

You know surrounding yourself with the right people will greatly affect your success, but Nuthology is interested in how you are perceived through some affiliation or lack thereof. You may be a thousand times better than the company you keep, but it looks like what your mother said was right: You are who you hang out with. You are who your friends are. You are who you surround yourself with. Need I say birds of a feather flock together? Whether it is fair or not, you are only as good as the company you keep as far as public opinion is concerned.

Expand Your Networks

It is always advisable to have some control over the kind of people you surround yourself with. Your network should include achievers in your target market. Join professional memberships and clubs that advance your mobility efforts. People you surround yourself with can make or break your happiness, success, and growth.

Control Your Information

How is this factor known? Employers and other gatekeepers are a microcosm of society. We know employers, for example, conduct thorough background checks of potential employees. It is possible they will come across personal information that may lead them to make biased conclusions, even when they are required to be objective.

Apart from the company you keep, there is published work, news, social-media presence, background checks, resumes, stickers, flags, symbols, hairstyles, dress, and body art. A means of transportation can put you in a certain flagged class. There are also universal symbols of thugs, gangsters, and rebellion. You may have family members who are politically exposed. You can be excluded based on ideas, belief systems, and opinions.

Professional Help

Some jurisdictions prohibit discrimination based on political affiliation. This is a global book, so I won't go into specifics. It is good to always consult with an attorney with the appropriate level of experience if you have any questions concerning affiliation or any other discrimination in your country.

Reducing Your Own Stereotype-Driven Aggression

Avoid spreading unfounded affiliation rumors about people. Occultism and secret society rumors, for example, can ruin somebody's financial or political life. Try running for office if you are rumored to hold an annual retreat in the foggy purple forest where you and your secret society seek wisdom from the giant frog and perform weird rituals.

Speak Up

Nuthology is an individual approach, but as a member of your society and the global human community you still have a duty to speak up. A lot of affiliation-related social exclusions are stereotypically and sometimes unconsciously propagated. We live in a world where people can be assumed to belong to a group based merely on physical attributes. Advocate for horizontal coexistence where no one is treated unfairly because of some perceived affiliation.

7

Age

Take My Advice. I Don't Need It

Mr. Waithood and his twenty-five-year-old son, Lolest Elmao Waithood, have been in bad books for the last three months. Both are currently unemployed technicians. Lolest argues that it is the older people who are causing the unemployment problems in the country. He has a job ad to prove it.

"Ten years of experience required."

His dad, Mr. Waithood, has a different take. He is convinced that it is the young people who are causing the problems. He also has a job ad to prove it.

"Great job for a recent grad. This is a great position for someone in their twenties or thirties."

Lolest's mother, Mrs. Arbitress Waithood, agreed to moderate a debate over dinner. The order was decided by a coin toss.

Arbitress: Lolest, you go first. You won the coin toss.

Lolest: If I was an employer I would be concerned about hiring older workers because of many reasons. I can name a few. Outdated workplace habits, higher health costs, lower job performance, higher accident rates and slow adaptation to change.

What about lack of updated technological skills and dynamism? Older workers are less flexible and harder to train, especially on technical skills. They may also lack speed. If a job is highly physical, one has to deal with chronic age-related health issues like arthritis, osteoporosis, and falls. That is not all.

Older people are always overqualified. They will want too much money to match their former job's pay. That means they are less satisfied because of the sudden pay cut and are likely to quit for better opportunities. I would assume they will not stay with the company; they will be waiting to retire or for their old industry to come back.

Arbitress: Lolest has laid out some serious concerns. How do you respond?

Waithood: Lolest, you should be ashamed of yourself. I raised you better than that. One day if you are lucky, you will grow old.

Arbitress: Waithood, can you give a response based on points.

Waithood: Older people are the perfect employees. Well, where do I start? Obviously older people are more experienced and have tons of transferable skills. They have a provable credibility trail. They are more dedicated. Mature workers tend to stay longer, less job hopping, numbers don't lie.

This is a kicker. They tend to attract other older workers who have disposable income and can turn into customers. What income do these parasitic punks have? Older employees require minimum supervision or training. They hit the ground running. They have better people skills and manners that are unquestionable.

Since we already have responsibilities, we are much more responsible, well, just look at me. We need less coddling, less constant praise, unlike today's fragile generation. Less whining about little broken affairs like you know who here. Better work ethics. Do I need to mention no gum chewing in the conference rooms? How about less drama and less social media at work? We are talking uninterrupted productivity.

Disciplined and committed. A direct product of growing up in the greatest generation.

Less distracted and exhausted with kids all grown up. We are not waiting for a school bus or reporting to a school nurse every waking minute. I would never hire these young bums to save my life.

Arbitress: Lolest, five minutes.

Lolest: Are all young people naïve and ignorant? Are all old people automatically wiser and experienced? Is being old in itself an achievement? In this country you are only in a protected class after you turn forty. I have to wait fifteen years for age discrimination laws to protect me. There is a structural pattern of youth discrimination. With age comes wisdom, said an old man. Where is a quote by a young man?

Waithood: Permanently tethered to their little gadgets, young people nowadays have no morals, ethics, or values. They are all arrogant, pompous, ignorant, and self-centered, starting with your own son here. They do not uphold faith-based values like we did in our day and continue to do.

Look at this ad:

"Great job for a recent grad. This is a great position for someone in their twenties or thirties." Aren't these code words for "don't even try if you are fifty-five"?

Lolest: No, look at this ad. "Ten years of experience required." How many twenty-five-year-old engineers do you know have ten years of experience? This does not make any sense at all. How do I get experience if no one will give me a job? Statistics show the unemployment number for younger people is always higher than that of older workers. You said it. Numbers don't lie. Let me get this straight. Young people who are healthier are paid less than older workers who are less healthy and slower. Go figure.

Waithood: I have to make myself look younger every day. I have to talk like I am social-media savvy. Who needs a thousand stupid fake friends who can't even help you move a table?

Lolest: I have to wear a stupid watch, fake reading glasses, conservative clothing, and carry an empty brief case to look old and hirable. I think the older workers who failed to save in their youth are having to delay retirement at our expense. And I get it: nothing is more boring than a retirement without income to enjoy it.

Waithood: Don't go there! In my day we respected our elders.

Arbitress: Stop, Waithood. Please, stop. I have to end this debate. We don't seem to be reaching a middle ground; if anything I think you guys are drifting apart.

Manifestation of Age-Based Social Exclusion

This is one exclusion factor that is quite universal. The risk of age discrimination exists at both extremes of the working population. There are tons of stereotypes to trade from each side, some of which are portrayed in the fictional case study above. This depends on your backdrop. Who is old anyway? The index does not define age because it will depend on your specific situation. If you are running for president at thirty-eight years old, you are technically too young. If, on the other hand, you want to be a world class gymnast at thirty-eight years old, you may be viewed as a dinosaur.

In most companies discrimination against older job candidates is an unwritten policy. It is an open secret that you can see from miles away. There are high occurrences of age-related unfairness in different industries.

Age discrimination and underemployment affects older workers in a special way. They have more responsibilities, including taking care of their young unemployed dependents. People are turned down every day for being overqualified; the older person is more likely to be in this category.

In a perfect world age should just be a number. That is utopia. This is the third rock from the sun. Welcome home. You just need to look at the attitude toward aging. How about the market for antiaging cocktails, injections, miracle pills, surgeries, creams, and dyes? The list is endless. Antiaging and longevity is multi-billion-dollar industry. Oh, the elusive fountain of youth can be expensive.

Youth Social Exclusion

Like I said before, ageism swings both ways. If you read books written centuries ago you will find complaints about the youth of the day. It is comical that every generation thinks the younger generation is full of suckers. They are social parasites that do not know the value of work and always glued to their new shiny pieces of rock.

In some regions youth social exclusion is considered a normal transition to adulthood. The reasoning behind the blocked transition to adulthood is that everyone goes through youth. "It is the elders' turn to eat. Sit down and shut up." These power structures organically marginalize the youth, leaving no legitimate energy outlet. Youth social exclusion is a major political, economic, and security problem in many countries today. Unemployment, underemployment and limitless youth energy is always a bad combination.

Then there is the garden variety catch-22. You need experience to get a job. But wait! You actually need a job to get that experience. How do you get experience if no one will give you a job? In most countries the unemployment number for younger people is always higher than that of older workers. Young people often lament the fact that they are paid less than older workers who may be less productive.

The youth also may face age-related contempt issues. Is being old in itself an automatically unearned privilege or an immutable natural phenomenon? In most cultures the authority and wisdom of elder people is held in serious reverence. It is beyond questionable by default. This can also mean that the older generation can wield enormous power. Is it possible to have old people who are not wise?

Most property and capital resources are owned by the older generation. There is some dictatorial authority that comes with that. Inheritance, retirement, and estate planning are also at the center of the financial battles between generations. The older generation often doubts the younger generation's ability to tackle the future. Their parents probably did the same thing.

Delayed retirement due to a change in economic environment or lack of planning by the older generation means the jobs that would naturally go to the younger generation will not be available.

Conglomeration of Exclusion Factors, NUBC

Age can make you less attractive in some industries. If you are a female who works in front of a camera or in some client-facing jobs you may find yourself at the congruence of age, gender, weight, and attractiveness exclusions. There are also age-related diseases, disorders, and disabilities that can come into play as time progresses. It is therefore not uncommon to see a combination of exclusion factors working harmoniously together.

Ageism
Attractiveness
Gender
Weight
Disability
Disease stigma
Long-term unemployment

This is just an example. If you add other factors like parenthood and shelter this becomes an even bigger challenge.

Nuthology Strategy

At the personal level, you are either old or young in a particular backdrop. There is no conflict there. Learning how age can be used to exclude you should be a part of your financial strategy. It gives you a wakeup call to think ahead and act preemptively. Ask yourself the right questions. What will happen if you lose the youthful look for which you were hired? Suppose you are a twenty-four-year-old female manager and all of your ten direct reports are sixty-year-old men. What soft skills would you need? These guys were thirty-six years old when you were born, for crying baby's sake! These are risks that may never materialize but they are concerns.

If you are young, find a way to network with the older crowd where there are more opportunities. It might require you to show some respect. A lot of elders have a lot to offer when it comes to character, etiquette, protocol, and personal branding.

Sooner or later you will discover that there is some wisdom that comes from having gone through an experience. Some of that experience can be passed down. That is efficiency for you because you don't have to go through it or you can use it to avoid landmines. As you grow older you will appreciate your elders more. I am reminded of a classic quote from an age expert.

"When I was a boy of 14, my father was so ignorant I could hardly stand to have the old man around. But when I got to be 21, I was astonished at how much the old man had learned in seven years." Mark Twain

Expand Your Network

Try the great-ships strategy from the SCHOOL section. Aggressively seek network relationships, mentorships, internships, and apprenticeships. You should try these early in life so that you can deal with the proverbial "chicken and egg" question. Which came first? The experience or the job?

For those getting out of college, I would say it is not wise to spend years waiting for the job of your life. You must start somewhere, especially if you are dealing with a tricky NUBC catalog. Every day that you don't work makes you less employable. In most cases it is far much easier to find a job when you are working than when you are unemployed. At the very least your nerves are calmer when you have gas money.

Reducing Your Own Stereotype-Driven Aggression for the Younger Generation

Remember that youth is temporary. Youth and beauty are fragile and quickly diminishing natural resources. If that is all you have to offer, expect some swift and accelerated depletion. That's planning that only you can do.

I hope Nuthology strategy will motivate you to treat the older applicants with respect and empathy. Although growing up is optional, growing old is inevitable. What will be your unique bias conglomeration then?

If you are lucky to live long enough, you will notice a few more wrinkles and thinning hair on the horizon. There will be dark yellowish teeth and other features that may come with aging, and, depending on the society, you may be viewed as not being attractive. Your exclusion conglomeration will change drastically. You will want younger people to respect you.

Even when taking care of immediate financial concerns, you should plan for the fact that you will get older. There are many other finance-related problems that are related to age. These will require proactive financial planning. The earlier you do it the better.

Try savings plans that offer an automatic component. I hope issues that are raised in this chapter will inspire you to prepare for later years. If you ask me, I would begin saving for retirement with your first job. Why? Assuming you get the job out of college starting early has big dividends. First, beginning to save early means you can save smaller amounts. It gives the money more time to grow and soak up impressive compound investment gains. You may have fewer major obligations like mortgages and kids.

The financial habits you develop when you are young are going to go with you into your adulthood. There is a great deal of information about retirement available on the web, so I won't bore you with schematics here. I have to admit that getting motivated to save for something that will happen decades from now is not easy. Thinking about aging and reading about the struggles that older people are facing is a good motivator.

If you are an older candidate, there are many things that are still under your control at the personal level. Let us start with toning down the vitriol, if any.

Reducing Your Own Stereotype-Driven Aggression for the Older Generation

"What's wrong with kids today?" This question is as old as mankind. There is always the risk that the older generation will see the new one in terms of fewer producers and more takers. After all, you have to feed, clothe, and provide them with shelter for at least two decades.

In most cases each new generation has had it easier than the last in terms of technology. The fact is you can get lazy people from any generation. We have millions of young people with great work ethics and intelligence and who are highly motivated. You also will find the whiny, entitled, parasitic, spoiled, and selfish ones. You can say that with any generation.

The kid isn't all that different than you when you were his age. There is one thing that has been the same for thousands of years: the young will grow up and become productive people just like all the generations before them.

Are all young people a bunch of selfie-taking, gadget-addicted, self-absorbed, and narcissistic crybabies? Are they all sitting in the basement trying to develop an app that will one day make them a sandwich and fund their retirement? Of course it is not fair to categorize a generation of people with one stereotype.

Expand Your Networks

Naturally the young have more cultural dexterity than the older generation. In today's diverse world you may have to change approaches to life. Getting stuck in what was normal in your youth may work against you. I would suggest you develop networks that go beyond your generation. That is what great leaders have always done. Develop a partnership mentorship that benefits both generations.

Address Gatekeepers' Concerns and Dilemmas

It is your duty to research gatekeepers' fears and needs. Finding ways to satisfy them is the way you will get compensated.

Information Control

Avoid calling attention to age itself unless experience is a plus. Are you slowly developing some rebellion against the present generation and an increasing longing for your wildly romanticized youth? Avoid starting all sentences with "Back in the good old days," especially in an interview situation with a younger manager. Romanticized view of the past can be very limiting. If you really miss steam engine typewriters, keep it to yourself. The more you paint yourself as a dinosaur, the more others will believe it. Underscoring your age can increase the distance between your values and those of the young gatekeepers who are charged with determining if you are a cultural fit.

Perform some research on the commonly asked and unasked questions in your industry. We don't have many employees who are your age, would that bother you? Will you be comfortable working for someone younger? What are your salary requirements?

Be careful about bringing up health concerns unless it is very necessary. The company is looking for help when they call you for interview. Keep in shape if possible. Looks shouldn't mater but they do. If you live in an ecosystem where the older generation is known to disregard the new technology or that is the stereotype coming in, this automatically creates a risk that your technology skills might be examined more than normal. Refresh your skills, keep pace with technology, new processes, and social avenues.

If you are facing long-term unemployment, you might consider volunteering instead of sitting at home. You can put that experience on the resume instead of a yawning time gap.

Go where you are wanted. Some businesses are very demographic oriented even when they have no official policy on age. It is your duty to read between the lines. Avoid age-biased job listings that may end up wasting your time and energy. Seek companies that value employees. Forward-looking employers know that an age diverse workforce is effective, productive, and motivated.

Other Age-Related Financial Concerns

Some people find themselves abandoning retirement involuntarily. There are many things that cause this. Financial planning is one of them. How you spend your retirement funds is as important as how you built them. Knowing your "decumulation" number is critical. Factoring in taxes, entertainment, and basic expenses, what percentage of your nest egg could you afford to access each year? How much do you plan on spending each month?

Take advantage of technology and avoid being uninformed to an extent that you are forced to turn over your finances to someone else before you are ready to.

The fountain of youth can also swallow your precious coins. Some antiaging procedures are not only harmful to your health, they also drain your wallet and retirement funds. Learning how age can be used to exclude you should be a part of your financial strategy. At the societal level, you should find ways to contribute to the ageism debate. Speak up against this and any other exclusion class. Advocate for horizontal cross-generational relations rather than your age-group superiority.

8

Alma Mater, Credentials

What School Did You Go To?

It is not often that you find kids scrambling over a school. But there is a reason students cry to go Elytate University. Elytate is not your father's garden variety college. This school has produced more presidents, more world leaders, more Nobel Prize winners, and more fortune 500 CEOs than any other college in the world. It is the place to go if you hope to make top management in your first fifteen years or earn a salary worth writing home about in this country.

Elytate hires the best leaders in every industry as faculty and pays them handsomely. However, most of the value is on reputation, perception, and hype. They call it goodwill. This school is literary the congruent of what you know and who you know. Let's face it, who you know in this school is not your regular lame backyard tricks six-pack draining Uncle Joe. These are the children of "who's who" and the grandchildren of "get out of here."

The school costs an arm and a leg if you manage to get the ridiculously high score required for those without valuable connections. One years' tuition is higher than double the country's median income. It is therefore reserved for the children of the wealthy. The intimidating admissions and financial requirements ensure that the low-income crowd is, for the most part, kept at bay. They still make sure to throw in a few low-income students to hide their footprints and create some smoke screen.

Elytate's name on a resume makes a recruiter freeze on his way to the trash can. Companies demand that management hire consultants from the Elytate. If you are a CEO, you better recruit from Elytate. That's the unwritten policy. If you decide to hire a consultant from a mediocre ranked school and the company underperforms even for totally unrelated reasons, your decision will be questioned. The poor performance will be attributed to the apparently poor hiring decision.

The alumni-loaded endowment pipeline ensures Elytate will remain on top of the coveted school rankings with generous faculty salaries and an unparalleled student standard of living. The value of connections in this school cannot be ignored. It is this in-group favoritism that creates inequality far beyond the steel gates of Elytate University. If you don't want to retire a worthless cube dweller, go to Elytate.

Manifestation of Alma Mater or Credential-Based Social Exclusion

When most people think of bias, the first thing that comes to mind are the popular classes like race, religion, gender, age, or disability. In some industries, however, where you went to school makes a big difference. Since most students go to college in order to get better jobs, the financial impact to the affected candidate is huge. When combined with other exclusion factors, alma mater bias can stealthily produce a permanent underclass.

Does your Alma Mater Matter?

Naturally we're more generous in our perceptions of fellow members of our own in groups. School happens to be one of those groups. We know cases where parental bias for their alma mater may have crossed the line of civility. We are more likely to donate to the schools we attended. Using the same thinking, is it possible to have unconscious biases related to alma mater? One of the assumptions of Nuthology is that gatekeepers are a microcosm of our society. They may have unconscious biases. What a gatekeeper might see as gut instinct may just be a gut overflowing with preconceived judgments.

It is common to hear blanket statements on the street about people who went to certain colleges behaving in a certain manner and the gatekeepers believing that to be the gospel truth. "Oh, that is a party school, no education happens there. I love the other school, everybody is well behaved."

In major corporations, alumni from same school can form watercooler cliques to discuss common issues and alma mater sports statistics. These groups later play a big role in middle-level management decisions, which include hiring, promotion, or layoff. That may cut out the crowd that did not go to the same school as that group.

Like many other biases discussed in this book, it is all about perception as opposed to the ability to perform the job. If the general sentiment moves toward a certain aspect of a candidate, the gatekeepers will naturally pick the perceived winners.

Let's look at the numbers for a minute. Is it a coincidence that a majority of the biggest company CEOs in the USA are products of less than fifteen colleges? Is it a coincidence that for the last three decades the USA has elected mostly Ivy League graduates as president even when a top school degree is not a job requirement?

One of the clearest forms of this bias are college rankings by magazines. Emphasis on school rankings creates outright discrimination against graduates of lower-tiered schools. There is even a pejorative term for the graduates of third-tier schools. We have reached a point where school rankings have become more important than the individual graduates' personal values. In some countries school rankings are so subjective that they are just status symbols, not unlike beauty pageants.

First of all, these rankings are misleading to parents, students, and potential employers. There are students who abandon their individual goals in pursuit of the highest rated school. The fixation creates confusion and disrupts the personal career planning processes. I have to add that some rankings have very suspicious weighing criteria if you look at them seriously.

It is hard for most institutions to ignore the rankings because of their ability to create an artificial halo effect and revenue sources.

Some majors are more school sensitive than others.Wall street investment banks and big-name law firms, for example, still place a great value on Ivy League graduates. A lot of connections are made while in school. It is therefore not surprising that the graduates are able to get top positions. It is worth noting that some of these graduates already come from very wealthy and well-connected families to begin with.

Please note that this can have an opposite effect depending on your backdrop. Ivy leaguers can also be stigmatized as elitist, demanding, and lacking that "fire in the belly." There is a sizeable group of hiring managers out there who can't stand elite school graduates. They may be perceived to have high salary expectations, which may scare away employers.

National Origin

Another form of alma mater–related double standard is directed to the foreign educated. None feels the bias against alma mater more than foreign educated immigrant graduates. Most degrees from developing countries are perceived to be worthless in developed nations. There are thousands of university-educated immigrants working dead-end, low-skill, or low-pay jobs. They are unable to find any sort of employment in their fields due to their credentials not being recognized. Even considering that a small part of that group is trying to pass licensing exams in their fields, an MBA from Blalalaland may not be worth the paper it is written on.

Credentials

If the number of people with college degrees is high in your population and you don't have one, it may not matter if college education is necessary to perform the job tasks. In this case, it will be necessary as a filtering mechanism.

Schooling can act as a perfect filter, especially in areas where a marginalized group did not receive adequate basic education to begin with. When schooling is used as a method of elimination rather than a qualification, it becomes a subtle form of exclusion. The credentials are therefore being used primarily as mere exclusion tools.

In this backdrop, gatekeepers may require an academic degree for a job that can be done perfectly without formal study. This over-emphasis on credentials when hiring ensures only the educated get job, which ends up being the current dominant group. How convenient?

One of the assumptions of the Nuthology Index is that a candidate must be qualified to perform. Since that credentialism ensures that the candidate does qualify in the first place, it becomes a perfect for bias gatekeepers.

What about the election of future policy makers? Even with financial success, one may face education-related bias when looking for an elected office job. An example would be a candidate running for an elected office where the lack of a college degree may not be a disqualification by itself but may be a potentially powerful distraction. Is it a coincidence that the last time the United States elected a non-degreed president was seventy years ago even when college education is not a job requirement? If it is hard for everybody, it will be harder for a conglomerate to be elected to a high office without a college degree.

Grade

There is a lot more subjectivity in grading than we like to acknowledge. This also makes room for unfairness. A gatekeeper who absolutely hates "your kind" may have a final decision to something that will change your life. There are lenient institutions that dish As like peanuts. Why are so many of the students getting As? Should the professor be intentionally inflating grades just to keep students in his program? There are schools that set limits on how many people should get what grades. They may set an arbitrary limit. They might say, for instance, that there should be no more than four As per class. Why shouldn't you get an A if you earned it? Why shouldn't there be a lot of As? All these students are expected to compete for graduate school, a professional opportunity, internships, or jobs as if all As were the same.

Conglomeration of Exclusion Factors NUBC

In a workplace backdrop, alma mater–based and in-group favoritism can go undetected. It is viewed as harmless fun when employees support their old school's sports team. Nothing is inherently wrong with that. When this factor is added to others like place, race, social class, gender, or national origin it becomes a very effective exclusion class.

Nuthology Strategy

Learning how alma mater and credentialism can be used to exclude you should be a part of your financial strategy. It is not whether your school was good or bad. The distance between your values and those of the gatekeepers will determine the cultural fit.

Alma mater and credentialism are just concerns. Do not let them stop you. They are risks that may never materialize, but they are concerns that need to be addressed. There is no such thing as one best college for everybody. How well you do in college is often more important than which college you attend. It is not necessarily performance but personal growth.

It is important to educate yourself on career and school choices. Remember, school admission advisers work for the school. You should do enough research for yourself. Find the college that matches your capsule of talents, ambition, abilities, and all of your unique exclusion concerns with the realities of the job market. In this context, you must research if your college major is alma mater sensitive. There are also other things to consider when choosing a college, like cost, climate, proximity to family, and the size of and type of school.

How much this factor matters will depend on your field. There are times this factor can work for you, especially if the potential employer is familiar with the school's coursework.

Addressing Gatekeepers' Concerns and Dilemmas

Credentialism can also work the opposite way. People who are very educated can be forced to hide or downplay their credentials to get into a wage earning occupation, especially in a recession. Try getting a simple cleaning job when brandishing three PhDs. You just want an entry-level barista job after a sudden lay off? The gatekeeper may view your academic qualifications as a flight risk. You will be out as soon as the economic condition improves. He is not stupid. He knows you didn't get the two masters to clean toilets or deal with the hostile morning crowd. Do you see the gatekeeper's concern? Again, it is your backdrop that dictates your NUBC at a particular context.

Speak Up Regardless of Status

Become an advocate for horizontal coexistence where no one is treated unfairly because of his or her alma mater.

9

Astrology

The Annual Baby Boom

"Gemini, Libra, and Aquarius wanted to work in city gyms, libraries, and aquariums!" screams the billboard sign. August ushers in the best season for the kids in this town. Well, only if you are a Virgleones. This is a lucky group of kids who were born either under Virgo or Leo star signs. Forty-five percent of people in this city are Virgleones.

This acceptable star sign prejudice is based on the dominant zodiac signs. Little attention is paid to educate kids that are not Virgleones. They have limited prospects for opportunities or meaningful relationships.

Most companies will never hire other candidates unless they cannot find a qualified Leo or Virgo. It is not a coincidence that all mayors for the last one hundred years have been Leos and that the county seat symbol is a lion.

"August is the time of the year that the sun is in line with twenty-eight celestial bodies," says Galileo, a senior hiring manager at the biggest company in the city. "Virgleones are very industrious and loyal employees, unlike those born under other zodiac signs," he adds.

Not everybody is happy with this arrangement. Patrick was born in April, and he is becoming a big campaigner against this prejudice. He is especially disturbed by the fact that hiring managers like

Galileo openly support a practice that excludes 65 percent of the population.

Patrick believes in astrology but opposes Virgleones supremacy. He recently presented a simple explanation to a human rights body that has attracted the world's attention. His argument was simple.

"November is a month of harvest, festivals, graduations, marriages, and weddings in this city. December's brutal winter forces people to stay indoors. Things happen when you lock newlyweds in the house for weeks. Obviously, nine months later we have the annual baby boom. Well, that will be August. It is grade school biology, stupid!" Patrick opined. His theory has attracted researchers' attention from across the globe.

Manifestation of Star-Based Social Exclusion

One of the oldest, most durable, and most popular human prejudices is discrimination by star sign. Many cultures have attached importance to astrology dating back thousands of years. Do the heavens rule over one's destiny?

In this book, the words horoscope, Zodiac, and astrology are used interchangeably. That is how most non-experts understand them. Other sources may carry very different definitions. Almost every country has some version of astrology. Some very successful people have been known to consult personal astrologers. Some prominent politicians and government leaders around the world have been known to consult the stars before holding elections, declaring wars, or toppling governments.

Is it Rational to Deny the Power of Irrational Forces?

Like any other immutable factor in the Nuthology Index, gatekeepers may use astrology to classify individuals according to stereotypes. If these people are denied opportunities or freedom based on this prejudice, it cannot be fair. It is a fate-of-birth-based discrimination like race or gender. You are still prejudging an individuals based on generalized beliefs about a group.

Astrological Sign Motivated Negative-Stereotype Confirmation

Negative-stereotype confirmation is defined in various sources as the experience of anxiety in a situation in which a person has the potential to confirm a negative stereotype about his social group.

Suppose your sign says you are not trustworthy and have a quick temper. You are impatient and impulsive, stubborn, bullheaded, moody, and hypersensitive. Your star also says you are indecisive. Is there a risk that you may internalize this analysis, become less productive, and consequently confirm the prophecy? Don't ask me; I am just a clueless Orion!

Horoscopes have been used to explain aspects of a person's personality and even predict future events. This often opens room for partiality and favoritism. It also can give a false sense of connection. In some cases zodiac bias promotes confirmation. Is it okay to use astrology as part of the hiring process? Should we use candidates' horoscopes instead of their qualifications and experience?

If this was not about denying people a chance to earn a living, it would be a good joke. Forget education, skills, talents, abilities, or any individual merits. Under what sign were you born? You are hired! Consider a person already classified as a pathological liar according to ethnic stereotype whose blood type is work negative and per the zodiac was born in the year of the snail. He has this strange handwriting that shows he cannot be trusted. His scull dimensions indicates that he may not be the hirable kind. Okay, take a chuckle break.

There are no better examples of immutable attributes than your ethnicity, blood type, and birthday. Surprisingly, these over-the-chart discriminations happen in modern economies.

Conglomeration of Exclusion Factors NUBC

In the countries where this factor is a big issue, it can add to other exclusion bases. Consider a conglomerate who is already facing gender, age, and attractiveness exclusion concerns. She reads that her star says she is moody, hypersensitive, and indecisive. There is a risk that she will sell herself short or make low-ball goals for herself. Astrology can be the factor that confirms the others.

Zodiac
Gender
Attractiveness
Age

Nuthology Strategy

Learning how astrology can be used to exclude you should be a part of your financial strategy. This might also save you time. If you know that a company uses this method to recruit, you might decide not to waste your time pursuing them.

Conglomerate all your concerns, including this factor, when setting your goals or planning a career. You have your capsule of talents and abilities. It is not whether astrology is good or bad here. You don't have to believe in astrology for this exclusion to be a concern. It can have an indirect effect on your decisions.

Consider a war general dealing with enemies who believe in astrology. The general may hire his own "star" experts for prediction advice. This general does not have to believe in astrology per se. But this is where it all makes sense. If the enemy is making decisions based on zodiac signs, wouldn't you want to know? In fact, you can use it to predict their moves. This is the point of our discussion here, not whether astrology is accurate or not.

Speak Up Regardless of Status

No child chooses the day he or she was born. At the societal level, be an advocate for horizontal coexistence where no one is treated unfairly because of the day he or she was born.

10

Attractiveness, Lookism, Grooming

Facial Discrimination

Helen MonaLiza of New Sparta City, an aspiring gospel singer, has been waiting for this interview all her life. The trucking company's call center is the perfect job for her sweet voice. She can rest her 450 pound body on a chair all day and let her mouth do the walking.

This company likes hiring "beauty challenged" people. The manager argues that since ugly people have less perceived value in the marketplace they are cheaper, work harder, and are more likely to stay with the company. Unlike job-hopping beauties who elope with the truck drivers, the aesthetically challenged generally concentrate on improving their skills. The manager, who likes to remind people that she is not actually Miss Galaxy herself, has been with the company for thirty years. She claims that if you treat unattractive employees well, they're usually loyal and hardworking.

With such weight, an unusual hairline, rainbow teeth, and standing barely four feet tall, the forty-year-old Helen understands that in this shallow world she is not Marylyn Monroe. Her left foot is a few inches shorter than her right foot, making her lean slightly on one side. This makes her face appear asymmetrical, a feature that throws her into the ugly bucket in this city.

The interviewer's forced smile did not put her at ease. She learned early on to read minds. In school she was mostly excluded frm the in-groups. The dating scene has been predictably rough. She gets weird looks on the street.

There is one thing that she has in abundance. She is a believer. She realizes it is still up to her to either become dispirited or embrace the other million and one personal strengths she has. Does she have any control? Yes. Helen has developed a go getter attitude over the years; she makes every effort to look sharp and dresses well. When the dust settles, it was the time she spent on self-development and her excellent personality that eventually carried the day. It was a long journey, but she got the job.

Helen's story reads like a romantic novel. She later met a guy who worked on radio. Troy LaZeus had the same issues because of the "Elephant man disease" that made him unsightly in downtown New Sparta. He had a great sense of humor, probably a coping strategy. He used to joke that he will never work on television because of its overreliance on outward beauty. But with thirty million weekly listeners, who needs TV?

Helen left the trucking company to join her husband on radio. This worked like magic because she was able to release her dream album. Her musical talents took the city by the storm. Ironically, they both ended up working on a TV program, *Helen of Troy*. They both looked stunningly beautiful. In this town, most celebrities with money look beautiful.

Manifestation of Attractiveness-Based Social Exclusion

The concept of beauty is relative. Every society has its own definition of beauty. We know attractiveness is very subjective and that it is rather arbitrary, not an absolute. Of course this depends on many factors, including popular culture, industry, location, community, and even era, but it is out there. In some communities you remove some teeth to look beautiful, in others your gaps are frowned upon.

Nuthology is not about undefined operational variables. It is about what the "market" aka society considers good-looking. When it comes to opportunities, the ugly truth is that ugliness is in the eye of the gatekeeper. This is the open secret. The more attractive get higher salaries, better performance evaluations, higher levels of admission to college, better grades, more votes when running for public office, more favorable judgments in trials, higher chances of getting a partner, and the list is endless.

I saw in a recent study that feminine-looking women are seen as more attractive than masculine-looking women. Feminine-looking women tend to win elections more than masculine-looking women. Feminine-looking women get better breaks in the hiring office down the hall. It is not just women: tall, handsome men get better paying jobs and are elected to office more often. In a perfect world we would keep beauty pageant mentality out of the voting booth and hiring office. Tell me when we get there.

We live in an era where beauty industry players must keep the masses obsessed about their looks to stay in business. How much time, energy, and resources are spent on cosmetic camouflage and nonmedical cosmetic procedures? This factor has spawned a multibillion-dollar industry. Cosmetic products dealers, beauty experts, and cosmetic surgeons are busy cashing in.

There are studies out there showing that attractive people are perceived as better, smarter, more successful, more important, and even more valuable. Feeling unattractive may lead to low self-esteem. Low esteem people earn less than high esteem people.

First of all, I don't know why we needed a study to show that pretty people get better breaks. Most people I talked to when I was researching this topic knew somebody who got ahead not because of qualification but looks.

Social Exclusion of the Beautiful

How many people choose to be born beautiful? I am guessing as many as those who chose to be ugly. It might be true that some beautiful people still enjoy a significant edge. However, beautiful women face discrimination in certain jobs. We are talking about jobs that are seen as more masculine and behind the scenes where beauty is not a big factor.

Do attractive people have any positive inner qualities or do they rely primarily on their looks? There are situations where attractive people can be stereotyped as not smart, egocentric, dishonest, and other negative traits.

Conglomeration of Exclusion Factors NUBC
There are many variables that go into the definition of attractiveness. Some are freestanding exclusion factors such as age, height, and weight. Dressing and fashion are also contributors. That means wealth can make you look more beautiful either by halo effect or being able to afford things that make people beautiful. Sometimes it is both.

My point here is that if you add exclusion factors such as gender, weight, height, disability, age and even race you better believe this factor carries a heavy punch at individual level. I want to note that age-related exclusion weighs unequally when it comes to gender because the attractiveness yardstick is not gender neutral.

A short middle aged woman who has been working in a male-dominated ugly averse industry may have concerns that include:

Attractiveness
Gender
Age
Weight
Height

Nuthology Strategy
For the most part, what defines beauty around the world is dictated by the cultural perceptions of the day. Based on the microcosm assumption, Nuthology strategy is interested in whether gatekeepers, not necessarily other beach goers, are influenced by the societal aesthetic preferences. If that is the case in your backdrop, this will be a risk that will need to be mitigated.

It is easy to shrug off this factor as financially inconsequential, and you might be right. Well, who cares? But this ostrich-head-in-sand strategy may not work, especially if you are depending on the same shallow crowd for food, shelter, and clothing. Jobs that require face-to-face client contact or being on camera may be more sensitive to this factor.

Learning how attractiveness can be used to exclude you should be a part of your financial strategy. Friends and family may always tell you how beautiful you are. I guess that is why they get to remain family and friends. It is your duty to research the target industry.

This is tricky when you spend decades investing your passion in a looks-obsessed industry only to be disappointed. How many things can happen to change you from beautiful to not conventionally beautiful? Age, disease, accidents, and weight gain are just examples. If you get attracted to jobs that primarily require feminine and beauty attributes, you run a risk that you will be laid off based on the same when your image naturally changes. That is a fact that may only exist in your financial intelligence. The gatekeepers will make sure it is never officially declared.

Take Control

Conglomerate all your concerns as one. I hesitate to state what should be obvious, but sometimes the obvious must be stated. When you lose control of yourself you will find yourself struggling with an unattainable standard of beauty. Nuthology strategy is about identifying stereotypes. Find ways to isolate stereotype-effect and groupthink-effect risks before they affect your self-esteem. There are many jobs out there where attractiveness has little or no bearing on job performance. Keep both your energy and esteem up.

Addressing Gatekeepers' Concerns and Dilemmas

Most gatekeepers may not care about beauty but grooming is a big factor. Do not let yourself go to prove a point. Like all of us, employers and investors are visual beings. They scan you within a few seconds of meeting you. They get that good feeling or bad vibes. It might be your dress or those perfectly shined shoes that gets you the second interview.

It is not whether you are attractive or not. The distance between your values and those of the gatekeepers will determine the cultural fit. Letting yourself go may indicate laziness or a don't-care attitude.

First Impressions, Lasting Impressions

Grooming is a major player in this category. It gives away your character and decision-making skills. Like it or not, clothes and grooming are part of your likability package. Traits like honesty, likeability, and smartness can be unconsciously perceived from your wardrobe choices. The gatekeepers will want to see their future employee in you at first sight. Do you look the part?

Long-Term Planning

Those who get hired based on age and conventional beauty will be fired based on their age and beauty. It's the media that gives the allusion of beauty as a sole advantage to success. Statistically, there are more companies looking for soul-deep beauty than those looking for the skin deep kind.

Based on the laws of Nuthology, if you get hired based on youth and conventional attractiveness, you must develop some other competitive advantages before your youth and beauty expires. The expiration date on these two factors is nearer than it appears on the side mirror.

They say growing old is inevitable but growing up is optional. One day you will be formerly good-looking, highly educated, and highly experienced. Or, if all you have is good looks, well, you will just be formerly good-looking. You get to decide.

You might even apply this to other facets of your life. There are very handsome guys that are made of bad husband material. As time progresses, a six-pack-abs displayer with no job will appear less attractive than a confident and intelligence person with some scattered age scratches.

While most people may not admit it, income plays a part in how you may be viewed. People with advanced degrees and impressive assets may appear more attractive even with aesthetically challenging features like a six figure body mass index.

Reducing Your Own Stereotype-Driven Aggression

Don't hate others just because they are been declared more beautiful than you.

There are many people who are conventionally attractive but did not get where they are because of their beauty. That beautiful brain surgeon who can also design space rockets had to read some books. Don't be jealous or envious. This will consume you and reduce your networks.

Speak Up Regardless of Status

You would think people should be judged on merit and not looks. We are all so much more than our faces and bodies. Become an advocate for horizontal coexistence where no one is treated unfairly because of his or her physical attributes. There are millions of people with scars and deformities as a result of diseases, accidents, and conflicts. There are millions of people who were born with deformities or unique physical features. Some of these people continue to face bullying and ridicule at school, in the streets, in their homes, and at their workplaces. Their physical scars are converted into mental scars for the rest of their lives. These people need a voice. Join others in eliminating lookism and other forms of bias in society.

11
Body Art

Is That Real?

The emergency crew rushed in with 'guns' drawn. Nobody move. It was like an old Western movie. An old lady had fallen in the shower. She was unconscious. Nobody knew her name. Somebody in the facility had called for help in a panic. Within sixty seconds the first responders had a full medical report. It turned out the lady had two small tattoos on her left shoulder as the crew had hoped. One read "No CPR" and the other was a bar code. The crew scanned the bar code with their wireless guns.

Within five minutes the patient was up and mingling with the crowd. The computer had wealth of life-saving data as well as end-of-life instructions. Ottiz was the lady's name, and her son was the local geriatrician, Dr. Arthur. She was not only diabetic but also allergic to penicillin and peanuts.

When Dr. Arthur and a group of health professionals started Medical Tattoos Research Institute, he didn't know that a day like this would come. His efforts literally helped save his own mother. He had tried dozens of medical jewelry and tags on her. They all ended up getting misplaced, lost, or broken. There was no greater indication that his project had a promising future medical potential than this incident.

This emergency scare gave Dr. Arthur the much needed validation and emotional juice. His organization's research had been met with heavy resistance due to the underlying social stigma surrounding tattoos. In that city, tattoos and body piercings were associated with certain antisocial lifestyles. Those lifestyles were related to unsafe drug use, forbidden sexual practices, and prison alumni.

Dr. Arthur's dad was one of the fiercest critics of the medical research. He would not eat in a restaurant if the server or cook had visible tattoos. There was a chance he would change his mind now that the tattoos had helped save his wife's life. Only time would tell.

In this conservative city, women with tattoos tended to be viewed as less physically attractive, promiscuous, and heavier drinkers. A tattooed man in TV or movies is often associated with the criminal element. He is always the bad guy.

Dr. Arthur and his medical cohort became unstoppable. There was a list of issues that still needed to be ironed out. They had prepared a proposal for medical authorities and Congress.

- Medical standards to create some uniform medical coding and styles
- Creating conventional and legal guideline, including addressing privacy concerns
- Licensing of tattoo artists and facilities
- Training emergency crews and first responders
- Raising awareness to reduce body art stigma
- How to include other forms of body art in the medical world
- Developing advanced applications to handle the fast data
- Developing scanning technology
- Incorporating other medical technology in the system

Manifestation of Body Art-Based Social Exclusion

Body art is one of the earliest forms of art. It goes back more than 5000 years ago. There have been many uses of body art in the past and present.

Rite of passage
Status symbol
Mystical, religious purposes
Beauty, fashion, and decorative
Record keeping after hunting
Protection from evil spirits
Identification and affiliation
Inventory of prisoners and slaves
Self-expression
Counterculture and rebellion
Cultural identity

This factor includes tattoos, body piercing, and other modifications. This may include scarification, sub-dermal implants, scalping, and body painting. If you are in the performance art industry or you are a tattoo artist, having a tattoo may be considered a plus. You should count it in the index only when it is a concern. If body art is mainstream enough to be acceptable in your backdrop, this discussion is not relevant to you.

Body art perception has been changing with the times. Public institutions and businesses keep revising their policies. In a perfect world, body art shouldn't matter to people anyway. While tattoos are much more common today than in the past, they are still not acceptable in some professional settings. Obviously, the art means something to you. Nuthology strategy is interested in how the art is interpreted and how that interpretation affects your achievement, not whether it is okay or not. Some communities do not accept modified people as normal. Every community has its reasons as to why tattoos are not respected.

Stigma

Keep in mind that most social exclusions are stereotypically, unfairly, and, sometimes, unconsciously practiced. People with multiple tattoos are often stereotyped as being bad, outcasts, or criminals. Some body art is believed by law enforcement to signal the wearer's criminal resume and bragging rights. It doesn't have to be factual, but if your art is interpreted that way, there is a risk for exclusion. Profiling may follow this kind of perception whether it is based on facts or not. The art may end up costing you your freedom.

Conglomeration

A young person dealing with other exclusion issues such as age, character, protocol, credit history, affiliation, and place may risk exacerbating his situation by getting an obscene facial tattoo and a loud nose ring. All the initial exclusions could have been mitigated easily. The new NUBC becomes more interesting:

Body art
Age
Character
Protocol
Credit history
Affiliation
Place

Nuthology Intelligence

Learning how body art can be used to exclude you should be a part of your financial strategy. As far as the Nuthology is concerned, it is not necessarily about right or wrong, it is about acceptance and exclusion of decorated people. It is your obligation to study patterns of data. This will help you to measure the public opinion in your backdrop. Most people do this organically anyway. This is the main reason most people have tattoos on body areas that they can easily cover when in certain environments.

In the USA, for example, over 60 percent of high school dropouts have tattoos. Ninety percent of convicted felons have tattoos. Fewer than 5 percent of those with graduate degrees have tattoos. There is a gender bias too. In some communities, a woman cannot be a lady with a tattoo.

Addressing Gatekeepers' Concerns and Dilemmas

Gatekeepers are part of our society. They carry our perceptions to their gates. The distance between your values and those of the gatekeepers will determine the cultural fit. This time is about appearance. What might be a hiring manager's concerns?

Do companies have the right to demand that their employees look professional? Some careers do not accept body modifications at all. Employers may be hesitant to hire someone with visible tattoos that would reflect poorly on the company, especially in the service industry.

It is a good financial strategy to research cases involving tattoo discrimination in the workplace in your backdrop. Is this an industry where body art is regarded as being in bad taste, a distraction, and offensive? Is the corporate culture conservative or creative? Is body art considered fringe and unprofessional?

If you already have some permanent art, look for a company where your career advancement will not be stymied by the art. Search for jobs that align with your personal expression.

Subject, Size, and Quantity

Does the art depict extremist, indecent, or offensive content? What is the size of the art?

Some gatekeepers may not object tattoos but may not like the subject. Obscene, political, or gang-related tattoos may be frowned upon. Since some tattoos are personal, this is very subjective. It will depend on how the subject is interpreted. If the body art seems to celebrate violence against a certain section of the population, people may not want to be associated with you. Some gatekeepers may not object tattoos but may not like the quantity. It is the excessive tattoos, not just the art itself that is the problem.

Location, Location, Location

Is the art on the head, face, neck, or hands? Some gatekeepers may not object to tattoos but may not like the location. Very distinctive facial tattoos, for example, are just a different ball of wax entirely. Most conservative workplaces won't give you a chance. Even people who don't hate body art can try to misjudge your decision-making skills based on the tattoo or the fact that you have a tattoo at a particular spot. What was your thought process?

Rebellion Perception

How risky a prospect can you be? How will you fit in the company subculture? Religious tattoos may erroneously signal fundamentalism. Tattoos displaying extreme political views are frowned upon in most corporate settings. Is it art or an ego boost? If the art is viewed as counterculture, the wearer may be perceived as a difficult person to work with. If it gives an impression of dissatisfaction with your natural appearance, then your art will be regarded an insecurity label. Is it attention-seeking art for those who need constant validation from others?

Right to Self-Expression

Chances are your body art is meant to express your individuality. We communicate verbally and nonverbally as human beings. Body hardware is one way we do that. What happens if it succeeds in reducing your pool of jobs, customers, and potential partners? Since you will be judged, and sometimes you won't even know, then this becomes counterproductive.

You may be embracing an "identifier" that puts you in a category that makes society suspicious of you. Tattoos may not be a bad thing per se. But that's the way it is in business, at least for the foreseeable future. You may be limiting your potential income. They may cost you a much needed opportunity.

First Impression

Body art can rob you of the chance to make your first impression based on your personality and intelligent conversation. At the very least, body art may give away your decision-making abilities before you have time to present it to a gatekeeper. Body art is a self-expression practice that can ironically rob you of other forms of expression.

When in Doubt

When it doubt, cover it up. At the personal level, you may have to remove all visible piercings and cover any visible tattoos during the hiring process. You may have to a wear a long sleeve shirt at a job interview. You may have to remain covered in the corporate setting. The question here is whether it would be acceptable in the circumstance in question. In some industries it is an open secret. If you really want to limit your earning potential, show off your tattoos.

Tattoos Are Permanent

A lot of people regret their tattoos, especially if they were products of an impulsive decision. Getting a romantic partner's name tattooed on you, for example, is all fun and games. Well, until there is a nasty breakup or some changes occur. Okay, so you got a face tattoo on a dare during a drunken escapade. Tattoo removal is painful, costly, and a big business today.

Future Planning

Circumstances change with time. Picture yourself as a sixty-five-year-old with a bunch of tattoos that you got when you were fifteen during some revolution. You can't even tell what they were. They have changed into ugly faded smears as the skin ages. You may have to wear a long sleeve or turtleneck in a hundred degree weather. Pins and other hardware may leave ugly holes when removed.

Voluntary Exclusion Perception

There are schools of thought that argue that since tattoos and piercings are voluntary, employers have the right to exclude decorated people as long as the art is not considered religious or an ethnic belief. Unlike race, nationality, gender, or disability factors, body art is a choice, so it gets few sympathizers. The thinking is that you dug your own hole. You may not create a storm and then complain about the weather. Regardless of your opinion on this subject become an advocate for horizontal coexistence where no one is treated unfairly because of his or her body art.

12

Character, Taboo, Weird

Trimming of the Deadwood

Desechable Gente, a publicly traded company, has failed to attract any revenue for the fifth year in a row. The news hit everybody like a ton of bricks. That means costs must be cut or the stock will take a nose dive. In layman's terms, the company bigwigs up the food chain must decide to let some people go. The middle management will have to present names.

Last year's layoffs were easier. The choices were clear, at least to Mr. Schadenfreude and the other middle managers. For him it was time to take out the trash. He did not bother using performance reviews as expected. He had his list ready:

The weather guy who rules the water-cooler station rumor mill
The guy who liked to bark orders at coworkers
The Bluetooth fairy, hooked on the earpiece
The "caps lock" guy
The guy who chews gum loudly
DJ wannabe who blasted loud music in the parking lot
The guy who dressed down to pajamas for casual Friday
Forward and clearer of unfunny e-mails, her pets, and kids—some distasteful
Gossiper in chief, company's unofficial tabloid
Gullible pyramid scheme vendor

The guy who would call for a food day for any reason
The worker who hums all day- the serial "hummer"
The worker who loved to hear himself talk. Mr. Verbal Diarrhea
Monday afternoon quarterback who says nothing at staff meetings
Negotiator on small things: Who borrowed my paper clips?
Son of the whistler's mother, Mr. Arrhythmic
Outrageous expenses guy: billed company for two toothpicks
The Emotional time bomb
The Emotional vampire
The Shouter, son of old yeller
The quixotic dreamer, bridge to nothingness
The backstabber, walk backwards everybody
The "high priority" e-mailer
The "reply all" gal
The "stinky lunch", Casu Marzu anyone?
Munching and crunching gravel eater
The aggressive self-promoter
The clueless,
The coaster, Happy Friday, everyone
The cologne Olympic swimmer
The company's official wet blanket: "It will never happen."
The complainer: Mr. Constant Kvetcher
The condescending know it all
The control freak. Bossy to insanity
The slob. Biscuit crumbs and small animals in his beard
The habitual late comer: "The dog ate my alarm clock, again."
The hermit, killer in the next cube
The idea drone,
The idea thief
The just awkward
The curator of bad breath
The loud talker
The loud thunder laughter
The minimal effort guy. Mr. Buck Passer
The narcissistic, constant ETA requester

The free energy deflator
The nosy rubberneck
The parasite, credits on other people's work
The dumb questions guy.
The rock next door. No sense of humor
The selfish and the self-absorbed
The senior slacker. "Not-my-job" nut job
The serial braggart, who owns great lakes
The stupid practical joker. Growing up, optional
Too much information. Guess what?
The swearer of every second. Drunken sailor
The emoticons enthusiast
Musically inclined but not talented
Drama seekers and company
The team leader with an "authoritarian" streak
One with toxic competitive syndrome
Curator of petty grievances

That was last year. Something smelled fishy this year. Schadenfreude had his vendetta list ready. But nobody seemed to ask the middle managers for a list. Every one hoped the list will be shorter this year. Then the list fell directly from the top with a loud bang. It is the middle managers who were, surprisingly, being laid off. Twenty-two of them in a single sweeping move. Schadenfreude was one of them. His secret list is still in his pocket as security escorts him out like a hardened criminal.

Schadenfreude turned off years ago anyway, according to his boss, a senior VP. They'd made him manager because of seniority in years. The fallen log was once brilliant. "He now talks more and works less. Say hello to him and get ready for the longest speech reenactment. That group of managers had been draining energy and resources. They had been generating a very stagnant atmosphere. I'd tried donuts and ice cream in tanks. Written warnings meant nothing to those zombies. Those one-time company assets had become the main source of customer complaints. The cohort had to go."

Who knows what next year will bring. There are no signs of new revenue anywhere on the horizon. Mr. Terminador, the CEO, is a black belt, hyper efficient bean counter who lost his soul in a skiing accident. The doctors apparently replaced it with artic ice. His eyes are trained to see people as only numbers and cold cash. He is one of the few managers who can survive by attracting absolutely no new revenue for five years. He has a simple model. He joins a big company and cuts costs by closing facilities, conducting brutal layoffs, and aggressively outsourcing. The market responds well to the perceived efficiency, the stock goes up, and, consequently his pay doubles. This is repeated for a few years. When he senses that the cuts are near the bone, he stealthy moves to the next publicly traded giant with his good reputation and premium pay. And the cycle continues.

Manifestation of Character-Based Social Exclusion

Almost everyone I talked to about this subject has an acquaintance or a relative that they will never refer for a job. I am sure you know one too. Recall that cousin of yours who is so uncouth that you will never refer him to your job? First of all, you can imagine him drunk at an office party. Picture him trying to one-up your boss in some small petty way. Imagine his creative handshakes. Picture him body bumping the interviewer. Hell will freeze over before you introduce him to your company.

Character can be a major block to personal improvement in terms of career or small business. When it comes to making decisions about who to hire, promote, or fire, qualifications are only part of the equation. Hiring managers are usually on the lookout for counterproductive work behavior and antisocial behaviors in candidates.

There are observable behaviors in your society that may flag you as a risk. Most of the times it is the body language and nonverbal communication that makes the employer recoil. It is the first thirty seconds rule that gives the interviewer bad taste in the mouth. I am thinking of facial expressions, gestures, eye contact, and tone of voice, street lingo, swagger, and body posture.

There are behaviors that generate tension, mistrust, and confusion unconsciously. Employers are human. They have the self-preservation mechanism in them that may work against your dreams. As a society, there is a meeting of the minds that agrees that assessing your character is fair game.

This is a factor that is able to carry other factors. In most places, a criminal record is considered an indicator of character. In some industries, credit history is used as a measure of character. Protocol and etiquette can also be character red flags.

Taboo and Weird

This is another deviation from societal norms that can make one socially excluded. Weird is a relative word. Peculiar behavior comes in many forms, but who decides what is normal? Weirdness will depend on the backdrop.

Depending on the context, some beliefs can flag you as the weirdo next door. Do you believe in superstition, numerology, astrology, mysticism? Are you obsessed with seeking the truth using a non-scientific or an anti-intellectual worldview? Do you lick your fingers during a meal? Society also frowns on various addictive behaviors and odd obsessions.

The guy with ten pounds of hair
The guy dating cars
The one who loves bee stings
The guy who eats only month-old road kill.
The hoarders
The owner of 112 starving cats

Certain gestures may be considered obscene and taboo. Offensive language that includes obscenity or vulgarity is not normal. In some settings you may not mention some bodily functions in front of polite company if your mom did not give you "the eye" already. Do you recall that driver who insists on backing into spaces even in wide-open parking lots? Or the customer who insists on paying with a stone-age personal check at the grocery store and takes ten minutes to balance her book while the line has thirty people in it? I am hoping that was not you.

Sometimes weird is just living your life. Your fifty-five-year-old uncle who lives with his mom and never dated may be characterized as weird. In some places shoes are not worn inside a house. If you do, look in the mirror, you are the weirdo; a person whose dress or behavior seems strange or eccentric.

Conglomeration of Exclusion Factors NUBC

Chances are if you have other factors your little foibles will be augmented because they are feeding an existing stereotype. When character as a self-standing factor is added to organically occurring factors such as race, gender, height, and weight it adds fuel to the fire. The output may be unemployment, adverse credit history, and negative law enforcement encounters; another group of exclusion factors.

Nuthology Strategy

Learning how character can be used to exclude you should be a part of your financial strategy.

Mitigating Character Exclusion

Unlike some of the exclusions in the index that you cannot change, character is one of those factors that you can play a big part in adjusting. No one is born with good character. Take your time and do some research on trustworthiness, respect, responsibility, caring, and fairness to others. People notice the little things but might not say anything because they don't want to start a third world war with you or hurt your feelings. You have to proactively perform the research and seek guidance. Most of character issues are common sense.

When should you wear clothing with vulgar, offensive, or violent language?

When should you wear clothing with vulgar, offensive, or violent images?

When does your right for expression allow you to offend the gatekeepers or everybody else? When should you create a storm and then complain about the bad weather?

Addressing Gatekeepers' Concerns and Dilemmas

In the court of public opinion personnel is policy. The employer will expect to see the company's image in the candidate it hires. This is a marketing strategy to some extent. It should not be sold as aggression.

The distance between your values and those of the gatekeepers will determine the cultural fit. This time it is your character. If you appear uncouth and disrespectful, even when you don't mean to, why should a gatekeeper convince himself otherwise? This is not a mountain sermon on how you should behave. It is about how your behavior can be seen as a risk preventing you from achieving your goal. Many jobs require that some etiquette, protocol, tradition, honor and decency be observed. That should never be misconstrued with bona fide social exclusion.

Commitment is not complete without character. You can be committed to the wrong things. Most of our workplace character-related personal skills develop over a lifetime. No school can effectively teach you integrity, reliability, punctuality, and diligence. You have to want it.

Dress for the Job You Want

I hope you will take a big picture approach. We know flossing and brushing your teeth will save you thousands of dollars in medical costs down the line. But who knew taking a shower was part of financial planning? Tangible and intangible characteristics of personal branding including attire, hair, makeup, behavior, verbal, and nonverbal communication are part of greater basic financial literacy.

Disposition

In a job interview, you may not act like work is a distraction from your life even when you believe it is. You are there to present yourself in the best light. Nobody is perfect; we have to tolerate each other's little foibles. I will give you that. But in this section we are talking about self-created obstacles. Get out of your own way.

Self-Expression

We are all encouraged to be ourselves. As valuable as self-expression is, anything that would cast a shadow over your character is damaging your chances. You might be within your legal rights to use extreme foul language, for instance, but should you use it regardless of circumstances or company? Your behavior may cost you networks or job referrals. Don't allow yourself to be one of your obstacles. Actions speak louder than words.

Control Personal Information

You enjoy drinking socially, says your online profile. But the larger picture from the online footprint does not support that argument. There are tons of videos of you passed out cold.

Be the Best Copy of Yourself

A lot of entertainers have routines that are part of their business models. You cannot cut and paste that without considering your career route. An entertainer may curate a tough guy persona with body art and swagger as part of his shtick. That is how he positions his entrepreneurship and creativity. You cannot curate the same persona and try to be a first grade teacher or another job that requires a soft landing.

Seek Guidance

It is always important to understand the cultural taboos, especially when visiting a different region or country. We are constantly learning when it comes to this factor. There is always a chance that the education you received at home or in school did not prepare you for the world outside your neighborhood. Some behaviors are perfectly normal in one place but frowned upon elsewhere.

The employer will have his own pattern of data. How come you call in sick only on Fridays and when the weather is good? Good weather sickness? If you are young and starting out, it might be the small things that get you:

Forgetting your manners at home and claiming your dog ate them

Not being intuitive of other people's needs.

Not respecting other people's time

Talking over others

Forgetting your grandmother's golden rule: listen, process, and then logically act

Understand that you may have to work in environments where profanity and vulgarity are not entertained, even if you live in a place where they are normal. Releasing a torrent of vile verbiage in the wrong company will put you in the bad books without realizing it. The immediate reaction may be laughs, but the long-term damage may be irreparable. Your colleagues may not have enough courage to tell you. Companies that deal with sensitive clients may view the behavior as a risk. This becomes worse if due to a group attribution error you were already expected to be crass.

Avoid Anchoring

There are instances where stupidity, lack of manners, and rudeness are repackaged as discrimination. If, for instance, an inconsiderate neighbor conducts a forty-piece orchestra training in her driveway at 3:00 a.m. in the morning or let's her eight dogs bark continuously all night, should others complain? What about cruising like she is on the autobahn on a five miles per hour children's zone? Should she then repackage a valid character complaint as gender, racial, ethnic, or another popular bias just because she happens to have different physical attributes? That kind of tethering is a major problem in a lot of areas.

Is there an expectation of civility in your backdrop that you are overlooking? A sense of decorum and decency goes a long way in most public environments, even when not explicitly stated.

Advocate

Most social exclusions are stereotypically, unfairly, and, sometimes, unconsciously practiced based on negative group attribution. In real life, no group is all bad, nor, conversely, all good. Gatekeepers who have had or heard about bad experiences with a class of people may be reluctant to hire their members. A racial-character stereotype, for example, may become a threat to the individual achievement of every member of the affected race.

As a member of the civilized society, advocate for horizontal coexistence where no one is treated unfairly because of his or her group-attributed negative character traits. What would Martin Luther King, Jr say today in his blog? "I have a dream that all people will one day live in a job market where they will not be judged by the content of their sub-group attributed character traits."

13

Class, Caste, Descent

Because of Fate of Birth

For the last thirteen years Bobby has mastered the art of parenting. He has answered all those tricky questions with flying colors. Or with flying white lies. Why does Santa pass through the chimney? Where do babies come from? Is that man pregnant forever?

But there is one question that Bobby hoped he will never have to answer. It involves his birth name and genetic lottery. He'd hoped his now thirteen-year-old daughter would never ask. He had always avoided discussing the subject at home or at community gatherings. It was only natural then that when his daughter came home crying one day that Bobby had a feeling the cat was out of the bag.

The immigrant community at New Diaspora City has been mum on caste identity for the last decade or so, at least publicly. The caste is a social group system developed in his motherland that divides people into separate groups based on birth, marriage, and occupation. It is a fate-of-birth discrimination whose toxicity is only rivaled by that of racism.

Bobby moved to West Nation to escape caste-based bullying, intimidation, and harassment in his homeland. Back home caste prejudice is rampant in the workplace, health care, and education. Economic disenfranchisement of the lowest caste almost always led to increased vulnerability to poverty, hunger, and violence. Both Bobby and his wife belong to the lowest caste.

Bobby changed his name on arrival so that it wouldn't reveal his ranking in the caste hierarchy to the immigrant community in New Diaspora City. The lowest caste was the rock bottom of the social ladder in so many ways. Most "lowest" casters back home remained uneducated and poor. They were restricted to mostly menial and degrading work. They were excluded from all political and social rights. Bobby's parents were never allowed to drive cars or ride horses. Driving was a privilege reserved for the upper castes.

Bobby lied and cried whenever his daughter asked about his birthday. The day was never recorded because he was born a "non-full person". The last fifteen years had been good. But a new crop of upper caste immigrants had joined New Diaspora City. They brought the old bias with them. There are signs in the air. Recently a close neighbor had to quit her job when her bosses found out that she was marrying down. She was subjected to harassment and humiliation. She was skipped over for promotion and had her benefits reduced. Inter-caste marriage is a forbidden practice in this system.

Now his own daughter was being harassed. She was being asked about her caste by other children in the community. Bobby took out his best weapon, a brand new notepad. This fight was going to the highest law making body of the land. Yes, there were strict anti-discrimination laws on the books. There were rules on bullying and harassment in schools. But caste bias was still a foreign concept to the West Nation justice system. Bobby wouldn't allow caste labeling and name-calling to follow his children to this corner of the globe. He took a deep breath and started writing.

Because of Fate of Birth

What would you do if because of fate of birth you were considered a nonperson?

You are considered unclean and your shadow as pollution to environment.

You have to sit in a separate area in restaurants and at public functions.

You are prohibited from wearing certain footwear.

You are prohibited from riding a bicycle in certain areas.

You are prohibited from using some public paths.

Your remains are prohibited from certain public burial grounds.

You are prohibited from certain public amenities.

You are restricted to menial and degrading work.

You are excluded from all political and social rights.

You are not allowed to drive cars or ride horses.

Your children are prohibited from attending some public schools.

Just because of fate of birth.

Ladies and gentlemen, this is about human rights, equality, and justice.

Caste has permeated the diaspora community in this free nation.

It is time to act decisively and swiftly.

Do not allow this exclusion practice to be imported.

My children will not be judged by a social group where membership is decided by birth.

I will not be a non-full person.

Manifestation of Descent -Based Social Exclusion

When we talk of caste, a specific subcontinent comes into our minds. This section, however, covers any environment where hierarchical order is determined by the family you were born into. It is not hard to find a social stratification in other parts of world that resembles some aspects of caste system. Almost every nation has communities that are traditionally treated as outcasts.

There are groups working to ensure that discrimination on the grounds of caste is against the law at least in Western countries. Laws are changing in different countries. In some communities it is unlawful to call someone an untouchable, nonperson, un-person, or any other derogatory names associated with this kind of social stratification.

Since some laws can be morally and ethically questionable, human rights should be a guiding principle when deciding on this factor, whether we understand the underlying traditions or not.

There is a gender twist to the fight against caste bias. Expansions of urban centers and capitalism continue to reduce caste hierarchies. Men were first to move to cities where there was less caste exclusion, while women stayed in rural areas. Women are also negatively affected by colorism associated with this social stratification.

Conglomeration of Exclusion Factors NUBC

Consider an older female immigrant from a lower caste whose skin color is different from the other immigrants from the same ethnic group. She may have simultaneous concerns on:

Caste
Colorism
Race
Gender
Social class
National origin
Age
Ethnicity

Nuthology Strategy

The first thing you do is to conglomerate these classes and develop a personalized approach that factors in both the NUBC and the unique capsule of talents. Learning how descent can be combined with other factors and how it can be used to exclude you should be a part of your financial strategy.

Reducing Your Own Stereotype-Driven Aggression

Don't take your anger out on innocent children who were born in upper castes. Nobody ever chooses where they are born or their family or their inheritance. The child did not choose to be born in royalty or the upper caste.

Speak Up Regardless of Status

Like I said in the beginning, the guiding light for Nuthology strategy is human rights. Using that as a litmus test, it is obvious that in many ways caste discrimination and racism are analogous. They both encourage segregation in housing, schools, and public services. Both are obstacles to civil, political, economic, social, and cultural rights that are based on immutable characteristics.

At the societal level, become an advocate for aggressive investment in children's education and economic empowerment. A level playing field cannot be achieved if education and training are denied. A combination of capitalism and education will be a major step in combating discrimination based on descent.

If you live in diaspora, educate the local authorities on discrimination on the basis of caste in areas of employment, housing, education, and other services. Become an advocate for horizontal coexistence where no one is treated unfairly because of his or her fate of birth, either through race, caste dimension or any other inherited status,

14

Colorism

Just Not That into Hue

Statuesque City is one of the most interesting places in the world. If you venture into the belly of this predominantly black neighborhood you will be surprised to find out that nobody is actually black. Well, at least this rule applies on the dating scene. People are described by the shades of their skin tone. They are, yellow, chocolate, caramel, walnut, mocha, mahogany, blue-black, midnight-black, light skin, Nubian green, or some other hundred shades of chocolate. Some terms may not be acceptable, so don't try this at home.

The older folks and opinionated scholars believe that these are visible residues from dark eras of humanity where lighter-skinned slaves had unearned privileges over their darker counterparts. But this phenomenon is global. There has to be a better explanation. Hue-ism is not limited one race or country.

The mayor of Statuesque City decided to convene a color summit. Soon she had the backing of the governor. Intra-racial colorism involves a member of one racial group making a distinction based on the skin color of members belonging to the same racial group. Discrimination occurring among members belonging to the same racial group is just as damaging as interracial-grade colorism.

It is the first international meeting of its kind. A global debate on the effect of intra-racial colorism in dating, the workplace, and other facets of society was long overdue. The governor has witnessed this bias at the state level. It is producing what she calls "minority minorities."

There was this bi-racial man from Africa who could not qualify for a scholarship because he was too light to be considered African. A group of fair-skinned Hispanic men were not considered minorities or non-minorities. A group of fair-skinned, light-eyed native Tunisians were not considered Africans, Asians, or Caucasians. Then there were aboriginal immigrants from Australia who looked like sub-Saharan Africans, but they were genetically 100 percent Asian. They wanted to be Asians but they were not accepted.

Statuesque City had created a monster. The central government and the world body joined the conference. The venue had to be changed. Dark-skinned Hispanics in the Dominican Republic who faced discrimination apparently caused by anti-Haitian sentiment called in. Dozens of albinos from Tanzania seeking refugee status wanted representation.

A delegation from India wanted a speaking spot. There was an underground war between the "dusky, fair and wheatish." It was so serious that some women had committed suicide. They attributed this to anti-darker skin sentiment in the water.

Some light skin women in sub-Saharan Africa had allegedly also benefited from this unearned privilege. Many dark-skinned black women had bleached their skin to conform to societal standards of beauty. They also wanted to send delegates. Is skin tone now a marker of beauty, merit, or intelligence? This conference had to decide.

Manifestation of Colorism-Based Social Exclusion

How much do you deviate from the normal complexion? If you have not already figured it out, Statuesque City does not exist. That is the length I have to go to get your attention.

Colorism, at least in our discussion here, involves favorable or disparate treatment of individuals based on the lightness or darkness of their skin.

Intra-racial colorism is an issue that continues to separate and divide people of color who, ironically and sadly, are still fighting color-based exclusion known as racism. Most discussions about skin color–based exclusion are lost in race discussions.

We know interracial colorism involves a member of one racial group making a distinction based on the skin color of members belonging to a different racial group. In a way, one can say intra-racial colorism is a franchise of racism since it also involves distinctions based on skin.

Historically people of color have encountered both interracial and intra-racial colorism. A light-skinned complexion has been linked to greater probability of marriage, higher earning, and higher chances of employment among people of color.

This form of color-soluble exclusion is more complex than inter-racial colorism but results in similar preferential, prejudicial, or disparate treatment. Since this can be practiced intragroup, it usually receives little attention; but the effects are damaging. This is especially detrimental to the psychological well-being of bias conglomerates because it creates a double punch.

Light Skin Exclusion

In most cases, lighter skin is sold and perceived as more beautiful. There are, however, cases where light-skinned individuals are subjected to ridicule and exclusion. This includes biracial children who are seen as not dark enough to fit in a certain sub-group.

Colorism is also found in many races and ethnic groups. This comes to play if you are considered lighter or darker than others with the same ethnicity group. There are stereotypes about tan skin, pale skin, and bleached skin. Hair color and eye color are usually not far behind in this exclusion. The effect can be damaging at the personal level when internalized.

There is a multi-billion-dollar industry that depends on this factor. Bleaching creams, darkening products, tanning products and equipment, hair extensions, and plastic surgery are just the tip of this iceberg.

Conglomeration of Exclusion Factors NUBC

The damaging effects of cultural beauty standards related to how dark or how light the skin is are usually left to the conglomerates. You can combine this exclusion with a lot of factors. Young women, for instance, are bombarded with images of the perfect complexion. This is bound to have direct impact on their level of confidence and self-esteem. This exclusion is often combined with hair to rob people of their identities. As an example, the beauty expectations of a location can demand long, flowing, straight hair on top of light skin. The risk of negative-stereotype confirmation goes up tremendously with each additional factor:

Colorism
Racism
Gender
Attractiveness
Hair
Ethnicity
Age

Nuthology Strategy

Most social exclusions are stereotypically, unfairly, and, sometimes, unconsciously implemented. One of the assumptions of the index is that gatekeepers tend to mimic the society that they come from. Our main concern here is whether gatekeepers buy into the media version of beauty definition. It is worse if these gatekeepers are using this to exclude some people from opportunities.

Capsule of Talents

Learning how colorism can be used to exclude you should be a part of your financial strategy. Understanding how media marketing campaigns work should be a part of your financial intelligence. It shouldn't take the media to tell you that you are beautiful. You are a piece of your creator; this should not be a negotiable issue at all. Conglomerate all these factors and design a personal strategy. These are risks that may never materialize, but they are concerns that you may need to factor in.

Speak Up Regardless of Status.

Prejudices and misconceptions associated with light and dark skin often go unaddressed, probably because they are perpetuated intra-race and within the same social economic block.

The people in a civilized society cannot stick their heads in the sand and pretend things are not happening. There is a growing debate across the globe from India to the United States of America about the effects of colorism in dating, in the workplace, and in other facets of society. Skin-tone bias has served to promote power inequalities and to perpetuate negative stereotypes.

Avoiding Overcompensation

Advocate for horizontal coexistence where skin tone does not decide who gets an opportunity. Every tone is beautiful. Campaigning that your skin tone is better just replaces other people's skin-tone supremacy claims with yours. It is counterproductive; even if it is meant to motivate a marginalized group.

Reducing Your Own Stereotype-Driven Aggression

Assuming that a person got to a certain position because of the complexion of his or her skin is also a low blow. One can be considered conventionally beautiful while also having great integrity, intelligence, and character. These are not mutually exclusive attributes.

Most people did not choose their complexion. It is also insulting to assume without facts that a person received unearned privilege because of his or her skin tone.

15

Credit History

Miss Fixer-Upper, Flip This Man

Angel Maninvestor is going to therapy for three months thanks to her local church. She is addicted to dating fixer-uppers. She needs a way to sniff out the deal breakers before she gets exclusive with another "project."

It all started with a guy named PO (Project One). The guy had low self-esteem, multiple addictions, and a very questionable character. But she took him anyway. She gave it her all. He turned out to be a lemon inside and out.

Then there was the prince of nothingness. The second project was a braggart who had nothing to his name. When the dust settled, it turned out Mr. Charming was all hat and no cattle.

Project number three had no motivation to improve his life. Mr. Deferred Success was a total failure-to-launch transaction. He was stuck in teenager mode. In his free time he mostly played video games. I take that back. What free time? Free time means when he wasn't sleeping.

Angel's last "project" was a success. Well, sort of. It was not his fault that he was in such financial ruin. His mom "borrowed" his identity when he was growing up, opened eighteen credit cards, and maxed them out. There were twenty-four judgments on his credit report by the time he turned eighteen. He was the lucky one; his other three siblings had more than thirty each. The mom was a high roller, living large a mile wide and an inch deep.

Last project could not get an apartment to save his life. He couldn't get a phone, electricity, or water in his name. Angel came to the rescue and used her clean credit history. He couldn't get a car loan or store credit card in his name. Angel used hers. You get the drift. Angel helped him through his college days. When he received a shiny MBA and a job to boot, he bailed out. What was his reason for bailing out? She was below his class.

Angel was left to nurse her debts. Her credit was no longer pristine. If she wanted to buy a house, she would have to come up with a big down payment and agree to pay a hefty interest rate. She wanted to date again. Today she's going to therapy before she yokes herself to another soul draining parasite.

Manifestation of Credit-Based Social Exclusion

Discrimination by an employer or a landlord against a person that is based on the candidate's credit history is a very hot topic. Those who use credit history to make decisions about employment argue that a low credit score is a sign of inferior morals. Credit information provides insight on an applicant's integrity and responsibility toward his or her financial obligations. What about white-collar crime by people with high credit scores? Silence.

Are all people with damaged credit automatically poor job risks? It is not that difficult to hit a sticky patch. This factor can be inherently unfair. Not all people with bad credit made immature choices. Long-term unemployment, divorce, medical emergencies, accidents, or a bad economy have nothing to do with character. A credit report in this case is not a fair measurement.

What about those on the receiving end of identity theft? Are they also bad security risks? The fact that credit agencies that compile these reports are known to make their share of mistakes makes this even worse. If these erroneous credit histories are then used by employers in hiring, could this unfairly shut qualified people out of the job market? Wait there is more. If you live on cash you might not have a credit history. You belong in the same inferior moral bucket.

Conglomeration of Exclusion Factors NUBC

This is an exclusion factor that keeps on giving. Landlords may require credit history. This can force you to live in an area with no opportunities. You children may go attend subpar schools.

Credit history
Unemployment
Place
Social class

Nuthology and Financial Education

Poor debt management is a major cause of credit history issues. Conglomerates face the temptation to keep up with peers when their incomes don't allow it. Learning how credit history and credit scores can be used to exclude you should be a part of your financial strategy. Good sources are available for those who want to learn basic financial literacy.

Addressing Gatekeepers' Concerns and Dilemmas

Understandably, there are a few cases where credit checks are required by law, especially in areas related to the banking industry. Educate yourself on your industry and how this factor can cost you opportunities.

Identity theft by family, friends and close neighbors is very common. It is also very complicated especially when it involves close family members. Consider a case where parents misuse their child's information. This will have impact on every aspect of the child's financial life. Sometimes it takes decades before it is discovered. What if this child spends many years successfully pursuing degrees to get in a specific industry only to discover that candidates must have pristine credit?

Anticipate Dilemmas

This factor creates a catch-22 for job seekers. You are unable to secure a job because of damaged credit. You cannot improve your credit because you cannot get the job. What gives? You may also find yourself pondering how to respond to a clueless interviewer's illegal questions. A question like "Do you have any outstanding debt?" may be illegal in some countries. Taking the fifth may mean you have something to hide.

Establishing Credit

The credit world can seem confusing. Every positive incident will seem to be minimized, while small negative items get augmented. A secured card is one way that can help you establish credit or even repair damaged credit. The way this works is that you "buy" credit by putting up your own money as collateral. The bank usually sets a spending limit equal to your deposit.

The advantage is that the issuing bank reports your payment record to the credit bureaus. Use the card for routine purchases, and then pay the balance in full each month. This helps you to build a credit file. It is still your duty to make sure the card reports to all major credit bureaus.

Make sure to put fraud alerts on your credit files to stop anybody from opening up new accounts under your name. It is your duty to keep a close eye on your credit report and manage your money wisely.

Speak Up Regardless of Status

Be an advocate for horizontal coexistence where no one is treated unfairly because of his or her credit history. Narrowing job opportunities based on credit is damaging to marginalized communities. To begin with, marginalized people are likely to be poor. Poor people are known to have credit issues because they do not have enough money to pay all their bills on time. Is the ability to pay bills now a part of job merit?

It also makes self-employment difficult. Business capital and self-improvement loans become either too pricey or entirely unattainable. Trouble qualifying for new lines of credit may force some people to use predatory lenders. Payday loan interest rates can be up to thirty-five times as much as the interest rates for credit cards.

As if that is not enough, you get high car insurance premiums, high interest mortgage loans, and high interest credit cards.

Be an advocate for financial education subjects in elementary schools, especially for upcoming communities. Most of the responsibility of teaching financial literacy often falls on parents. We have a lot of grown-ups who as kids were not taught how to manage, grow, and protect their money. Essentially we are expecting potentially financial illiterate parents to teach money management to kids.

16

Criminal Record

The Tale of Celipo-Gettar Pizza

Both Gettar and Celipo were living in an abandoned warehouse with other social misfits when their stories collided. They were both doing odd jobs in Rikoka City, desperately waiting for yesterday to come back.

For Celipo, life came to a standstill ten years ago on one of those uneventful hazy summer nights. Celipo had just attained his CPA license after six attempts over a period of five years. On that fateful night he was driving from Rikoka City to Cagochi a four-hour middle-of-nowhere route. Despite his recent prostatitis diagnosis, he was determined to make all of his auditing assignments that year. He wanted to prove to his bosses that he could be a dependable full partner.

It was two hours into the journey that his ailing bladder started acting up. It was 2:00 a.m. and he was two hours from any civilization. The interstate was virtually deserted. He parked his vehicle hurriedly on the freeway shoulder and went down an embankment behind the bushes. It took a minute or so but he felt much better. It was a decision he would later come to rue. Two more hours and he would be in a cozy hotel room. That never happened.

Parked behind his car were two marked state trooper units with lights on full Christmas mode. Soon a third one joined the motorcade. His heart skipped a beat. What happened next would never leave his mind. Celipo was manhandled like a rabid lion. Public urination in that state was a sexual-related offense. He spent the next two months fighting for freedom and his CPA license.

There was no way he could manage his health condition in prison. He knew the conditions in the local jail. He even owned some stock in the company that owned the prison system. He had audited the company books as part of his assignment a few months before. With that in mind, he decided to cut a deal with the state to avoid prison time. He would have to register as a sex offender for the rest of his life. He lost his job, his CPA license, his dreams, his dignity, and pieces of his heart.

Gettar's story had its own unique drama. It involved his high school sweetheart who was three days younger than him. For some weird reason, the girlfriend's mother disapproved of the relationship so much that she called the police on him. His girlfriend was visiting him to prepare for his birthday party. The police showed up a few minutes after midnight. He was arrested on his birthday, the morning he turned eighteen. His girlfriend was still legally a minor. He was a two-hour adult sexual offender.

His girlfriend's mother later admitted that it was a calculated move. Her initial call was for underage alcohol consumption. She felt deep remorse and even tried to join his family to have Gettar's record expunged. It was too late. Gettar cut a deal and did three years in prison. The newly minted sex offender had to register for life and live at least two miles from a school or a playground.

In that city, landlords, both private and corporate do not accept convicted sex offenders. So getting a decent apartment was out of the question. Homeowners, especially those with small children, are always on the lookout. It is also about numbers. The presence of a convicted sex offender can hurt property values big time. A registered sex offender living nearby can reduce a home's value by 40 percent. In this country the law requires that people convicted of sex crimes notify local law enforcement of any change of address or employment. That information is then made public via various online databases. Homes near registered sex offenders can take more than 80 percent longer to sell. That pressure alone made Gettar's family kick him out, even though they believed he was never guilty.

A year or so after leaving prison, Gettar met Celipo at the only place those excluded from society could find some peace: a crumbling Great Depression–era abandoned ammunition factory. They braved ice-cold winters and simmering hot summers. Celipo came up with an idea to sell hot dogs at a local flea market. With the help of Gettar's mom, they bought their first hot dog cart. One cart turned to twenty-five. They bought a small ranch in the middle of nowhere and started families. They would later buy their first restaurant with cash. That is how the multimillion-dollar Celipo-Gettar pizza chain empire started.

Manifestation of Criminal Record–Based Social Exclusion

To a bias conglomerate, a criminal-record stigma attaches itself with a grip of an until-death-do-us-part magnitude. In most developed nations people with criminal records are now categorically barred from working in thousands of occupations because of the way laws and licensing rules are structured.

Society struggles with this factor every day. Should ex-cons continue to carry the burden of guilt regardless of what good deeds they have done since their release? Does a change for the better in their lives count? We live in a world where politicians won't address issues relating to the rights of ex-convicts. It is a very unpopular territory and one many politicians don't want to venture into lest they lose votes. Your opponent will eat you alive. He will paint you as the defender of felons.

Is Everybody with a Criminal Record Guilty?

Every country has its share of corrupt cops, detectives, prosecutors, judges, and other justice-system gatekeepers. It is therefore likely for innocent people to be convicted. It is not uncommon for innocent people to take a plea bargain, especially if they are low income citizens, because the "deal" sentence is usually less harsh than that of an unfair trial. Not everyone who gets a record is guilty, according to many humanitarian reports.

In some regions a district attorney has to maintain a certain conviction rate if he or she wants to get reelected. District attorneys are lawyers who want to win their cases. These players are obviously more legally shrewd than most street-level suspects. Authorities can threaten witnesses by trying to take their kids away or bringing unrelated charges. They can reward dubious witnesses with sweetened deals to testify against a "bigger fish" defendant.

There are many cases where money and power decide if a person is guilty or innocent. Do you have money to pay bail and pay a good attorney to be on your side? The poor are unlikely to have family members who can bail them out and afford legal representation.

Impressions matter whether you care or not. That's a fact of life. Those with inadequate legal representation are likely to go to prison for a simple infraction of a court protocol or a legal technicality.

There are policies and laws that clearly put some members at a disadvantage. In some areas, the business of crime is a normal activity. Its works like a factory assembly plant: police arrest people without proper cause, and the public defenders tell those charged to plead to a lesser crime or they are going to get convicted for a big one. It is a quick win for the prosecutor, the judges, and the police, who claim to be solving crimes in the headlines. Arrest records mean those charged have to "check the box" on job applications.

Conglomeration of Exclusion Factors NUBC

Criminal and bad credit records after paying the penalty may lead to unemployment, no place to live, and no transportation. Diminished access to transport may force the affected not to report to the probation officer. This leads the person back to jail or results in more criminal activity. Feel free to repeat this metamorphosis several times. It becomes a vicious cycle. For marginalized members of society, it is even worse. This is because it has almost a multiplier effect on the naturally existing bias factors and stereotypes. A combination of race, place and social class can lead to unequal treatment in the justice system.

NUBC
Criminal record
Credit history
Character
Transportation
Unemployment
Place
Shelter
Social class

You will find that the penal system disfavors racial minorities more than any other segment of the population. Where tribalism is the issue, you will find that the penal system also disfavors tribal minorities more than any other segment of the population.

Criminal record
Credit history
Character
Transportation
Unemployment
Place
Shelter
Social class
Racism

Prisoners are known for body art and questionable affiliations. Lack of education and skills may be an issue. The resulting grinding poverty and the blocked entries into productive social roles drastically increase incarceration rates.

Criminal record
Credit history
Character
Transportation
Unemployment

Place
Shelter
Social class
Racism
Body art
Affiliation

For foreign prisoners, society has no incentive to rehabilitate them because they are not coming back to it. Some are jailed because of language, lack of family and a social network, lost travel papers, and other foreigner-related barriers, not necessarily because their crime was prison worthy. Anyone can end up in prison abroad because of mistaken identity or a road accident. That NUBC can get long fast.

Criminal record
Credit history
Character
Transportation
Unemployment
Place
Shelter
Social class
Racism/tribalism
Racism/tribalism
Body art
Affiliation
National origin
Language

Nuthology Strategy

For a conglomerate, learning how a criminal record can be used to exclude you from opportunities should be a part of your financial strategy. This should happen long before it becomes an issue.

Handling this factor will depend on your backdrop and many other moving parts. There is no one size fits all.

As with many problems, the first step should be prevention. You have to do your best in this department. Teach your kids to avoid negative interactions with authorities early in their lives, even if your demographic is unfairly targeted.

Educate Yourself on Local Laws

Learn how to stay on the right side of the law. Minorities in urban areas usually move in groups for instance. They are usually young, not very educated, and have fewer options as they navigate the transition from adolescence to adulthood. This culture of moving in groups makes them good candidates for common-purpose legal doctrine that is available in many jurisdictions. For example, if eight men rob a liquor store and one of them shoots the cashier dead, all eight may be tried for murder. It is treated, understandably, the same as if all eight pulled the trigger. There will be cases where a person was just riding along or had not agreed to the killing part. Another example is a riot or club fight where one uses a knife to assault a rival and the other participants in the fight knew he might use it. Even if these participants did not actually have knives themselves, they will likely end up in jail or with adverse records.

Addressing Gatekeepers' Concerns and Dilemmas

The distance between your values and those of the gatekeepers will determine if you are a cultural fit for their organization. Gatekeepers' worries, however unfounded and unfair, should be addressed somehow. Expect that conviction question, even when you hope it won't come up. What questions are in an employer's mind when he or she looks at you or your resume? Suppose this guy steals? Suppose he has an outburst with another employee? Suppose he comes in stoned and crashes my fork lift? And if he hurts someone, do I get sued? Is he off drugs? The fears are based on whatever stereotype is floating around the community.

This may never happen. You are just strategizing and assessing risks that may never materialize. Develop strong talking points and skills to mitigate such risks.

Appearance Issues

Deal with appearance issues that reinforce stereotypes and dress appropriately. This could include tattoos and body rings if the market is sensitive to them. The public knows that convicts acquire affiliation tattoos to show allegiance or for protection in prison. Gatekeepers are part of this society.

Look for patterns of data and apply common sense, especially when you are representing yourself in court. Shrewd lawyers make sure you don't show up in offensive attire, nontraditional hairstyles, and incriminating body art. When do you make eye contact with the prosecutor, jury, and witnesses? When do you drop the lemon chewing attitude? Does your facial expression give a sense of innocence or portray a cold-blooded sociopath that should be locked away forever? How do you react to testimony? Good attorneys make sure you arrive early and understand court entry and exit protocol.

Today, dressing defendants is an art; some defense attorneys even hire fashion experts. Minor appearance issues can make a difference, especially in a close case or where jurors have fewer charge choices. Should a jobless defendant who lives on food stamps wear a $5000 suit to court when facing drug dealing charges? A body hugging mini dress may be seen as disrespectful to the judge. What about the writing on the T-shirt and the beer company logo when facing DWI (driving while intoxicated)?

Set Realistic Expectations in the Market

When your record is known at the workplace, expect that your sincerity may be questioned and tested. Your reaction will be monitored a little bit more, even when your case had nothing to do with violence. There will be temptations to counter aggression with aggression. How do you deal with insults and arguments? Do you walk away or resort to violence and confirm the stereotype? Prior records will be the lens through which your reactions will be observed for some time. People will doubt your character. You should approach the skepticism with a sense of equanimity and aim to regain trust. You may have to work harder to earn or reestablish trust.

Establish Meaningful Networks

Expand your networks beyond people with issues like yours. Seek to develop marketable skills. Learn how to sell yourself and market your job skills. Find ways to present your case in a way that puts you in a good light.

Capitalism sometimes works in a strange way. Find occupations where you can be the person in charge of your own enterprise and work with folks you trust. Do work as an independent contractor if you have to. Start your own business. Make your mess your message.

Confront the Past as Data and Discovery

Learn from any negative decisions that you made in the past. Learn from your family members' negative decisions if that is the case. Let this be the wind behind your wings. Find ways to stay positive and keep your spirits up. Study about your rights.

Concealing pertinent information will work against you in the long run. Should you disclose the information on your resume, cover letter, and application, or during the interview? Work with a professional counselor in your backdrop to establish the correct way to present your situation. Learn and practice how to positively frame past experience. Seek help from individuals, groups, and organizations that help people with criminal records.

Speak Up Regardless of Status

Become an advocate for horizontal coexistence where no one is treated unfairly because of stereotypical negative group attribution. Some crime-related social exclusion is stereotypically, unfairly, and, sometimes, unconsciously propagated. We still live in a world where gatekeepers can recklessly and wantonly target one group for arrest, put them in jail, and have the chutzpah to present that count as a statistic to prove that the group commits more crimes than its share of the population. It is the equivalent of false math and the epitome of naked injustice.

A real or perceived criminal record is a big problem in marginalized groups around the world. When low-risk convicts and nonviolent offenders receive overly harsh penalties instead of counseling, they come out of the system hardened. It is the economically disadvantaged people who are likely to encounter denial of legal protection, arbitrary arrest, and detention. Recidivism and joblessness create an orbit with its own magnetic field for the rest of a convict's live. Crime and the reliance on prison for its reduction are both burdens to law-abiding taxpayers.

The most painful kind of criminal record is the one you didn't even know you had. It is the economically disadvantaged who are likely to be perceived as having a criminal past based on negative group attributed stereotypes. We have seen cases where gatekeepers assume you are on parole just by the color of your skin, age, gender, place, or social status.

17

Disability

South Paw Sinistrality Club

When Mr. Seaside was invited to testify before Congress in support of disability rights legislation, he couldn't sleep for days. He had been waiting for that moment all his life, and he did not disappoint his audience. He knew every word of what he wanted to say. Mr. Seaside was a university president and also the chairman of the South Paw Sinistrality Club, a worldwide body that aims to increase public awareness of left-handedness.

"Ladies and gentlemen, what I have today for you is the story of my life as a left-handed kid. I grew up when left-handed babies were strongly encouraged to switch to right-handedness. The mothers would go to great lengths to make sure their kids did not write or eat with their left hands. Mothers would often tie their kids' left hands or impose punishment for using the wrong hand. Most of you know that all schools officially required students to write with their right hands. Teachers would encourage bullying against kids who used the wrong hand.

"It is not a secret that I was suspended from school nine times for cheating during exams. It is also on record that I was the brightest kid my school has ever come across. Today my record has not been broken. How was it possible that I was looking at other kids work during exams? It was simple.

"You all know that classroom desks are designed in such a way that the writing surface is attached to the right side and does not extend enough to the left. I was never able to write using my right hand, so I had to turn my body ninety degrees to use the writing surface. Exam rules dictated that a candidate had to face forward all the time.

"At one point I dropped out of school due to bullying and the institutional unfairness. All musical instruments and sporting equipment in the school were designed for right-hand use. The computer mouse was for the right. Even a small thing as a pencil sharpener was designed for right-hand use. How did I get back to school and become this scholar that the world knows today?

"First of all, I have always liked reading books. I started reading about great left-handed people. When I discovered that left-handiness is not even a disability, I was on fire. It was just a minority status with a surprising advantage in many areas. I also found out that for some unexplained reason, left-handed people are overrepresented among geniuses. My yield point was when I learned that my idols, Albert Einstein, Benjamin Franklin, Isaac Newton, and Charles Darwin, were allegedly left handed. I was unstoppable at that point.

"I had an uncle who understood my problem very well. He grew up when right-handed habits were so strictly required that most of the left-handed kids of his generation became ambidextrous. This uncle helped me to design a left-handed desk, but the school would not allow it. I used it at home and it still sits in my office today.

"Predominance of right-handedness is an extremely old phenomenon in this country. Many left-handed kids in my time dropped out of the school system because of bullying and the hostile environment. Those who stayed like me developed severe back, neck, and shoulder problems because of sitting and writing in a twisted angle for decades. In this country, left handers still earn less on average than their right-handed counterparts. There is an increased rate of illness among left-handed people. It is ironic that we become disabled because of a perceived disability.

"I use left-handedness as an example because I can relate to it. But the disability issue is big and wide. Ladies and gentlemen, we have not had a single left-handed elected member in this chamber, ever. We are light years behind other nations. More than 10 percent of world's population is left-handed".

"The school policies and the public attitude toward people facing real and perceived disabilities have not changed an inch. That is why I am here today. Spinal cord injuries and other disabilities don't discriminate against people. Anybody can end up in a wheelchair. Please pass this bill today."

When Mr. Seaside stopped talking, there was not a dry eye in the whole chamber. The disability act was passed by an overwhelming majority.

Manifestation of Disability-Based Social Exclusion

Disability exclusion is a global problem. Some countries have laws on the books that classify the disabled as a protected class. When people talk of disability, it is physical disability that comes to mind. We don't think of people who grow up with dyslexia, attention deficit disorder, or other learning disabilities. What about those with sight, hearing, speech, smell, and sense of touch disabilities? There are also people with mental health problems. The list is long. This factor covers all kinds of disabilities, including perceived future disabilities, as related to genetic discrimination.

There are also technical details and differences within each class of disability. Muteness, for example, describes people who can hear but cannot talk. A person can be born mute, or become mute later in life due to injury or disease. Muteness is often associated with deafness, especially for people who were born mute. I can write volumes on this subject alone, but I hope you get the idea. The topic is huge.

This book is about the ability to achieve your potential. Let us talk in terms of opportunities and negative-stereotype confirmation. Since most social exclusions are stereotypically and often unconsciously propagated, you should also educate yourself on disability-related stigma as exclusion. Users of mental health services, for example, may find themselves excluded from opportunities.

Lack of resources can be ruinous to your health and sanity, both of which are important in earning and getting more of them. In this state, you are stuck in the doldrums; a convergence of the predictable winds of poverty.

Conglomeration of Exclusion Factors NUBC

Disabled people have very low rates of employment when disability is accompanied by other exclusion factors, such as single parenthood, ethnicity, race, gender, age, or social class.

Nuthology Strategy

Learning how disability can be used to exclude you should be a part of your financial strategy. Look for patterns of data in an industry, company, or area in terms of hiring, assignment, promotion, performance reviews, and layoffs for people with disabilities.

Nuthology is about how you can direct the contents of your unique capsule talents in a way that benefits you. You can do this either by entering a profitable profession or starting your own business. There are many questions about what to do in a workplace backdrop. Since your disability and backdrop will be different from anybody else's, there is no single answer that will cover every situation. Your research and consultations with qualified professionals will guide your personal strategy. There are questions that can only be handled at the personal level. One such question, for instance, may involve disclosure of information. Should you reveal that you have special needs during the job application process? If so, should you disclose it on the resume, cover letter, during the interview, or the during onboarding process? The needs are also diverse.

Special Hardware or Software
Special Accommodation
Accessibility Needs
Adjusted Scheduling

Can disclosing information about your disability during the job application process work against you?

When should you be forthright about a mental disability? Should you reveal an invisible disability? What are the most common questions ignorant interviewers will ask? What is a lawful and inappropriate line of questioning?

Predictive Planning

The planning will depend on what concerns and backdrops you are analyzing. There are jobs that require you to endure long hours of physical labor, for example. You will factor in this assessment when choosing a career field, even without disclosing it to people.

Age-Related Disability

Something might look good when you are a teenager but become a burden as you grow older. A good example is a physically demanding job and aging. At this point, age becomes a perceived "disability". Even if you might be perfectly capable, the gatekeepers may look for ways to get rid of you. Depending on the industry, this factor should be a part of your planning.

Keep Up with Technology

Though not enough, there are many ways technology has helped the physically and mentally challenged improve their lives. Wheelchairs, elevators, braille, hearing aids, medical implants, and software programs continue to enhance people's lives. The ability to network with other people is a big plus.

Addressing Gatekeepers' Concerns and Dilemmas

Society needs a lot of education about dealing with people with disabilities. Consider a person speaking loudly to people in wheelchairs as if their physical disability affects their hearing. Another may use a preschool teacher's voice as if using a wheelchair affects mental capacity. These are common complains.

Some of the education will ultimately come from disabled people themselves. The first thing that most people think when they see a physically disabled person is to go out of their way to help. There are times when the well-intentioned action ends up offending the person being helped. Are you trying to patronize me or diminish my capability? You think I can't do this by myself? It can lead to a dilemma. When should one help?

Speak Up Regardless of Status

There is a continued need for society to improve quality of life and access to opportunities for people with disabilities. Representation in policy-making bodies is a good step toward that direction. Who knows better about a specific disability than the people living with it? There is a lack of representation in most law making bodies for the blind population, if I have to give an example. How many blind people are in your government? Become an advocate for horizontal coexistence where no one is treated unfairly because of his or her disability.

18

Disease, Genetic, Blood

The Journey to Hell and Back

A lot of water has passed under the bridge, but Mkena will always remember the year from hell. It was one of those times in her life that etched itself on the roof of her brain like a lightning fingerprint. It was the year she and her husband were both diagnosed with unrelated terminal diseases. They were both written off and forced to dig their own graves.

Mkena's husband, who worked in the city and came home only on weekends, was the first to receive the shocking diagnosis. He had prostate cancer. Fortunately he worked for a healthcare company that encouraged screening, so it was caught quite early. But he was worried about the heavy stigma related to lung and prostate cancers in the village. That was mainly due to the prevailing cultural myths and taboos.

The two cancers did not receive equal compassion and dignity as other cancers. Lung cancer was seen as one's own fault. Although most research studies show that more than 15 percent of lung cancer patients have never smoked cigarettes in their lives, patients didn't receive the benefit of the doubt in that region.

Prostate cancer patients faced even worse stigma. The body parts affected by the disease, the symptoms, and the treatments' side effects helped to add fuel to the stigma. There was no local language name for this disease, so it was only known as PC. In the village, men were so concerned for their manhood that they delayed seeking treatment. Mkena's husband was lucky since he spent most his time in the city.

Like other men with that diagnosis, Mkena's husband faced embarrassment. He swore his wife to secrecy when he first broke the news. But soon his hair started thinning due to the drugs, and the cat was out of the bag. It was in this backdrop that Mkena learned of her own nightmare. It was like adding fuel to a raging inferno. She had gone to the health center because of a mild case influenza.

She did know she that was pregnant with twins. It turned out that the combination of pregnancy and influenza was able to stimulate the immune system to produce antibodies that cross-reacted with HIV antigens and produced a false positive. It also appeared that there were rampant cases of clerical errors and contaminated specimens. It was discovered later that the lack of adequate staff training created numerous incidents of misinterpreted results. She was not aware of the false positives for months, which bring us back to our story.

Getting a false positive HIV test result can be stressful for anybody. In the village it was a hundred times more stressful. She did what everybody else in the village expected her to do. She prepared two graves at the corner of their farm: their final resting places. This was not only normal but mandatory. The graves were inspected by the local chief. She also paid a carpenter to make two identical wooden coffins at a discount. Can life ever get lower than this? The answer is yes.

In this country women are held to a different moral standard than men. They are often disproportionately blamed for the spread HIV in their communities. Arguably, it was all her fault. The internalization of the stigma lead her to experience unimaginable self-blame. She believed it though she could never figure out how she got infected in the first place.

By July her husband's health was improving. He was still thin and had lost most of his hair, but the results of his tests were very promising. Her influenza was gone. It is the villagers that were the problem. By now nobody would dare shake hands with either of them.

Neither of the two diseases are contagious, but the people believed they were. The belief in the village was that cancer was not only contagious, but it was a punishment for past sins. And HIV carried an even worse stigma. Two yawning graves in the backyard were not what anybody wanted to see when they woke up in the morning. The couple decided to move to the city permanently.

Within a month of settling in the city, three tests showed Mkena was HIV negative. To say that she was immensely relieved to hear the news is an understatement. Who wouldn't be? It was like having a seventy-ton rock removed from her neck.

Mkena's husband missed a lot of work days because of treatments; he had to constantly beg his boss not to lay him off. But the effort was worth it. It did not take long for him to be declared cancer free. They both regained their health. And when their bouncing twins were born later in the year, it was just icing on the proverbial cake.

Manifestation of Disease Stigma Based Social Exclusion

According to experts, this stigma happens when others devalue a person because they are associated with a certain disease. There are many reasons why people may crucify you for having a disease. It will depend on the disease and your backdrop.

This factor is all over the place. Some people may sympathize when you have one ailment but not another. You may be stigmatized by others based on assumptions about your moral integrity, lifestyle, and behavior. Did you engage in a questionable lifestyle?

There are myths and belief systems associated with different kinds of diseases that may result in social exclusion. A belief that a disease is contagious when it is not is a good example. Fear of contracting a disease, for example, can make others discriminate depending on the information out there.

A disease may be seen as a punishment based on cultural beliefs. People may delay being checked for a deadly disease solely due to cultural myths and taboos. In some countries the stigma exposes patients' vulnerability to physical violence.

Our concern here is how disease stigma affects one's ability to earn a living. We know this leads to increasing dependency and poverty. There are many ways that society suffers due to stigma. Disease stigma undermines prevention, treatment, and care of people to begin with. It may force people to hide infectious diseases and ultimately endanger the whole community.

Genetic Discrimination

What if a gatekeeper uses genetics to make decisions, such as hiring, firing, promotions, pay, and job assignments? The gatekeeper may be an employer or insurance company who is looking to see if you have a family history of a disease or some other genetic disorder. Some countries have even enacted laws on genetic discrimination. This can work against you if you are found to be a future liability, even after investing in education in that field. It's a good idea to research your target industry and contact qualified professionals in this subject.

Discrimination by Blood Type

If this was not about denying people a chance to earn a living, it would be comical. "You really don't want to hire type-F blood. That means failures. You really don't want to hire type-L blood types. That means losers." But this is a serious exclusion class. Since blood type distribution may be different for specific racial and ethnic groups and even nations, this exclusion can be a front for racial discrimination. Consider a situation where the gatekeeper insists on a certain blood type, knowing too well that people from other ethnic groups or from certain regions will be disqualified.

Conglomeration of Exclusion Factors NUBC

This factor is worse for groups who are already marginalized based on gender, sexual orientation, ethnicity, race, or any of the other exclusion classes. It only accelerates the negative spiral.

The rich and famous people may not be as excluded as poor people with the same disease, so social class also plays a role. It is not uncommon to find homelessness, mental illness stigma, and ageism factor exclusions together. Compare two people who are HIV positive. One is a rich celebrity while the other is an old, poor homeless person with a mental problem. Their NUBCs will not be the same. The former has some credits working for him while the later may have concerns with:

Disease stigma
Age
Shelter
Social class
Employment
Place
Character

Nuthology Strategy

Nuthology is about optimization of your talents in a challenging backdrop. In this case its disease stigma. You will agree that every patient is different and the backdrop will also differ when dealing with this issue. That is the main reason society cannot craft a perfect solution for everybody.

Learning how this factor can be used to exclude you should be a part of your financial intelligence. Your strategy should include how to seek professional help and control private information. If the factor is combined with other exclusion factors, use the strategy in our mitigation section and other sources of education to create a strategy that puts all the ducks in a row.

You should know that you are always in control. This realization empowers you tremendously. You can now live for yourself and not for others' approval.

Like most social exclusions, disease stigma is stereotypically, unfairly, and, sometimes, unconsciously applied. Your plan should be executed in a way that you avoid exacerbating the issue at hand. Do not delay seeking help because of the stigma. Move if you have to. Perform some good research. Chances are somebody else has gone through what you are going through. Develop networks and join groups that will enrich you.

Speak Up Regardless of Status

History shows that the general public's misconception about a particular disease is major contributor to this exclusion. The way leprosy stigma has been handled by states and churches over hundreds of years can give you a good picture on how this factor manifests itself.

At the societal level, become an advocate for horizontal coexistence where no one is treated unfairly because of his or her disease status or perceived risk of an inherited disorder.

Mental illness and drug addiction are also some of deviations under this class that will require society to come up with a better approach. Let us not forget that marginalized groups are more vulnerable to mental disorders than well-to-do groups to begin with. The constant fear of physical and financial insecurity is a major source of depression. Nobody wants to live in a situation where he or she can lose control at any minute. What may seem to be a non-catastrophic event, such as temporary unemployment, lost crops, or a short-duration sickness, can be a major blow to people with low incomes. There is no buffer zone.

19

Ethnicity

Ode to the Wandering Third Rock

Of the eight spinning, revolving and often tilting rocks, the third one from the gas giant was the only one with living things. The rock had enough space and food for each occupant. That was before the man came out and started shouting:

My family is the greatest.
My clan is the greatest.
My tribe is the greatest.
My people are the greatest.
My race is the greatest.
My religion is the greatest.
My God is the greatest.
My part of the rock is the greatest.
My, my, my, my.

His name was Mr. My.

Oh my. Then all the inhabitants of the third rock came out shouting. Each one of them was proclaiming the supremacy of some in-groups. Different criteria were used organically to form the groups. Membership on the major groups was based on shared physical attributes, cultural heritage, ancestry, history, and language. Symbolic systems such as religion, mythology, and ritual, as well as food, dressing style, and physical appearance were also used. Social stigma was born.

The tension grew. Some Third-Rockies started designing experiments to prove their inherent superiority. There were pseudoscience reports and revised historical documents. The lines were drawn on the rock with blood.

In-group favoritism was replaced by aggression. Each group had meetings on how to exclude other Third-Rockies. Some people started hoarding resources and spaces on the rock. Rock pieces were used as weapons to attack and defend. The need to have more superseded the need to keep inhabitants alive. Hunger appeared on some parts of the now demarcated rock. People died of hunger on one part of the third rock. People died of overeating on the other side.

For the billions who call the third wandering rock home, life would never be the same. Between in-group favoritism and hate-filled aggression, compassion had taken the backseat. Greed became the new religion.

Manifestation of Ethnicity-Based Social Exclusion

If you followed any world news today you will agree with me that ethnicity is one of the dominant themes in conflicts around the world. Our history has major scars to show from these conflicts.

Most sources define an ethnic group as a social group of people who identify with each other based on common ancestral, social, cultural, or national experience.

In this book we will use ethnicity as it is generally used without dwelling too much on semantics. The same definition can fit other natural-based exclusions like racism and tribalism. In this case, a race includes a vast variety of ethnicities. We all know it is more complicated than this.

Most ethnic-based stigmas and social exclusions are stereotypically, unfairly, and, sometimes, unconsciously promulgated. Negative stereotypes may be a joke to some people, but we have seen them lead to ethnicity-based discrimination and state-sponsored mistreatment of people.

Nuthology is interested in ethnic nepotism and how it affects your ability to earn a living. Like in tribalism or racism, this involves in-group favoritism applied toward people with the same ethnicity within a multiethnic society. Anti-ethnic sentiment often entails modern-day derogatory stereotyping and discrimination. Relationships between the major ethnic groups are often complicated. Jokes based on stereotypes about certain groups and their work ethic may lead to fewer job opportunities. There are even jokes that generally stereotype certain ethnic groups as being of inferior intelligence.

Conglomeration of Exclusion Factors NUBC

Consider an immigrant who is internalizing concerns about race, ethnicity, tribalism, colorism, national origin, alma mater, language, and protocol all at the same time without a proper strategy. His NUBC may be as follows:

Ethnicity
Race
Tribalism
Colorism
National origin
Alma mater
Language
Protocol

The economic importance of this convergence cannot be ignored. At the very least it will be inefficient to do that.

Conglomerate

You should first remember that these are risks that may never materialize, but they are your concerns. Bring them all together and design a personalized strategy that factors them all. Learning how ethnicity can be used to exclude you within various specific backdrops should be a part of your financial intelligence.

Addressing Gatekeepers' Concerns and Dilemmas

Let's refer back to the microcosm assumption of the Nuthology Index. If you are new to a community, for example, chances are that the gatekeepers are part of the local society. The distance between your values and those of the gatekeepers will determine the cultural fit. You have to build enough skills, networks, and character to reduce the gap. Since this will all depend on your backdrop, educating yourself on this subject is a great start.

Index

Feel free to include any bias that is based on actual or perceived ancestry in this category if it is not covered under another admitted class.

Reducing Your Own Stereotype-Driven Aggression

Catch yourself not supporting prevailing negative stereotypes in your area, such as people from this ethnic race are lazy or people from that ethnic race are bad drivers. How would you feel if there was a negative portrayal of your ethnic group as a backward or lazy group? Ethnic slurs and negative stereotypes are all meant to disparage and put down a group of people. It is a form of bullying and harassment.

Speaking Up

Become an advocate for horizontal coexistence where no one is treated unfairly because of his or her ethnicity. Many ethnic organizations have been formed to challenge the negative stereotyping of the people once prevalent in media.

20

Etiquette, Protocol

Hippo-Grade Yawner and Sons

After thirty years in this business, Greg has become a student of interview room behavior. But this particular candidate was out of this world. He was very qualified on paper. It took Greg decades to learn not to form an opinion based on a candidate's appearance and the impression it made. Every time a candidate walks in the room, he has to catch himself.

The law requires that candidates get a fair chance to showcase their talents and qualifications. But the interviewers are human beings. These mere mortals are bound to come across a candidate who reminds them of the guy who cut them off in traffic and flipped them multiple birds.

Matt, the candidate showed up an hour early. You could smell his cologne from the parking lot. During the interview Matt moved from rubbing the back of his neck and nose to slouching back in his seat. He yawned and checked the time. He answered one question in ten minutes. He was not waiting for questions to be completed. He cracked inappropriate jokes, either trashing his previous bosses or previous jobs. Several times he stopped to take a call and check messages.

The interview took an eternity. The company had been sued before, so Greg let the interview run its course. Then it was the candidate's turn to ask questions. All hell broke loose. "What does this company do again? When will I have my first vacation? Do you guys do back-ground checks?"

One good thing came from all that mess. That night Greg launched Greg Mock Interview Services. In his new company veteran interviewers worked part time doing paid mock interviews using generally asked questions. They trained candidates on interview protocol and business etiquette. The candidates received guidance on basic interview etiquette and entry behavior. Their main concentrations included body language, resume preparation, and pre-interview research. The world was ready.

Manifestation of Etiquette-Based Social Exclusion

Different cultures maintain different etiquette and protocol. This includes corporate culture. Different industries maintain different etiquette and protocol. You may have all the qualifications, but this factor can sink your ship in a jiffy. Body language and personal space may cost you an opportunity often without your knowledge.

Let us take body language, as an example. What message do you communicate the moment you walk into a room? What are your eyes, hands, and shoulders saying? What information can people gather about you before you ever say a word?

Etiquette and protocol change every day. Just a few years ago it was a capital offense to interrupt people while they were on the phone. Depending on the background, nowadays you may be forced to get people off their phones; otherwise, Jesus will come back before they do. Phone time is now an eternity. You just need to look around to see Homo sapiens tethered to ear-pieces or with thumbs glued on the small screens.

Many actions that are considered jest outside of work can be perceived as inappropriate or even harassment in the work environment. You have to be flexible and a good student of your environment.

You may recall what happened to your ears when you were caught misbehaving in church when you were a little kid. That was church etiquette that you broke. Here are some more environments:

Interview
Formal and non-formal dining
Gym
Business
Funeral
Phone
Cinema
Family reunion
Weddings
School
Diplomatic
Grocery line
Bathroom
In-laws house
Court
Church
Public pool
Beach
Other social settings

Conglomeration of Exclusion Factors NUBC

Since this book is a financial literacy book, let's look at the workplace backdrop as an example. Let's consider kids who grew up in certain marginalized areas who may not know how to act in a business environment a few blocks from their street. The combination of concerns may produce a mobility-blocking strain of NUBC:

Etiquette protocol
Ethnicity
Race
Place
Affiliation
Age
Employment
Character

Nuthology Strategy and the Capsule of Talents

Learning how etiquette and protocol can be used to exclude you should be a part of your financial strategy from the get go. Each of us is endowed with talents. You have to find ways to utilize those talents, and that includes interacting with people in a civilized manner. This can include manners, business etiquette, and even international protocol. This will vary from profession to profession and culture to culture.

"If a child washed his hands, he could eat with kings." Chinua Achebe

Addressing Gatekeepers' Concerns

In a dating environment people may not have good insight into what attracts them to others, but they have a good idea what does not attract them. The job environment is the same. Even when armed with a lengthy job description, the recruiters may lack insight into what exactly attracts them to a candidate, but they have a good idea which candidates never to hire. They still remember the gum-chewing missy from ten years ago.

The distance between your values and those of the gatekeepers will determine the cultural fit. In most cases, when you visit someone else's home or place business, that person's wishes take precedence in terms of the dress code. You are the one who came looking for a job.

Employers and investors are visual beings, not unlike us all. They will scan you within a few seconds. They will get some preliminary vibes from you, good or bad. Sometimes appearance can indicate laziness or attention to detail. It might be as simple as that perfectly shone pair of shoes or a pressed shirt.

You must not act like the interviewer owes you something. Forgetting your manners and claiming your dog ate them is one of the best ways to exclude yourself. Being intuitive of other people's needs is a good start. Respecting other people's time and not talking over others follow close behind. There is a good old rule of thumb that demands that we listen, process, and then act.

First Impression

It is good that you are comfortable with whatever you are wearing. For most jobs you just need to dress accordingly. Limit your application of colognes and perfumes. What to wear on your interview seems like common sense to most of people.

It is not necessarily about the clothes themselves, because different jobs require you to dress in different ways. It is about the art itself. It is about playing that future employee that the employer wants to see. If you are looking to be a lumberjack, a designer suit and a well-manicured face might work against you. If, on the other hand, it is a Wall Street hedge fund job, facial hair with small animals and rugged dressing may not help.

Tardiness

If you are going for an interview, it is obvious that you must be punctual. Even better, arrive early. Not too early or you will be pushing it. Anticipate traffic, road construction, and parking delays. This is your one chance.

Personal Space

Establish a comfortable amount of personal space between you and the interviewer. You have to research this. In most places there are established personal air spaces that may activate fighter jet looks. The interviewer may not want to know that you ate garlic and probably Naphthalene mothballs the previous night.

Handshake

Give a strong handshake. Avoid the milky handshake. Don't make the interviewer feel like he is holding onto a moldy wet noodle. On the other hand, don't be a bone crusher. That flesh-grinding cinch may work in high school practical jokes but not here. Reserve the creative handshakes and bumps for the happy hour at Joe Blows tavern.

Interviews are actually voluntary full-blown interrogations. Pretend you care for a minute. You are also reading the interviewer.

Who is better, an over-talker or the stone-faced interrogator? Show your enthusiasm by keeping an interested expression.

Lack of passion or visible boredom is a deal killer. Sit up straight and lean slightly forward in your chair. Don't rub the back of your head or neck. Don't sit with your arms folded across your chest. Don't slouch back in your seat. Mind that constant hippo-grade yawn; it is an interview not a dental exam. No taking a call or checking messages unless there is an actual earthquake at your mother's house.

Catch Yourself

Trashing your old boss or previous job may be tempting when talking to a potential new boss. Never feel like you need to disparage past employers. It almost always makes you look bad. Avoid overselling yourself to the interviewer. It may come across as cheesy.

Asking the Wrong Questions

Forget what they told you: there are wrong or stupid questions. Don't ask questions that can be answered by a quick online search. This is not 1800. In this technological age, asking what the company does shows that you are grossly unprepared. Avoid being seen as focusing too much on the benefits the company provides over the value you can bring to the company. It should be the opposite. That's why the job was under "help wanted" not "who wants help."

Etiquette and protocol don't not stop when you get hired. There will be reviews, promotions, and terminations. You have to decide when to use exclamation points instead of periods in your written communication for example. Not everyone appreciates emoticons and the smiley faces on your e-mail. You might love that winking or big smile emoticon, but the use of emoticons in professional e-mails is frowned upon in some industries. It is not what you say; it is how you say it. You may not overshoot or embarrass your boss in meetings. There is a firing app for that.

Seek Education

Employers look for manners, self-respect, discipline, etiquette, and protocol on top of qualifications when deciding who to hire. These are lessons that are naturally considered part of parenting obligations. What about the kids who grew up without those vital lessons a few years back and who are now the new parents? We are expecting parents who were never in the job environment themselves and who may be ill equipped to dispense income generating advice to do just that. Consequently, their kids may grow up to be non-earners. That cycle can be maintained by geography alone and needs to be broken. Research your target industry and environment. Find networks and mentors outside your comfort zone.

Reducing Your Own Stereotype Driven Aggression

There is pressure in some locations for the youth to view obeying laws, business protocol and self-improvement in a negative way. This not about conforming or duplicating other cultures. Decency expectation is not conformity. Learning to live where opportunities are and improving yourself should not be sold as being a "sellout." Just because somebody has cleaned up well and networked outside his comfort zone makes him a monster? Give me a break! Independent thinking and problem solving are part of the quest for social, political, and economic equality.

Speak Up Regardless of Status

Some of the social exclusions related to etiquette are stereotypically, unfairly, and, sometimes, unconsciously applied. If a negative group attribution perception is that a certain community suffers from character, etiquette, and protocol deficiency members may be subject to discrimination by affiliation. Become a good advocate for horizontal coexistence where no one is treated unfairly because of his or her perceived affiliation.

21

Gender

Conundrum of Success

Mary is the first female chief engineer ever for this company. In this part of the world, beautiful women are not expected to excel in a science field. Culturally driven gender differences in education and upbringing tend to steer women away from engineering careers in this town. She holds two PhDs in nuclear physics and a ton of experience to boot. There are few women engineers working for the company due to the underlying stereotypes in the city.

Mary's teething problems as leader were predictable and started early. To be a leader you have to be assertive. Well, women are not expected to be assertive in this neck of the woods. That would be considered being bossy. Dealing with 5000 egos will call for guts. Mary is cut out for it. But she had bigger man problems.

Her father wants her to meet somebody before she turns thirty. In any other world she wouldn't be in a hurry, but this society's unwritten rules are clear. Step one after you finish school is to get married, have children, and procure a newer model minivan. The acquisition of a dog and a house with a picket fence should not be far behind. Cats are optional but will definitely earn you extra brownie points. That's the normal order of things as defined by the neighborhood watch. Any deviation from this process will be met with social stigma.

Mary is willing to play along, at least to please her dad, but her last few dates have been catastrophic. She had met a few great eligible men but all had the same problem. They thought she made too much money for their comfort. That would be a good thing in other places but not here. Even the mere thought of a man depending on his wife is emasculating.

In this society women who bring home bigger paychecks have a hard time dating and are known to have marital issues. She sold her house recently to cut her "baggage" down. Her desires did not align with what women are supposed to want.

Last Monday was an even bigger disaster. She went on her first date in almost six months. She had met this thirty-three-year-old freelance consultant online. He was fine with any financial arrangement and the dinner date went well. After the dinner she had to pay for their meals because the man had "forgotten" his wallet at home. The basement dweller called his mom to pick him up, borrowed five dollars from Mary, and went on his merry way. It was nothing unusual. Mary had found a keeper, or so she thought.

When her father heard of the encounter, hair blew off his bald head. He was so apoplectic. He didn't like the football field–size red flags generated by the date. "Let me get this straight. You want a jobless guy who lives in his mother's basement, doesn't pay for his date's dinner and has the gall to borrow five bucks? Are you kidding me?" Even her usually supportive mother was a bit cheesed off too. She thought the guy sounded like a garden variety "deferred success."

Well that was another false start. For now Mary will continue wearing a wedding ring to deflect the single status stigma. With such a hostile cohort at home, this might require a brand new double enhanced thesis. She will call it "The Conundrum of Female Success in a Male-Dominated Ecosystem."

Manifestation of Gender-Based Social Exclusion

Gender exclusion is a well-documented factor. It is a product of in-group favoritism, out-group derogation, and negative-stereotype all mixed up. Failure in both gender and social class relations almost always go together. This leads to a widening gap in distribution of resources, benefits, and responsibilities. We have places in fairly modern nations where people cannot be executors of estates based on gender. That puts one gender at an economic disadvantage right off the bat. That is just one example.

Gender roles in society provide a setting where gender inequalities are both manifested and sustained. Most traditional attitudes and beliefs that drive gender exclusion in education, property rights, inheritance, and opportunities are way past their expiration dates. Social pressures, for example, can be used to explain the gap between minority females and technology professions more than race.

Since gender roles and barriers are institutionalized at a very young age, this issue must be confronted from the root. If you want to balance gender diversity in the technology industry, for example, then you have to improve computer science education to women and girls.

Gender discrimination is a major reason women choose some careers and not others. This ultimately determines what they earn and contributes to the ever-growing wage gap. Gender bias continues at other gateways such as admissions, hiring, and promotion decisions. This can also lead to double standard where everything is measured in terms of the dominant gender. A woman is seen as a leader only if she displays a masculine leadership style. A behavior that would be seen positively in men may be seen negatively when women do it. In an effort to appear ladylike, women are tempted to downplay their success. It becomes a dilemma.

There are also many stereotypes that work against men that can result in emotional and financial consequences. Since this a personal strategy, it is appropriate to look at examples where a man can face unfair exclusion. The risk of a man getting the short end of the stick in a divorce is very high in some countries. In a contested divorce scenario a man may have to fight a little harder to be awarded primary custody. By default women are seen as the nurturers in most societies.

You can also find gender bias against men in many child support rulings. Bigger men can be abused by smaller women, but it is hard to convince the court or law enforcement of that. Men can also be judged based on things that are determined by genetics, such as height or baldness.

Nuthology strategy is not about putting one gender over the other. Are there cases where men are overlooked because the company wants more female employees? Yes, off course. If you are a man looking for a job in this backdrop then the gender exclusion will count.

Society creates pressure for boys to be aggressive at an early age. Sometimes it is the females in a boy's life who creates the monster. "Be a man. Don't hit the ball like a girl. She makes you wash dishes?"

The above examples are not meant to side with any gender. Since this is a personal book, you will decide when the risk of exclusion is apparent. Let us remember the gatekeepers are not always of the opposite gender. Although men are usually seen as the main obstacles, some female employers will not hire a woman that is better looking than them. There are also men who may prefer hiring women based primarily on gender.

Conglomeration of Exclusion Factors NUBC

Consider a newly divorced single mother who is jobless and has no credit history of her own. She lives with a relative in a bad neighborhood and lacks reliable transportation. Society may help dealing with gender-related concerns but other concerns such as marital status, parenthood, long-term unemployment, credit history, shelter, transportation and place may still block her mobility. The society may see a gender concern only. Her NUBC shows:

Gender
Credit History
Parenthood
Marital status
Parenthood
Social class
Place
Transportation

Consider the same a single mother as above only this time she is an older disabled minority woman. Her NUBC shows.

Gender
Credit History
Parenthood
Marital status
Parenthood
Social class
Place
Transportation
Race
Age
Disability

Nuthology Strategy

Nuthology is a strategy aimed at helping you to take control of your financial destiny. Gender discussions tend to get caught up in the unitary concept lens. At personal level you are able to see the full picture. This is not something new. Most people do this organically. The first thing you do is to conglomerate all of these factors when creating a personal strategy.

Most gender-related social exclusion is stereotypically, unfairly, and, sometimes, unconsciously propagated. You have your unique capsule of talents. Be the best original copy of yourself. Negative stereotypes can lead to underselling yourself either by choosing low paying careers or by not displaying your achievements.

Even without the Nuthology Index, people's perceptions of the way things are really influences how they act. The risk that you may even judge yourself based on these stereotypes must be addressed first. You will need to develop a plan of engagement that promotes your abilities and self-worth. You will need live for your own and not for others' approval.

What if you brought in the biggest client that netted the company tons of revenue? Provide facts and details if you fear coming off as arrogant. Do not be afraid to take credit for things that you have done.

Gender exclusion is a risk that you may have to mitigate when choosing a career. Should you go for that modeling contract or a professional degree? Can you do both? Should you do both?

Be realistic as you fight equality. Equal opportunity does not mean being a cheap replica of someone else. Recognize that biological differences between women and men are considered in relation to hazards they may face in some industries. There are many other factors that contribute to gender-related issues that we are not covering here. Some women leave jobs to raise children. Some never return to the workforce. Some never enter the workforce at all.

Reach out and expand your networks beyond your bubble. Even as you design your own goals, you are still part of the larger community that is fighting for equality. Encourage social inclusion with inclusion of your own wherever possible. Men and boys are often the untapped resource in many gender initiatives for instance.

Reducing Your Own Stereotype-Driven Aggression

Discourage casual sexism in the workplace and public life, which includes insensitive remarks toward the opposite gender. Overcompensation and blanket blame only reduces your network. Be aware of activism that crosses the line and becomes counterproductive. Gender equality for women should be a question of equitable access and equality as human beings, not a question of substituting unfair patriarchy with unfair matriarchy.

Speak up

Become a global advocate for policy changes regarding gender inequities regardless of your gender.

22

Hair, Baldness

Hair Today, Gone Tomorrow

Half of the waiting crowd was already in tears even before the returning soldiers started disembarking from the gigantic aircraft carrier. Bruce Jordan's mother was wailing uncontrollably. Her son had survived two major wars. The first was the "hair war" at home. It was easy to be fooled by Bruce's demeanor as he strode confidently from the sea vessel. The clean shaven head, bulging muscles, and sharp military uniform made him look like a human wrecking ball. Five years ago it was a different story.

Three weeks before his first deployment, the nineteen-year-old marine received $20,000 from his mother for an "as seen on TV" hair transplant procedure. He had not asked for it. Bruce's mother was convinced his early hair loss would affect his self-esteem, so she had mortgaged their house. She had endured receding hairline stigma in her teenage years a few decades earlier. It was the early nineties. At that time men would go to great lengths to hide their baldness, which ushered in a multibillion-dollar hair loss industry.

Bruce had taken the money to please her and even went ahead and set up an appointment. He was never really sold on the idea. Was baldness a disease that he had to do something about? Then deployment happened. A close friend gave him a humorous plaque that said, "God made but a few perfect heads. The rest he put hair on." That was not all. He convinced him to buy a cheap technology stock until he was ready for the procedure. The cycle of deployments took longer than expected.

In those short five years, a cohort of wildly successful bald athletes and movie actors swept the nation like a storm. Hair was no longer considered to be the main thing above the neck. Most balding men were no longer spending sleepless nights thinking of artificial means to cover their heads. It was now cool to have a shiny head. As a matter of fact, many young men with full heads of hair were shaving just for the look. The clean cut head made them look sharp and tough like the celebrities they adored.

The homecoming was magical. He didn't have to say anything about the hair issue. Bruce's mother already had a sense that her son was no longer pursuing the transplant procedure. But she was not ready for the surprise that would leave her speechless. The stock that Bruce had "accidentally" bought was now worth $150,000 dollars. He had a hard time convincing his mom to accept at least $50,000 of the gain. Since marines don't give up easily, she agreed to take $10,000 to clear the last portion of outstanding loan.

Manifestation of Hair-Based Social Exclusion

I am sorry if I made you cry. The story was not meant to be an episode of *The Bald Soldier Prince.* In all seriousness though, I hope you agree with me that the above hair-raising fictional case study is not that farfetched.

Hair world is a multibillion-dollar industry for a reason. Hair infomercials work, otherwise they wouldn't air them every night. Treatments for hair loss include medication, replacement, and restoration. Stores have thousands of products that are meant to enhance hair. Wars have been fought over hair. Well, domestic civil wars!

Hair is considered a part of first impression and appearance. Your backdrop will dictate how hair-related social exclusion manifests itself.

It is unfathomable, but research and casual observation indicates that hair-related social stigma exists worldwide. It is a great concern to the affected people. This book is about those real or imagined concerns.

First of all, let's play a game just because today is hair judgment day. Who is considered more beautiful? Who is considered smarter? Who is considered this and that? How shallow can we get?

Afro puffs
Animal hair
Auburn locks
Bald
Blond
Birds nest
Brunette
Chest hair
Colored hair
Comb-over
Dead hair
Damaged hair
Dreadlocks
Dyed hair
Ethnic
Extensions
Facial hair
Faddish styles
Faux-hawk
Funky cuts
Ginger,
Gorgeous hair
Gray hair
Half shorn
Head covers
Head ornaments
Human hair
Male-pattern baldness
Mohawks

Natural hair
Nontraditional hairstyles
Partial hair
Ponytails
Rat tails
Salt and pepper
Sandy hair
Shaved designs
Short hair
Small twisted braids
Tattooed head
Thinning hair
Toupee
Treated hair
Twisted braids
Unnatural
Widow's peak
Wigs

Lack of Hair and Excess Hair

As you might have noted, I am also including lack of hair in this class. Balding or thinning is a major concern for some people, even where it is not considered a mainstream bias class. Baldness has also been confused with aging in men. Premature baldness can be hereditary and have nothing to do with age. In some areas bald is becoming cool now because of celebrities and other thought-leader interventions.

There are people who have excess hair or hair in the wrong places. A woman with visible or excess facial hair may face a stigma depending on her backdrop. She will count this as a concern when planning.

Facial Hair

We all know people who like to look like the Old Testament patriarchs. Many employers have established strict policies on facial hair.

I have seen reports where people have been fired or suspended for sporting a run-away goatee. These reports do not account for cases where a gatekeeper uses a contrived excuse to push you out.

There is a growing advocacy against beard-ism. Unlike immutable factors like race or gender, having a beard is seen as matter of personal choice, so it is not as protected in most countries.

This is a factor that works well with other classes of social exclusion.

Age Factor

Gray hair is considered one of the most common signs of aging. Of course, heredity and other factors play a role, but remember we are talking about public opinion here not science. There are people who get gray hairs in their twenties. You want science? Here is the rule of fifty. By the age of fifty, 50 percent of the population has 50 percent gray hairs. I made the rule up but the facts are true. Gray hair is supposed to make you look distinguished but it's also known to attract age discrimination.

Social Class Factor

Another rule: if you are rich and famous you may look distinguished with whatever style you may choose. What if you are not? You may not be able to pull it off. Can it lead to age, shelter, or attractiveness concerns? You may appear more like a homeless stereotype than a celebrity. We are talking about prevailing perceptions in your ecosystem.

Race and Ethnicity Factors

There are issues with what is not written down, especially if hair style, texture, or color are viewed through a bias lens. This creates pressure to change from a natural hairstyle to a copy of somebody else's.

Affiliation, Lifestyle, and Character Factors

Hair can be used as way to express oneself or it can be viewed as so. Some hairstyles are predominantly worn by people who live certain lifestyles.

Wearing a hairstyle that is different from the norm in the corporate world can be a cause for subtle exclusion. You may be ultra-hip and ultra-cool, but your hairstyle may galvanize negative perceptions against you. Some faddish hairstyles may be unacceptable, even when that is not explicitly stated in the policy.

Attractiveness and Gender

Too much emphasis is placed on beauty in this world. Hair is a central player in this, especially for women. Male-pattern baldness in females can be tough in the aesthetics department. Millions of women in the world live with a concern of unwanted, male-pattern facial hair growth.

Colorism Factor

There is no credible research that shows any link between intelligence level and hair color. This does not stop some people from positioning themselves as inherently superior beings just based on hair color. You have heard those jokes where ones hair color is correlated to dumbness. Should you share that "supposedly harmless" deprecating humor? This leads to hair-based, in-group favoritism and sometimes out-group derogation.

Religious Factor

Beards can be ritual in a religious backdrop. Workplace discrimination against those who wear beards falls in this category. Some people wear hats or head covers for religious reasons.

Conglomeration of Exclusion Factors NUBC

Consider a poor woman with thinning hair due to a medical condition. If she had gender, age, weight, and disability concerns before, her NUBC may now be:

Hair
Social class
Disease stigma

Gender
Age
Weight
Disability
Attractiveness

Nuthology Strategy

Learning how the hair factor can be used to exclude you should be a part of your financial strategy. Each one of us is endowed with a unique capsule of talents. Do not give that power away. You should not, for example, let others decide if your natural hair type is beautiful or not.

You should design a strategy that factors in all these concerns to avoid wasting time and energy. This is just a risk that may never materialize. This is a career or business analysis efficiency move that many people make organically.

When combined with other factors, as we have seen above, hair bias can cement the stereotype-related threat to the detriment of an individual's achievement. A conglomerate with certain hair color, for example, might think her or she is not good at something based on negative stereotypes. The risk that you may judge yourself negatively demands that you deal with these issues proactively.

Addressing Gatekeepers' Concerns and Dilemmas

Think before choosing a style that may be considered too edgy and against company policy. Some industries have hair standards as part of the company dress policy. They may say, for example, that hair must be a natural color and must not be a distraction. You may have to get a haircut or dye your hair back to a normal color. Hair grows back, time doesn't. You have to decide.

Sometimes it is in the vibe you emit. In some areas men that are unemployed have little need to shave every day. Consequently, not shaving can make you appear homeless or jobless. In some backdrops maintaining a beard can be viewed as laziness. Imagine an older man with unkempt hair, a long beard, torn jeans, and an old dress shirt with the worn tails out attending a church, a wedding, or a funeral while everybody else looks sharp.

Gatekeepers' Concerns on Safety and Liability

Most companies' dress codes address what hairstyles, lengths and colors, are acceptable. Beside your job qualifications, the distance between your values and those of the gatekeepers will determine the cultural fit.

Some industries ban facial hair for functional or health reasons. An example is when beards seem to interfere with breathing apparatuses or masks. At food counters, factories, and commercial kitchens excess hair can be seen as a health risk.

Overcompensation Reduces Your Network.

Growing certain hairstyles or a beard just to prove a point means that you may have bigger issues. Catastrophizing and exacerbating limits your opportunities; try to see the big picture.

Reducing Your Own Stereotype-Driven Aggression

This book is not about causes, but I want to point out that there are many diseases and medical reasons that can cause loss or increase of hair. This is something to think about when you work on your own aggression footprint.

Empathize more than you sympathize. Be part of the solution. Do not hate on people because they just happen to have perceived perfect hair. It is not their fault.

Hair-based humor can act as an indicator or releaser of prejudice, mostly subconsciously. Hair jokes usually have gender, ethnic, or racial undertones. This can make any workplace toxic. Do not encourage hair-based aggression. How is a short, fat, bald guy portrayed on TV and in the movies? Is he always the villain? Cases of teasing, joking, and bullying based on hairstyle can indicate that this factor may be in play.

Speak Up

Most hair-related social exclusions are stereotypically, unfairly, and, sometimes, unconsciously propagated. There are no reliable studies showing an intelligence correlation between what is inside the scull and what covers it.

Become an advocate for horizontal coexistence where no one is treated unfairly because of his or her hair, lack of hair, head cover, or related variations.

23

Height

The Height Hierarchies

All young shepherds in the Nahye plains were required to wear stilts until they were of age. This was not only to extend their field of vision and to allow them to reach the delicate Matunda fruits but most importantly to avoid being killed by the ruthless Super Crocuta, a rare breed of horse-size hyenas. Trohsman was no longer a boy, but he was barely four feet tall. The village was worried about him. The elders of the Nahye plains made a difficult decision. Trohsman had to walk on stilts until other means were found to protect him. Considering the recent spate of Super Crocuta attacks in the last few gracing seasons, the elders meant well.

At first Trohsman was very unhappy. It was abnormal and emasculating for adult men to walk in stilts. Historically in this town lofty boys were admired, while the very short were caricatured. In Nahye, tall men were perceived as natural leaders. The legend was that a mean man-eating Super Crocuta trembles and ducks for cover when a tall man approaches. Harvesting Matunda fruits and looking after sheep were the main male occupations in the village. Women competed for taller men for those reasons. Men were protectors and providers.

Necessity is the mother of boundless ingenuity. Trohsman became a formidable expert in stilt walking. He could jump, somersault, and do cartwheels on stilts. He could not find a woman shorter than him to marry. Then he met Llat Manwo. The six foot tall gorgeous lady had her share of problems with height status in the dating pool. She had a problem getting a taller man. She was taller than most people in the isolated village. She couldn't be a shepherd or a fruit gatherer. Engaging in those occupations would bring a curse to her family.

The two started as partners during village dances. They made an odd couple. Trohsman adjusted his stilts to be a few inches taller than Llat. Dances were therapeutic. It helped that both were good drummers and dancers. For the first time Llat felt valued. It was during one of these dances that a group of city tourists and leaders started visiting the village.

Mr. Smith, one of the tourists, had seen the dance on TV. But it was not the dance that impressed him most. It turned out stilting was a very marketable skill in his home country. One thing led to another, and Trohsman ended up in Doarba as a stilt trainer. His wife, Llat, worked at the school. She taught occupational and therapeutic stilting. Students at the Smith Stilt Institute included painters, artists, circus performers, clowns, and even amputees.

Then Mr. Smith came up with an unorthodox idea that turned out to be a gold mine: stilt basketball. The Doarba Stilt Basketball Association (DSBA) started as a local exhibition team with Trohsman as the coach and talent recruiter. Nobody expected the sport to achieve cult level within two years, let alone make millions of dollars. When the first game went viral, the snowball effect could not be contained. Stilt teams sprung up across the land. The school started designing sports stilts. Training demand went up. The rest is history.

The Trohsmans became advocates against height-related discrimination. They built schools and hospitals in their home village of Nahye. Trohsman still had a small problem; no pun intended. When people meet the now famous person they still said, "I expected you to be taller." If he had a dollar every time a fan recited that statement, well, I don't know how one would finish that saying when one is already a millionaire. Llat's height was no longer an issue in Doarba. Ironically, she designed high heel shoes and counseled dozens of short Doarba women who had issues getting men just because of their height. In Doarba, fashion models are always tall.

Manifestation of Height-Based Social Exclusion

There are studies showing taller MBAs make more money than their height-challenged counterparts. One recent study by a labor department showed that taller people are more likely to land a job when they're up against a shorter, similarly qualified, applicant.

In cinema, a short, fat, bald old man is often the villain or a caricature. The war generals in movies are usually tall and beefy men. Is this a coincidence? In some communities, short men are perceived as pushy and seen as portraying Napoleonic tendencies. The stereotype is that they must be overcompensating for the height deficiency. It is not uncommon to find people who believe that a man has to be taller than the lady in a dating scene.

You can also tell about a society's perception by looking at the fashion industry. Most fashion models are not short. There are height increasing shoes and other fashion tricks to make you look taller.

On the Other Hand

You can also be considered taller than normal. The very tall are also given nicknames and ridiculed unless they are sports stars. In a general sense, very tall women face more discrimination than tall men. In some communities women over six feet may have a difficult time finding dates based on the underlying perceptions. For very tall ladies, you may either have to wear flats or avoid high heels to fit in some groups.

Technical Inconveniences

For those people on the extreme end of height spectrum, this factor can be a concern for other reasons besides perception. They may have to deal with a few nagging technical inconveniences because most products are created with some average height in mind.

Consider a case where a short person is unable to reach windows, shelf or perform some simple daily tasks. If you are very tall you may have to deal with your head hitting door frames, chandeliers, and light fixtures that seem to jump in front of you out of nowhere. Finding clothes may be a challenge while others can easily swap. Sitting on a plane or other mode of transportation with limited leg room is a common complaint that I came across when researching this exclusion factor.

Both height and weight are related to the attractiveness factor, especially for women conglomerates. Heightism is not permanent as far as the index is concerned. It all depends on the backdrop.

Conglomeration of Exclusion Factors NUBC

When heightism, gender, weight, and other factors converge, they may become a bigger threat to personal growth. Consider a man who wants to play professional basketball for a living and is are relatively qualified. He is four feet eight inches and 370 pounds. The man is already twenty-eight years old and have no connections to the headhunters at present. How does he deviate from a normal basketball national league candidate? His NUBC may show that the gatekeepers prefer people of a particular:

Height
Weight
Age
Affiliation
Place
Character

Nuthology strategy

If you are walking through the jungle, you want to know what the shortest route is, where the dangerous animals are, and what resources you will need. The alternative is to just charge through the forest and hope everything will be fine. Nuthology strategy is not meant to discourage you. It is just a decision-making tool.

Nuthology works with patterns of data. Height is not a requirement for American presidential candidates, for example, yet most recent presidents are around six feet tall, well above the average height of a citizen.

If you are looking to be a model, the gatekeepers may not say explicitly that a certain age, gender, height, attractiveness, affiliation, social class, and the right body shape are must haves. Your NUBC data will tell you that. From there you can decide where your energy and time will be invested.

Capsule of Talents

Learning how heightism can be used to exclude you should be a part of your financial strategy. Tall or short, we are all vertically perfect. Don't let any social stigma create self-doubt or shame. That will be giving your power away. There are many assumptions about people's height. You can create a strategy factoring in all your concerns.

Career selection is a delicate balance. You are trying to live as authentically as possible without burdening others. You have to be realistic and pragmatic. Work on skills and education. Join support groups and meaningful networks. Follow our "SCHOOL" strategy but do not let stereotypes define you.

Reducing Your Own Stereotype-Driven Aggression

Picking on someone because of their height may not be like mocking a disabled person or spewing racial epithets, but to most affected conglomerates it is a concern. Whether a factor is a major societal issue or not does not diminish those concerns. Although heightism is not as protected as other classes in most of the world, it is still a major concern for most people. We have cases where teenage girls have committed suicide after being bullied at school because of height. Is heightism the accepted discrimination? People dealing with this prejudice know that it is real.

Overcompensation and Blanket Blame

Do not promote your own height as the perfect one, even if your group has been marginalized. Replacing others' perceived height superiority with yours is a counterproductive move. Nobody chooses their own height.

Speak Up Regardless of Status

Most height-related social exclusions are stereotypically, unfairly, and, sometimes, unconsciously applied. Become an advocate for horizontal coexistence where no one is treated unfairly because of his or her height.

24

Language, Accent

The Battle of Otherners and the Localites

Maria had worked for her boss for two years. The company had a lot of Othernees speaking customers. She was the only Otherner in the company. Everybody loved her. She said little because people laughed at her Othernees accent. This made her appear introverted and shy.

The problem for Maria started when two women from Othernation were hired. Otherners were considered cheap labor and they didn't complain as much as the Localites. The three Otherners started conversing in their native language. Maria became talkative and extroverted. She would even laugh aloud in her Othernees squeaky manner.

The boss who spoke only Localitian started getting uncomfortable. He made a rule that no one was to speak Othernees on the job unless when talking to a customer. The three started speaking Othernees only during breaks. The boss made a new rule: no speaking Othernees on company property unless when talking to a customer. One day he heard the three speaking in Othernees on the street on their way home. The next day they were all fired.

When Maria got home that day, she was surprised to find out that language problems had already arrived there. Her son had been diagnosed with a learning disability.

Seven-year-old John had just joined his mom from Otherner two months prior. Because of limited Localitian proficiency, he was falling behind in school. The teacher assumed he had learning disabilities. What the teacher did not know was that he was a star student in his native country.

It was a local pastor who saved Maria and her son from anguish. Language was not a protected class, but a lawyer was able to use national origin protection to win a wrongful termination case against Maria's employer.

The next issue was dealing with the board of education. The pastor had to involve the media to force the board to reevaluate John and remove him from the learning disability curriculum. When he was tested in his native Othernees, they discovered the boy was a genius.

John eventually completed Localitian special classes and joined the general school population. This case exposed the lack of cultural awareness in the school systems nationwide and prompted drastic changes.

Manifestation of Language and Accent Social Exclusion

Most of the time language bias is an indication of both negative stereotypes and prejudice manifestation. This creates risk for discrimination in housing, employment and other backdrops. According to many sources, linguistic discrimination is culturally and socially determined due to a preference for one use of language over another.

There are almost 7000 languages in the world. We know talent and intelligence have nothing to do with geography, but the attitude and disdain toward people for the way they talk and the regions they come from shows how shallow people can be.

It is often the dominant group that organically defines what the standard pronunciation is. Speakers who deviate from the standard are often said to "speak with an accent." Everyone speaks with an accent when they are outside their standard environment. Can a language unconsciously give a perceived social status? Can an accent unconsciously give a perceived social status? Why do most villains in movies have foreign accents?

Certain accents are perceived to carry more prestige in a society than others. Even when two accents are similarly intelligible and arouse the same discomfort, one may be viewed as more sophisticated than the other according to most experts. This positive evaluation usually occurs when an accent is associated with an upper-class social stratification. People with accents associated with lower socioeconomic strata are viewed to be less intelligent, less competent, less educated, and are believed to have poor language skills.

Accent discrimination is a common way to launder the forbidden protected biases like race, ethnicity, and national origin. In a workplace context, an employer may claim that a person's accent impairs his or her communication skills, which are necessary to the effective business operation. This happens even in occupations where talking is very small part of the job. Are there people with interesting accents in your area?

Non-native accents
Foreign accents
Regional accents
Domestic accents
Deep urban accents
Up the mountains accents
Really thick unintelligible accent
Found tribes accents
Upper-class accents
No money accents
Smart-challenged accents
Polite society accents
Crack-head accents
Wise guys and charlatans accents
Inheritance scam accents
Drinking expensive wine accents
Drinking tea and biscuits accents

Business accent

Place

Every region of a country can have its own unique slang. Accents associated with lower socioeconomic strata such as those perceived to come from slums, ghettos, poor rural environments, or third-world countries are a major source of social exclusion. In the same exclusion prism, a regional accent stereotype within a country can play a role in the erroneous assessment of the speaker's intelligence and, consequently, affect economic opportunities.

Social Class and Race

Initially it is the economic powers that decide the measuring stick of what constitutes "standard" and "nonstandard" language. We have cases where bona fide languages have been classified as slang. Language exclusion reflects other sociocultural variants, even beyond middle and upper classes. The "ugliest accents" are often associated with low class regions or communities.

National Origin

Accent is used as proxy for discrimination based on national origin, ethnicity, or race. Foreign or ethnic minority accents are often associated with lack of formal education or even learning disabilities. This is ironic considering most accents are caused by learning and speaking multiple languages. The last time I checked, you don't speak seven languages fluently because you have a small brain.

It can also work the other way, even against the local population. There are accents associated with science or engineering occupations. There are accents associated with cheap labor providers. These are just examples.

Conglomeration of Exclusion Factors NUBC

Consider a poor, racial-minority man who has an accent that is associated with low income and marginalized place. He is looking for a job in an upper-class area. He wants to buy a car but has concerns about his adverse credit history.

Language
Age
Race
Place
Transportation
Unemployment
Social class
Credit history

Capsule of Talents

Most language-based social exclusions are stereotypically, unfairly, and, sometimes, unconsciously applied. An accent is a part of who you are. Don't let some stigma create self-doubt or make you sell yourself short. Your accent is not a disease or a bad trait that requires treatment. Think about that when you are tempted to judge yourself. In this global economy, I would suggest you concentrate on communicative effectiveness. Use the Nuthology SCHOOL of Mitigation strategy to create a career plan that considers all of the structural barriers on your path to self-defined prosperity.

It is a delicate balance to live as authentically as possible and negotiate these potholes at the same time. Learning how language can be used to exclude you should be a part of your financial strategy. It is your duty to understand the politics behind the regional or national hierarchy of languages in your backdrop.

The prevailing negative stereotypes and attitudes toward your accent can have an impact on you if they are used to deliberately or unconsciously portray you as:

Less honest
Less reliable
Less competent

Less educated
Less intelligent
Having poor language skills
Having poor character, etiquette, or protocol understanding
Unpleasant to listen to
Giving negative feeling vibes
Potentially dangerous

Addressing Gatekeepers' Concerns and Career Planning

Does your accent materially affect your ability to perform key aspects of a certain job? The distance between your values and those of the gatekeepers will determine the cultural fit. This time language is the catalyst. There is reason people take classes to eliminate their accents.

Both language and accents affect the hiring process. How do you converse during a phone call? How you converse during an in-person interview will sway the gatekeeper's decision. A heavy foreign accent in client-facing jobs, TV, radio, or front office may be frowned upon unless it comes from a preferred class. In a profession like teaching where your check depends on talking all day, the need to be taken seriously is real.

Please remember these are risks that may never materialize. Don't let them stop you. But you shouldn't ignore them when making career decisions and spending money on college. If you choose an oversubscribed major, for example, your accent may work against you. You might have to take a certain route to achieve the same goal. You might have to increase your take-off speed tremendously to achieve a clean vertical takeoff.

"Excellent verbal communication is a must," screams the advert. There are many cases where your language can be a disqualification and not necessarily a deliberate bias. Whenever possible, you should learn the local language. This can be for business necessity, such as communicating with customers, coworkers, and supervisors. In emergency situations there is always a need for common language to promote safety and smooth evacuation.

Language articulation is critical in situations like a hospital operating room or an air traffic control tower. There is a built-in unfairness whenever you are not speaking a language in which you are best able to communicate.

Your distinctive manner of expression is part of your communications skills package. Although we are just going to talk about accent and language prejudices, there are other aspects of language that can read exclusion, including how rich your vocabulary is. We all know people who found opportunities using of their superior oratory skills. Whether language is a qualification concern or a bias, as far as the index is concerned it is an exclusion factor.

Avoiding Petty Overcompensation

Is learning a new language conformity? Most networks today run across nations and cultures. It is easy to get caught up defending your little bubble in an exploding world economy. Every small foreign thing should not be sold as conformity.

It is possible to educate yourself while still retaining your identity, voice, and vision. You have something interesting to say to the world. Learning how to say it well can make a world of difference.

Expand Your Networks

Expand your networks beyond your ethnic group. Look for resources on how to improve your vocabulary and articulation. The best way to learn a language is from the horse's mouth. Take advantage of native language speakers' articulation. You can only do your best. Plan for the fact that you will have to repeat yourself if you have a heavy accent. It can be frustrating. This also exposes the local population to foreign languages and reduces the "otherness' fear. These are the same networks that will open doors for opportunity.

Reducing Your Own Stereotype-Driven Aggression When in a Dominant Group

Vernacular should not be flaunted like a PhD in rocket science quantum physics. It doesn't take a genius to learn one's own mother tongue. Spewing hatred on a group of people based on their inability to speak your mother tongue or for speaking it with an accent is despicable in my book.

Most people would like to speak the local language if only for their own survival. It gets harder to be fluent in a foreign language as you grow older. You probably had your own struggles with a second language in grade school. Try learning a new language and speak it fluently when you are forty. You will discover a small fact. Speaking any language acquired later in life without an accent is not as easy as flipping a switch.

Speak Up Regardless of Status

We all know deep down that language is a mark of regional or national origin, not an intellectual capacity measurement or an achievement in itself. Language has been used to promote some groups' racial, ethnic, tribal, or cultural supremacy for a long time. Be an advocate for horizontal coexistence where no one is treated unfairly based on his or her language or accent.

25

Lifestyle

The Potential Liability Asset

This is the third management meeting on what to do with Mr. Venturer Gutsy, the company's top salesman and holder of five Golden Employee awards. Venturer is a prominent member of Rolling Madcaps From Hell, a daredevil-themed boy band with no music plans. It is made of six thrill seekers with a serious case of appetite for zany risk.

They specialize in crowd-pleasing exercises that include competitive eating, binge drinking, chain smoking, parachute-free skydiving, and naked-skull bungee competitions, among other over the top stunts.

Venturer used to compete in jump bikes, but his weight and the multiple broken bones got in his way. He now likes chain smoking and quantity food games because he did those things every day anyway. Every now and then the team would sit down and brag about who had the most broken bones. Venturer had x-ray negatives on the walls as decorative art. Every member of the team had Olympic-size metal plates in their bones and doctors' letters to present to airport screeners.

During the previous season, Venturer came up with a new business plan. Rolling Madcap From Hell would be run like a professional partnership. Each partner would specialize in one or two acts and they would all share the spoils. Now, Venturer chose to specialize in eating and smoking roles. That worked well with his sedentary lifestyle. He could still participate in binge drinking bets. Their online videos and blog posts were generating worldwide attention.

Things started going south when a local news piece mentioned Venturer's day job. His boss was not amused. That generated red flags for the brand protectors and company insurers. This brings us full circle to the conference-room standoff: The managing director is waiting the result of today's meeting. It must not be a hung jury. This issue is creating a conflict between the sales department and human resources department. The sales manager is dug in: he wants to keep his best producer. HR manager sees Venturer as ticking time bomb. His is a huge potential liability.

Manifestation of Lifestyle-Based Social Exclusion

When you refuse to fit in a certain box, can you be socially excluded from opportunities? Then again, does the business have a right and duty to design policies that ensure the safety of other employees and customers? Certain risky activities are known to increase risks of illnesses or injuries, which ultimately may increase employers' costs. Does a business have a right to protect its bottom line?

In this dilemma, you may never know if your lifestyle was used against you. A company can find other contrived excuses to exclude you. Consider an airline employee who was considered attractive when she was hired. Don't ask me what attractive means. She was known to live a sedentary lifestyle and boasted about it online. She was terminated for gaining too much weight. The company claimed the overweight flight attendant was having difficulty getting through the narrow aisles of the commercial plane. She might block the aisles during an emergency or fall on a passenger. The attendant could also claim she was fired for appearance reasons. This is not a legal book, but you be the untrained judge.

Can a company legally refuse to hire, discipline, or fire you based on lifestyle? Like many legal issues, the first answer is, it depends. The next answer is, consult an expert in this field. The third answer is to research on your backdrop and the industry you are targeting. You might discover the company only hires nonsmokers or other classification. This may not be written down. The conduct need not be unlawful to count in this category.

I came across quite a number of cases when I was researching this topic. I am sure you may have more in your backdrop that are related to discrimination based on "lifestyle."

Off-duty tobacco use
Political activity
Political affiliation
Sedentary lifestyle
Activism
Obsessions
Public assistance dependency
Panhandling
Smoking
Skydiving
Excessive alcohol use
Competitive eating
Fitness fanaticism
Abnormal marital status
Homelessness
Nomadism
Taboos
Advanced mooching

Conglomeration of Exclusion Factors NUBC

What is your conglomeration? Lifestyle can work well with other exclusion factors to make a solid opportunity blocking convergence. Consider a disabled obese middle aged man who is also a heavy smoker. He is looking for a job a walking distance from the city homeless shelter because he lacks reliable transportation. There are not many job opportunities in that part of town. His NUBC may include his lifestyle.

Lifestyle
Place
Shelter
Disability
Age
Transportation
Weight

Nuthology Strategy
Learning how lifestyle can be used to exclude you should be a part of your financial strategy. You want to live for yourself and not depend on others' approval. It is a delicate balance to live as authentically as possible without burdening others. Questionable lifestyle is determined by your backdrop.

Career Planning
Take a preemptive career planning approach. What would make a potential employer concerned about your lifestyle? There are jurisdictions that prohibit employers from disciplining or firing employees for activities they pursue off-site. It doesn't hurt to do some research, consult a legal expert, or both.

Addressing Gatekeepers' Concerns and Dilemmas
It is not whether your lifestyle is good or bad. Even when factoring your rights and freedoms, the distance between your values and those of the gatekeepers will determine the cultural fit. Sometimes this happens unconsciously. Avoid activities that may embarrass your employer or hurt the company's sales image.

Voluntary Information
Nuthology is interested in how information can be used against you without your knowledge. Too many photos of you drinking may paint a different picture even when you rarely drink. There are tons of things that can reveal your lifestyle. It is unfair, but you will be judged. Your

choice of wardrobe, flags, and modes of transportation, hairstyles, body language, and online footprint will come into play. If you are a whistle blogger, there are some issues that may make your employer uncomfortable.

Reducing Your Own Stereotype-Driven Aggression

Are people less fulfilled in their lives because they choose a different path to find happiness than yours? I find that presumptuous, but isn't this book about presumptions? There are many unfair assumptions about people who choose certain lifestyles. Choose to reduce your own stereotype-driven judgments.

Speak Up Regardless of Status

This is a very subjective social exclusion factor. Most lifestyle-related social exclusion is stereotypically, unfairly, and, sometimes, unconsciously applied. Be an advocate for horizontal coexistence where no one is treated unfairly because of his or her group-attributed assumptions.

26

Marital Status

Why Aren't You Married Yet?

Polenta likes weddings but does not like the idea of getting married. She considers herself happily and perpetually single for better or for worse. She believes that the pressure to meet the societal deadlines clouds women's business decisions, career choices, and other life goals. "You don't even have the chance to decide if marriage is a good idea or not. It has already been decided. You just need to follow the normal template, right?"

Polenta's community has a different view. They see a promiscuous, immature, and lonely social misfit. Polenta can tell by the number of pathetic "hook-ups" and offers of help she gets from her extended family. If these referral offers were cash, she would be floating in money.

Polenta has two sisters who are stuck in abusive shotgun marriages. Shotgun is a scenario whereby the father of a pregnant daughter shows up with a shotgun to make sure the boyfriend scoops his bride like a bullet train, pun intended. Nowadays it doesn't have to be a shotgun; a simple surface to air missile will do the trick. It is usually done to save face for the head of the family. This is caused by the deep social stigma attached to out-of-wedlock births.

Polenta doesn't have a child, so she dodged the bullet on that route. It is the incessant barrage of intrusive questions that drives her to the edge of the universe. Why aren't you married yet? Where are your people? This is the main reason she dreads that annual emotional mine-field her family calls extended family reunion.

Ten years ago the family reunion turned into an intervention. Her grandmother announced publicly that everybody needed to pray for Polenta. She made it sound like she had some kind of incurable ailment. It was actually a little bit hypocritical. There were fifteen divorcees in that meeting, twenty-seven deadbeat dads, and eleven widows. How come it was being single that needed God's attention? Go figure.

"Since when did marriage become a fulfilment of humanity? Does the humanity level fall too much after the thirtieth birthday that it needs to be refilled?" She couldn't help wondering aloud. For a country with more than 50 percent divorce rate, you wouldn't think it would be a big deal.

This does not stop at home, it also happens at work. She gets e-mails and books on "how to find a man." Why was the man lost in the first place? She constantly receives articles from strangers on how married people are happier. "It is obviously married people who peddle the studies. Of course married people are happy. Why wouldn't they be? They chose to be married. It would be sad if they were not happy."

Polenta is compiling a list of ripostes to test at this year's family reunion. She will respond based on prepared remarks depending on the rank and age of the interrogator. She has a list of frequently asked questions down to a science.

"Why aren't you married yet?" The answers will range from "Was I supposed to? I didn't get the memo" to "I am just lucky, I guess."

Manifestation of Marital Status-Based Social Exclusion

One of the assumptions of Nuthology is that gatekeepers, including employers, are a microcosm of our society. From that we can argue that people may judge you by your family formation method or lack thereof.

This factor is wide and interesting. I can write a whole book on it. This exclusion can take any angle. Put your judgment robes on. I got a question for you.

Which family formation method is happier?
Arranged marriages
Beta marriages
Cohabitation
Come we stay
Common law marriage
Convenience marriage
Divorced, but living together
Divorced, not remarried
Economic marriage
Eligibly single
Endogamy
Exogamy
Forced marriage
Ineligibly single
Interracial marriages
Intertribal marriages
Married, but living together
Married, but separated
Monogamy
Natural marriage
Only and only
Polygamy
Poor person's marriage
Same gender marriage
Serial marriage
Serial monogamy
Singleton lifestyle
Traditional marriage
Unmarried living together
Unnatural marriage

Untraditional marriage
Unusual age difference
Weirdo marriage
Widowed

Every culture or sub-group decides the acceptable family formation landscape and any deviations from normal are dealt with. The exclusions we are talking about here are not just about being excommunicated from a congregation. History has a lot of examples in which nation states had regulations banning or restricting certain family formations. The social stigma related to certain marriages still exists in today's society in one version or another.

Even where society is free, there are serious social stigmas surrounding unusual formations. The stigmas and stereotypes drive the social exclusion. Children are usually caught in the middle. We have cases where children of divorced, same gender, or single parents are bullied for something they have absolutely no control over. Other kids may not understand the deviation from the normal family forming procedures.

Conglomeration of Exclusion Factors

Consider a young single mother of five who is looking for a job. She has concerns that some companies may refuse to hire unwed and single parent applicants. She lives in a bad neighborhood and doesn't own a car. If a company sees her as a burden or as one who doesn't represent their brand, she may not get an opportunity.

Marital status
Parenthood
Age
Transportation
Place

Nuthology Strategy

Nuthology strategy does not support any type of family formation over another. This personal-driven strategy encourages you to research your industry for social exclusion incidents. Learning how marital status can be used to exclude you should be a part of your financial strategy. Do not let marital status derail your individual growth efforts. You should not feel under pressure to be with someone before you are ready just to fit in. And you should not feel under pressure to avoid being with someone just to fit in. Neither is good for your financial health in the long run.

Addressing Gatekeepers' Concerns and Dilemmas

It is not whether your family formation method is right or wrong. Since the gatekeepers are part of society and not rocks, they have their personal beliefs, which shapes their attitudes. It is your duty to do research on your target industry. Some companies may prefer single young people while others may prefer married people. This can happen unconsciously as a trend. Some companies have policies on this, for example, you may not become pregnant if your status is single. The distance between your values and those of the gatekeepers will determine the cultural fit. This time it is your marital status.

TMI Tip

It is a delicate balance to live as authentically as possible and earn a living. Some companies may prefer you keep your unusual marriage as a private matter but may not put it on the policy. Personal information relating to relationship disagreements and divorce are better kept private. Avoid outlandish statements about people's lifestyles, especially in the workplace. It can cost you an opportunity. It takes two people to make a marriage work. There are many people who tried their best but were not successful. You don't know what another person may be going through.

Avoiding Petty Overcompensation

We all may have different ideas about what defines marital satisfaction, even considering that marital satisfaction is not a physical object or quantity that can be readily observed and measured. Touting your family formation as the only perfect one reduces your network.

Do not overlook genuine concerns just to get even. There are situations where living alone can be more expensive that living with another person. While nobody is saying you should marry for money, retirement planning may be influenced by marital status. The lack of a spouse's income, survivor benefits, inheritance, pension, or social security, for example, is something to consider. The high poverty rate for the single, divorced, or windowed in retirement can be partially attributed to this.

If you are single, your financial independence may be more sensitive to illness and sudden unemployment situations. If you are married, you may be rigid when it comes to entrepreneurship, changing jobs, changing schedules, or taking jobs that require traveling. Bias or no bias these are real issues that you will encounter.

Reducing Your Own Stereotype-Driven Aggression

Not all questions about marital status are a sign of aggression, even when they get a bit invasive. You don't want to alienate people who are trying to be friendly. "How come you never got married? Why are you married? Are you with someone in a nonprofessional capacity?"

It is your duty to differentiate between polite interest and just plain nosiness depending on the backdrop. Is it just small talk or an interrogation? Your response to your clients' five-year-old daughter will be different from the one you give to that water-cooler tabloid at your office.

You should learn how to throw the topic back to the questioner without sounding overly defensive or rude. Learn to change the subject with a personalized rejoinder, premeditated comebacks, and a breathtaking riposte. Create a retaliatory maneuver based on the nonmaleficence principle. Do no harm to your purpose.

Speak Up Regardless of Status

All people are valuable regardless of their marital status. Be an advocate for horizontal coexistence where no one feels superior just because of his or her marital status.

27

Military, Veteran

Saved By Number Two

It was still dark when he crawled out of the oily parking deck looking like a hungry silhouette. Colonel Stonie Riot, a short, fat, balding, single, openly gay man, had definitely seen better days. The quiet, heavily tattooed seventy-five-year-old war veteran was a fading shadow of his former self. Stonie had good benefits as a military officer with rank. But he lost all his pension to his ex-wife in a divorce settlement. As a noncustodial parent, the court took him to the cleaners. He ended up on the mean streets.

Stonie had recently made a decision to look for a job and a place to stay in a predominantly upscale area despite his well-documented criminal record, shoddy credit, and HIV rumors. Following valuable advice from a former panhandling buddy, he had bought a gym membership and obtained a library card. He was now able to take showers and research panhandling tips on the Internet using the local library.

This day was special to Stonie. He wanted to go to a new location. "Location, location, location. Avoid the upscale mall like plague," his adviser had insisted. The mall had too many exits, and the patrons mostly used plastic cards not cash. Now, Stonie made a right turn towards the island. Two blocks south of the church pantry he saw them. The two police cars were parked facing the tunnel.

Even where panhandling was not illegal, the police could always find some broken-tail-light contrived excuse for arresting you just to check for outstanding warrants. "Fig-leaf" frisk stops were a normal part of the day for the shelter-challenged city dwellers. Police in the city could make up any charges they wanted, including trespassing, loitering, or impersonating humankind. Who will the judge trust? A "barely there" human being in rugs or an officer of the law in a well-pressed, crisp-looking, and wrinkle-free uniform? Do the math.

Going back to jail after a two-year stint was the last thing Stonie Riot wanted. He made a hard left turn onto a closed street. Half walking, half running, he was determined to make it to the discount store across the bay. Per the "panhandling guru," most discount store patrons lived a paycheck away from begging, so they were more empathetic. The way the economy was going, the old man could just as well be one of them. They were also more likely to be carrying cash in lower denominations, not the stupid plastics like the mall patrons.

Running while looking back at the same time turned out to be a bad multi-tasking idea. Stonie did not have a chance. He saw the septic open manhole caution sign a few seconds too late. Gravity took over with a vengeance. He braced for impact praying that there was enough waste to absorb the shock thirty feet down in the darkness. Was this how it would end?

He laid halfway submerged in the fermenting acidic mess. Thanks to the city population, his bones were okay. Talk about being saved by the poop. The colonel was out cold.

Stonie was awakened by a loud bang above the sewerage tunnel. *Where am I?* A couple of bats flew by startling Jesus out of him. He could feel the itching from broken glass cuts and stale urine. He could see blurry shapes at a distance.

Stonie waded for two grueling hours through the stinky, sticky, and intoxicating tunnel before he could find an exit. Then there was another problem. The exit led up to a very busy downtown street. He prayed for rain. He needed heavy rain. He needed enough rain to clear people off Eighth Avenue and clean his messy clothes. He would pretend to be insane. He would laugh aloud and dance in the rain. But it was summer in the city. Rain was as scarce as compassion.

Then there was another loud bang followed by falling nuggets of daylight. His pucker factor hit acute levels. His life would never be the same.

Manifestation of Military Veteran–Based Social Exclusion

It is easy for society to underestimate the difficulty of veterans' transition to civilian life. Some veterans fail the transition to civilian life due to combat-related physical and mental issues. Blast or shrapnel injuries can also lead to physical appearance concerns for the affected. Think of facial, hand, and leg burns. Speech impediment is another issue that can affect quality of life. The list is long.

Most people are familiar with physical injuries when it comes to veterans of wars. Less attention is paid to emotional and mental injuries. It also creates a dilemma. Too much attention on health issues may lead to unfair group attribution assumptions. Some veterans have complained about stigmas and stereotypes surrounding post-traumatic stress disorder (PTSD). This may prevent some veterans from getting jobs even when they don't suffer from it Others just suffer from mild symptoms.

Homeless is caused by a combination of factors. The percentage of homeless people who are vets is often higher than their percentage in the population. In other words, veterans are overrepresented in the homeless demographic. The natural disruption or break in the civilian job market and financial life may translate into an exclusion factor.

People in the LGBTQ community (lesbian, gay, bisexual, transgendered, questioning) and minority classes will face unique challenges as they attempt to enter civilian life on top of being veterans.

Female veterans face unique issues too. Parenting is hard enough for many people. Parenting while at war can be very challenging.

Conglomeration of Exclusion Factors NUBC

Although the above story is fictional, what we see every day in reality is as disappointing. Despite not being a racial minority, Stonie Riot's list of potential bias catalog is impressive. Stonie Riot is dealing with a barrage of conglomerating bias factors in his financial and social life. He also lacks the offsetting "shock absorbers" like an affluent family background or friends in high places. His informal "minority-ness' can be seen from the space station.

While society will attempt these conglomerating factors in isolation, whenever there is a discussion about veterans a different picture may emerge when NUBC is applied, exposing frequently forgotten subsets of this factor. Let's look at some examples:

Consider a middle aged minority female vet. Her concerns might be:

Veteran status
Gender
Race
Age

Consider an unemployed homeless disabled female vet who needs a car to get a job. The single mother of four also needs a mailing address. Let's assume she has concerns about her facial burn scars and depression.

Veteran status
Unemployment
Shelter
Disability
Disease stigma
Gender
Transportation
Attractiveness
Parenthood

The conglomeration can be deeply personal and unique. Each of these are concerns that can stand on their own as exclusion factors at society level. Despite the oversimplification of the NUBC, this is not a work of fiction. It is something that happens.

Nuthology Strategy

Learning how veteran status can be used to exclude you should be a part of your financial strategy. There is no one answer for social exclusion. You will need to design a personal plan that includes not only veteran status but all other social exclusion classes. As an individual you will then have to look at solutions from your perspective. The Nuthology Index is just an analytic tool for decision making, especially suited for subject with complex and potentially conflicting variables as social exclusion.

Determine the jobs you want in the civilian job market. Identify specific core competencies and skill sets valuable to corporate world. Research military transition and job-search strategies; remember, you are also competing with other veterans for opportunities. Your personal plan might make all the difference.

"If everyone is thinking alike, then somebody isn't thinking." Gen. George S. Patton

Addressing Gatekeepers' Concerns and Dilemmas

Find ways to address communication breakdowns in interviews and on resumes. Describe military skills in a way civilian gatekeepers can understand.

Zero Dark Thirty. What?

The military also has its own foreign language. Not many people may understand the complicated lexicon. Definitely not everybody will appreciate being referred to as "a good piece of gear."

Veterans remain a small part of the general population. Not many people who make hiring decisions have been in the military or in combat. It is your duty to covey your skills in a manner that the potential employer will understand.

Seek Programs

There are jobs, housing, sports, recreation programs that are aimed at active-duty military and veterans. Look for military job fairs and financing arrangements for example. Seek professional help for issues concerning health or legal matters early enough.

Expand Your Networks

Build networks to include people outside of military circles. Engage trustworthy family and friends to maintain your financial structures while deployed.

Speak Up Regardless of Status

At the societal level, there is a lot advocacy work that needs to be done for this class. Recruiters should be trained to deal with combat-related disabilities and job descriptions. A better way of transferring military credentials to their civilian equivalents should be developed. There are many cases where this becomes a concern. If you were trained in a medical field in the military, for example, your credentials may not be recognized in the outside world. Become an advocate for horizontal coexistence where no one is treated unfairly because of his or her military or veteran status.

28

Name

Oh My, Romeo. What Is in a Name?

Naming a brand new human being is often an auspicious task. Sue and her husband argued over what name to give their son for months. He wanted the weirdest, wackiest, and most unique name while she was leaning toward familiar mainstream names. Her husband's name was D'youknow Who.i.am. The negotiations were getting out of hand. At one point police were called to their home.

Sue knew a lot about bizarre names. Her name was not actually Sue. She had been using the name "Sue" since middle school. Her mother thought since she was a divine gift her name should be Heaven Lee, to mean Heavenly. That was before Sue's mom married her step father, Papa Gawd when she was three. The name didn't mean a lot until she started school. Her official name was Heaven Lee Gawd.

It started as a joke, but Heaven Lee Papa Gawd became a caricatured name in school. Even the teachers thought it was hilarious. Her parents though it was not a big deal. But it was very tormenting for her. Then the boys started doing the sign of the cross every time she passed by. She changed schools three times, but since the kids came from the same neighborhood it didn't help.

There was frustration as family and friends misspelled her name. There were constant clerical errors on her official documents. Her diploma had to be reissued, twice. She longed for a normal name. Then she married somebody by the name of D'youknow. That made it even worse.

She would never allow anyone to make her kids go through a similar ordeal if that was the last thing she did. So when D'youknow suggested they call the baby "@DWho.i.am" she went ballistic. D'youknow had hit a raw nerve.

"Are you thinking about what the child will have to go through with that name? Is a baby the golden chance to show your stupid creativity? Is this baby your canvas to express yourself? Is he a tool for your counterculture rebellion? Parents who choose crazy names are those who care more about themselves than their kids."

Their marriage counselor had to fly in to save the state of their union. They were in for a lecture.

"I agree with both of you. At the end of the day, it is the parents' responsibility to name their child. The rest of the world does not get to weigh in on it. However, in real life the world will decide whether the child's name is unique or just plain stupid. The child does not need a name. The name belongs to the world for identification. Studies show people are often unfairly denied opportunities based on their names. Shorter names get bigger paychecks. Shouldn't you give your baby the best chance you can offer him or her? It is the baby who will live with the name, after all.

"You should seriously consider the ramifications of medical, financial, college, or employment records. You should consider teasing and bullying. What name would you give your baby if you knew he or she will run for office one day? What name would you give your baby if you didn't know if he or she will run for office one day? Will the name affect his income generating activities or quality of life? Will the name make him a laughing stock for life so that you can express yourself today? Will he be bullied because his name means something weird? Are you being influenced by the name of the day that will not make sense ten years from now? I know a kid named 'Genius' who never got better than an *F* in any subject. He is now in rehab."

It was Sue who won when Emma Sophia was born.

Manifestation of Name-Based Social Exclusion

There are many schools of thought regarding this factor of exclusion. How did you end up with your name?

Baby Naming Protocol

In some countries you can name your kid almost anything. That means kids have odd names that suit their parents' fantasy world. There are times when the trend is led by celebrities. People with trust funds do it all the time, so it must be okay, right?

Not all people have choices concerning names. Handing down a family name and naming someone after a favorite grandparent or distant relative is common in many cultures. Some cultures use seasons, daytimes, or whatever is occurring at that time to come up with a name.

Some countries have very strict rules regarding what you can name your child. Others have a preapproved list of names. You can even end up in jail. Some countries do this to prevent ignoble families from giving their children noble names.

Some of the laws involve conditions, such as you must be able to tell the gender of the child by the first name, and you must not negatively affect the well-being of the child. Others restrict numbers or characters on names. Creative spellings of more common names are also often rejected.

Nuthology strategy is interested in whether your name can prevent you from achieving your goals. I am sure you know people who are in high places just because of their family names. At least that is the general consensus. If a name is perceived to have the ability to open doors, can it also have the ability to close them? Can your name keep you from getting a job, a contract, a customer, or another money generating opportunity? There are many ways this can manifest itself. A name that:

Sounds funny in another language
Is profane in another language
Means something obscene in another language

Reminds people of bad things
Gives a foreign-enemy vibe
Is foreign sounding and off putting
Reminds local people of an enemy country
Reminds local people of an enemy religion
Is shared with a famous or infamous person
Sounds like a most wanted person
Reminds people of a notorious person
Everybody agrees is stupid
Sounds like a stigmatized occupation stage name
Reminds people of failures
Is hard to spell and pronounce
Makes local people puke trying to pronounce it
Is too short
Is too long
Feeds existing negative stereotypes
Reminds people you can't do math
Reminds people you can only do math
Is a too ethnic
Calls for unwanted attention
Is illegal in your host country
Sounds too common
Comes in a bucket of eight middle names
Feeds into negatively stereotyped occupations

There are many people either adopting or giving their babies "culturally ambiguous or gender neutral names" in hopes that their lives will be better. Some people drop some letters in their names on their resumes. I came across a lot of cases where candidates used initials instead of full names. This may get worse when combined with place exclusion. The combination of an excluded name and address on a resume may work against you.

There are cases where a name changes the tenor of the interview or turns the interview into a joke fest, which may work against you. In a high competition market, if your name leads to awkward mispronunciation incidents that embarrass the gatekeeper, things might not end well. Your name may lead to awkward misspellings; an incident that embarrasses the interviewer.

We should not forget that there will be some companies that look for ethnic names because they may offer advantages in terms of labor costs or union affiliations. For this reason I am not recommending any one strategy. Your situation will dictate your actions.

Conglomeration of Exclusion Factors NUBC

Name exclusion works well with other factors like race, ethnicity, and national origin. Let's take ethnicity as an example. An ethnic sounding name may make the interviewer assume you speak a foreign language and you don't. An ethnic sounding name may make a gatekeeper doubt your status and prolong the hiring or vetting process. Some ethnic sounding names may make people think you are less intelligent. An ethnic sounding name should not make people think you must be an affiliate of some organized outfit or non-state actors who make people disappear. Does that happen?

Consider a bad neighborhood dwelling female, a racial-minority foreigner who graduated from a third-world school. Let us assume her concerns include her gender, her bad neighborhood, and her easily mispronounced name. Her NUBC:

Name
Place
National origin
Race
Ethnicity
Alma mater
Gender
Place

Nuthology Strategy

Learning how a name can be used to exclude you should be a part of your financial strategy. Hiring managers and other gatekeepers are supposed to make decisions without letting unconscious biases interfere. If that is what happens in your backdrop, then this factor will not be a concern.

If you were teased or bullied because of your name, you probably identify with our discussion here. Most foreigners to any country can attest to name frustration. Misspellings, mispronunciations, embarrassments, calls for unwanted attention, and profiling are some of the bumps one might face. Your name alone may prevent you from getting a customer. There are cases where names can lead to perceived low intelligence depending on how water has been muddied by negative stereotypes.

Addressing Gatekeepers' Concerns and Dilemmas

Is the gatekeeper concerned that your name may scare customers away? Patterns of data in your backdrop may give you a better sense of whether this may happen.

How do people currently handle this exclusion? Some people use initials or select a part of their names to use on resumes. Having a sense of humor is also a mitigation strategy that people employ.

Nobody likes to hear their name being butchered by the local population. Changing a name to improve one's prospects is a very common practice in some countries. Many first-generation immigrants tend to pick the easiest name to go by at work. "Just call me Bob, and get on with it". People change ethnic sounding names to give the market what it wants. The same as a company would do with branding efforts. There are cases where people have changed names to avoid gender biases too.

The change does not have to be permanent. Some actors have adopted stage names that they think will give them an edge but they never change their actual names officially. That's the way they get to make a living. Some minorities shorten or abbreviate their names on their resumes. There are other ways people try to mitigate this exclusion.

Building Networks

When a candidate is referred by somebody inside the company, name pronunciation or other concerns are likely to take a backseat.

At this point the company will decide to meet you based on reputation and credentials. This is a sustainable mitigation strategy.

Laws of Demand and Supply

You will also notice the effect of superior or scarce skills in mitigation. If you are competitive in your field and highly demanded, your name becomes less consequential. People with high skills or talents face less name exclusion. If you have a unique service or product, most clients will not care about your name too much because the demand overwhelms the exclusion. If you make the best secret sauce in the world, your weird name becomes an asset. As a bonus, few people can claim to be you.

Some companies are switching to the blind resumes approach, which is a practice where documents are reviewed without an applicant's name or address. This will help some applicants with name concerns.

Exacerbating and Overcompensation

Previously marginalized people are more likely to give kids unique names. It is a way to express their unique identities and origins. That means they are also likely to slide into open ethnic stereotypes. How much should you use your baby to express your creativity? If you feel creative, draw a picture or something. This baby will be here long after you are gone. The favorite player that you named your kids after might turn out to be a loathed criminal.

Your child will have enough on his or her plate during his or her adult life. While there are no guarantees, you don't want to give your child a name that can hurt his or her employment chances. I will agree with you that in a perfect world name-based exclusion should not be happening.

Be Decisively Original

A lot of people in the entertainment industry are able to use creative names as part of their gimmick, comic routine, style of performance, or some shtick. This is for branding in their area of business and craft. Your baby is not one of them. Their kids may never work in their lives or may end up working in that area. Your kids may have to earn a living in one way or another. Fame can also transform the weird name into a household name to an extent that it becomes accepted. This is something you may not be able to do at present.

TMI Tip

Using e-mail names like "wild party animal @ not serious.com" when sending resumes or communications can be a deal breaker. This is more serious when looking for a job. Don't send a resume using a funny, stupid, or weird username unless it is a part of your genuine modus operandi or shtick.

Reducing Your Own Stereotype-Driven Aggression

Kids learn early the art of utilizing names to harm and hurt people. The negative labels are powerful tools of exclusion. Creating derogatory names has been used throughout history to devalue marginalized groups. People tend to create names for others as an act of aggression. If somebody doesn't like a name or nickname, do not use it. Respect other people's names. Do not assume that a name you've never heard of is obviously made up.

Speak Up Regardless of Status

There are a lot of world cultures where names are decided automatically using a predetermined legal or common protocol criterion. You should not make fun of anybody's name. It is always good to empathize more than you sympathize. There are kids who grow up to find their names on no fly lists, no horse ride lists, no hire lists, no apartment lists, no food lists, no oxygen lists, or other black book lists. Become a good advocate for horizontal coexistence where no one feels superior or inferior due to his name.

29

National Origin

Diminishing Papers

The resolutions passed by the Mean-O-Mart daily assembly do not have any binding force over the members. But the body meets daily for therapeutic reasons. There is no roll call or minutes. Today's meeting was well attended. Among the distinguished guests were an MBA, a dentist, a lawyer, a professor, psychiatrist, pediatrician, neurologist, district judge, and even a recovering member of parliament.

The lack of an agenda is not the main problem. It is the venue and the time of the day that tells all. It is a midnight smoking break in the Mean-O-Mart parking lot. The members of the half an hour assembly are shelf re-stockers.

Night stockers are an important part of Mean-O-Mart. They replenish items on shelves and perform diverse backroom duties. Most of the night restocking crew members have foreign advanced degrees that are probably not worth the paper they are written on. The agenda is driven by the top ten banes of the day.

Language and accent are constant agenda items. The day supervisor got tired of their scratchy accents and failure to use locally available language nuggets. He put them all on midnight shift. He was a yeller. "For the umpteenth time, this is not a chemist; it is a drug store. This not a tea biscuit; it is cookie. It is not Petrol its gas. She is not a billing counter; she is a cashier." One member was sentenced to cleaning bathrooms until he stopped calling them latrines.

Culture shock gets on the agenda often. One member was recently arrested for jaywalking across a twelve-lane interstate freeway. Another had an old lady almost swallow him alive for cutting a grocery line. Item number three is about a member who had been suspended from class for showing a college mate the wrong finger. It turned out that the gesture is a sign of respect his native country.

One issue that keeps coming up in every setting is about credentials. Educated immigrants often run in difficulties when trying to use their native colleges' certificates. Law degrees, for example, apart from being country specific, are often also state specific in this country. Not all foreign credentials are transferable to a local equivalent certificate. It varies a lot based on the country, the school, field of study, and other factors.

The chairman has to retake college courses because no local pharmacy will accept his foreign pharmacy PhD. There are also apparent biases. Foreign degrees from preferred countries are accepted more readily than those from "TV documentary" continents.

It is not all bad news. Some of the foreign re-stockers are going through board exams, while others are waiting for their credentials to be certified. But there is a chance that many will remain making minimum wage at the good old Mean-O-Mart indefinitely.

Manifestation of National Origin–Based Social Exclusion

"I love your heavy accent, what country are you originally from?" Obviously people are born into particular cultures and are brought up absorbing the behaviors of their cultures. They will develop a worldview that considers their culture to be the norm, making foreign cultures abnormal by default. Social exclusion based on national origin or perceived national origin is a major problem in many countries.

If your entire understanding of air travel is based on stories about plane crashes, hijackings, and shoot downs you will definitely hate flying long before you tried it. Most citizens learn about foreign countries from news stories and tricked-up TV documentaries. I am assuming you are familiar with those documentaries where the child has flies taxing and landing on her perpetually bulging eyeballs.

The work of a journalist is to constantly feed condensed and sensational content to his employer's insatiable news beast. Foreign journalists will look at a host country from their view and from the editor's view. Editors will only endorse reporting they think will sell. Selling mostly means shocking. This can create the lens through which the rest of the world, including investors, views a certain country. A continent becomes the land of daily unending horrors to the daily viewer. As a person originating, or perceived to have originated from such a country or content, you may be met with some preloaded contempt.

Underrepresentation

Foreigners tend to be in the minority, so they don't have much say in policy making. In most countries, aggression toward foreigners is considered fair game. Immigration involves people coming from outside with tons of "otherness." There are TV channels where bashing foreigners is a ratings magnet. It's a national pastime.

Social Class

Immigrants tend to be concentrated in particular sectors of the labor market with low wages and poor working conditions. They are also likely to be living in an area with relatively high unemployment rates and crime.

Immigration is a complex and emotional issue for locals. The local population may be worried about drained resources, increased expenditures, increased insecurity, or dilution of the cultural fabric.

Immigration may be seen as forced sharing of resources and a changing of lifestyle. The prevailing macroeconomic conditions can be a major driving factor. Animosity can result when foreigners are perceived to be in direct economic competition with the lower- and working-class of the host country. In such cases, rich foreigners or foreigners from high economic countries often face less resistance.

Hyphenated Citizens

You don't have to be a foreigner per se to experience this exclusion. You just need to look like one. There is a perception that hyphenated citizens have divided loyalties even when the "hyphen" is used to indicate ancestral origin. Any hint of foreign origin may imply the inability to be a true citizen or dual nationalism.

Conglomeration of Exclusion Factors NUBC

Foreigners are more likely to have additional exclusion factors: race, ethnicity, religion, language, etiquette, protocol and group attributed disease stigma. Consider a racial-minority young man who lives in a poor neighborhood and has no car. He holds a foreign MBA and is looking for a job. He may have concerns based on:

National origin
Race
Language
Accent
Ethnicity
Social class
Alma mater
Place
Transportation

Nuthology Strategy

Learning how national origin can be used to exclude you should be a part of your financial strategy. Nuthology is about optimization of your talents in a challenging backdrop. This means looking at situations and identifying new ways to do things depending on your backdrop. The first step is to combine all the risks when you are crafting your strategy. Always remember these are risks that may never materialize, so don't let them bring you down.

Career Planning

Do not blindly follow career advice meant for local students. There are many professional graduates with a migrant background are stuck in low-skill, low-paid jobs or precariously employed in fields unrelated to their training.

Do not rely solely on national employment figures. Foreigners may encounter very low rates of employment when the national origin factor is accompanied by other exclusion factors, such as belonging to an ethnic minority group, gender, or lower social class. You cannot afford to fall in love with some useless college major with all these variables in tow.

Gatekeeper Business Concerns

Language, accent, and articulation issues can be a problem when interviewing for a job. It is important to distinguish discrimination from business concerns. A foreign accent may be a disqualifier for client-facing, TV, radio, and front office jobs. In many jobs you must be able to speak clearly to customers, bosses, and first responders during an emergency.

Consider a patient who requests her doctor be changed because his accent is so thick that she can't figure out what he is saying. Is that an aggression or a genuine request?

Learn to identify patterns of aggression in local language. Every country has some epithets that are used to disparage foreign-born or foreign-looking residents.

Research Culture, Protocol, Etiquette, and Taboos

Body language based on one culture may be misconstrued as something else in another. In some countries, for example, good eye contact projects strength and confidence. Conversely, a lack of eye contact may indicate the opposite. It can also mean you are not telling the truth. If you come from a country where eye contact is a sign of disrespect, this may work against you. Showing a certain finger might be a gesture of endearment in your country but a rude one in the host country.

You might have to adapt some local etiquette. Do you maintain the handshake throughout a conversation? Do you engage in excessive and animated gesturing? Do you greet each other loudly across hallways, highways, rivers, valleys, and city blocks? Do you have no respect for deadlines, punctuality, productivity, and absenteeism? It is your duty as the guest to research culture, protocol, etiquette, and taboos of the local population.

Research on Negative Stereotypes

You want to be an actor but everybody thinks you should be a gynecologist just because you come from a doctor churning subcontinent. You might be expected to know the prince in exile who promised to share his vast inheritance with local residents but did not show up. You cannot run ten feet to save your life, but everybody expects you to be the team flag bearer because you come from a country that dominate most of the world's long-distance running. You worked hard to get the *A* in math, but everybody thinks it is in your blood. There are a lot of nationality-based stereotypes and group attribution sentiment floating in the world oceans. It is your duty to research and mitigate these assumptions.

Perceptions

How do you react when you encounter misinformed locals? Visiting or living abroad requires that you have sufficient mental preparation. It is common to find yourself appointed the unpaid ambassador. You may be the punching bag for your mother country's nefarious foreign policy. When you move around the host country, you will surprised by how many countries to which you will be assigned citizenship. You represent the country where citizens look like you.

Incoming foreigners have their own misconceptions of other cultures. Ignorance of history and geography is not a specialty of the local population. You will learn very quickly that the host nation's foreign policy and the few host nation tourists you have seen are very inaccurate reflectors of normal public life on the ground.

Create Meaningful Networks

Expand your networks to include locals. Seek for integration programs and educational opportunities. Aim for a good balance where you can live as authentically as possible without burdening the local population.

There are many cases where assimilation may be required. This does not mean you stop eating your food or listening to your music. But there will be laws in the new land that you are not used to. If you are being afforded the same security and opportunities as the local population, it is unfair to expect the host population to adopt your foreign culture. You may have to learn the language. You will have to respect local culture and freedoms.

Educate yourself extensively on the expected visitor protocol. Whose customs deserve dominancy? How much should the locals change to accommodate you? You should set reasonable expectations. It is unreasonable to expect the host nation to understand every culture in the world, speak your language, and follow your religious beliefs and ideology.

Flag waving abroad can also make the locals uneasy. Not everyone in the host country will appreciate the fact that you are touting your country as the greatest. Don't be that guy who goes to a foreign country and yells at people for not speaking your language or speaking it with an accent.

Respect cultural differences and sensitivities. Some behaviors may be acceptable and normal in one country but unacceptable in another.

Develop Custom Coping Mechanisms

Some immigrants are known to start vending ventures, gas stations, taxi businesses, and other small businesses to deal with this exclusion factor. In areas or industry where customers prefer to see their own as business owners, some business owners give them just that. The owner of a business hires a local guy to be the face of business and remains in the background. This is a coping mechanism that is found in many countries. It is also used to mitigate other factors like race and tribalism.

Reducing Your Own Stereotype-Driven Aggression

Acceptance and love should not be sold as zero-sum games: it is possible to simultaneously dissolve the borders between disparate cultures while preserving what's best and most valuable about each one us. Tone down the cradle superiority complex that goes beyond patriotism. This is more important if you are doing business at global level. Remind yourself that nobody chose where they were born on this rock. Nobody can change where they came from. Where you were born is not a personal achievement.

Speak Up Regardless of Status

There are media personalities who earn their living solely by making up stories based on xenophobia. National origin exclusion is a profitable "niche" for many demagogues looking to attract sustainable following. National origin–based aggression serves as a good front for other factors like race and social class

The "otherness" knowledge gap is often filled with misinformation that creates in-group favoritism and out-group derogation as a by-product. A foreigner makes the perfect boogey man for the politician facing performance questions.

The targeting of immigrants by law enforcement and the failure to provide language assistance to foreign migrants are major concerns. Become a good advocate for horizontal coexistence where no one is treated unfairly because of his or her real or perceived national origin.

30

Occupational, Professional

What Do You Do For a Living?

The trouble started when Mr. Digger wanted to be the chairman of the board of education in the rural county. The money was good. It was double what he was making in the city. He was the most qualified by far. But he found a little problem after he filed his application: his occupation.

Mr. Digger worked as a "headsman" before he started at the hospital. As a judicial executioner for ten years, he carried out death sentences ordered by the courts. In a country that was known to execute innocents and dissidents, he was not a local hero, to say the least. Headsmen were shunned and treated with the utmost contempt by most citizens.

At the hospital he was the chief expired patient specialist (CEPS), which was actually the head undertaker. He worked with world-respected pathologists. But it was the CEPS who emitted the negative zombie vibes. In this country, people used euphemisms when they talked about death. Was it to shield themselves from the discomfort? Nobody knew. They used words like "off with the angels," "gone to glory," and "at a better place," instead of passed away. It was a cultural thing.

Undertaker and executioner were the most taboo jobs in this country. Mr. Digger had held both, yet he had the audacity to run for office. When parents say "Become something respectable, my child," they mean one thing. You can be a chicken catcher, squirrel milking man, or anything else, but never be an undertaker or executioner.

Why is it that these occupations evoke such negative feelings? In the past, people who worked in jobs that were considered "unclean" were supposed to be purified. Traditional rituals were performed after the every task. In some communities the worker's head would be shaved clean by a flying witch doctor. With no such cleansing in modern times, the workers remain unclean. Then again, it might be just the mystical creepiness of these jobs.

Families have been known to check on the backgrounds of potential in-laws to identify and red flag such bad elements. If you work in these fields, you make sure not to mention it on a first date. The date will likely freak out and run out on you.

Since the Diggers lived in a different town than the one they worked in, it was easy to keep their careers secret. But education, experience, and occupation are part of running for office. Today's voters feel entitled to know about your personal life.

The new media makes it impossible to hide things like education and occupation. The first thing the electorate wants to know is: What is your background? You had better identify "skeletons in your closet" or the Internet will do that for you.

For Mr. Digger, the word skeleton was not a good metaphor. It was also expected that during the campaign the opponents would certainly attempt to dig up dirt on his past. Dig up?

He ran to the election office and withdrew the application. In an ironic twist of fate, Mr. Digger's wife submitted her own application and won the seat. She also worked with dead bodies on the same floor with her husband, but she had two magic letters before her name: DR! Mrs. Digger was a forensic pathologist. There may be a lot stigma that comes from handling the dead in this country, but it does not affect doctors and dozens of medical students who work on the same floor.

Manifestation of Occupation Social Exclusion

In a normal world people should not face shunning, discrimination, and ostracism based on what they do to feed their families. Tell me when we get in a normal world.

What do you do for a living? How do you answer this dreaded question? This is a question so deep that it often triggers "selective mutism" and uncontrollable mumbling. Awkward blank stares from those who do socially unacceptable jobs are also common symptoms.

There is always a temptation to give a short answer. "I just breathe." But what the stranger means is, "How should I judge you?" Either the stranger is looking for a socio-economic status box to put you in or just trying to make casual conversation. It is all contextual.

There are certain law enforcement careers where you will be mandated to hide your identity. It is already expected that you may face occupation-based animosity. It is common for some prison or judicial officials to conceal their daily job duties. Some careers have procedures that are designed to provide anonymity.

In some communities, police are seen as the ruling government's muscle who are there to serve their interests and protect their own. It is a career that is tough, dangerous, and stressful enough to begin with. These stereotypes only increase the occupational hazards.

This factor also comes to light when transferring from one industry to another. Most people work odd jobs during college. It is hard to transfer from some industries to another if there are no apparent transferrable skills. If you worked as an armpit sniffer or a vomit collector during graduate school, your resume may show gaps or unrelated skills when you are applying for teaching jobs.

Occupation is a topic that readily comes up during the dating and marriage process. Understandably, people find career success attractive. It demonstrates drive, focus, strength, and initiative. A recent study shows that three-quarters of women said they were unlikely to date a man who is unemployed. I am guessing this includes professional students and those occupied in advanced, prolonged business launches.

This leads to the next question. Does a potential date's occupation matter to you? Some people will argue it doesn't. This then begs for a follow up question. Why do people lie about occupation on their online dating profiles? There are careers that can lead to social isolation, even when they pay well. What will friends and family say if your date's work deviates from normal? What is abnormal anyway?

In a perceived immoral industry
A dangerous profession
Unusual working hours
Unusual over-the-chart schedule
Unusual travel demands
Extremely dirty
Man working in a traditionally female-dominated job
Woman working in a traditionally male-dominated job
Job with unusual occupational hazards
Job with reputation of low wages
Occupations that give people the heebie-jeebies
Jobs that are regarded as bizarre
Life shortening jobs

Occupational Prestige

Different occupations hold different admiration and respect levels in a society. Occupational prestige can create social class positions in the community that can lead to exclusion.

There are also people who think their occupation deserves unearned privileges. "Do you know who I am?" You are tempted to ask, "Why, have you forgotten?" Then again, you are decent person.

A lot of actors, musicians, and artists who are beginning their careers may deal with occupation contempt in their own families and community. Artists who work odd jobs for living expenses while they develop their craft are seen as slackers. "When are you getting a real job?" It is only when they hit it big that everybody comes running back.

Occupational Stereotypes

Both positive and negative occupational stereotypes can potentially warp your career path. Consider a case where one gender is stereotyped as less likely to succeed in science- and mathematics-related occupations. What about one where an ethnic group is stereotyped as likely to succeed in science- and mathematics-related occupations? Depending on your situation and talents, both these can be bad.

There are always some jokes on just about any conceivable occupation. It is just a little fun, right? Well, until it starts affecting people's livelihoods. People start taking the stereotype seriously and attaching stigmas. There are bad seeds in every industry. Notorious incidents can generate bad publicity about people who work in a field.

In movies, people in some science and technology fields are portrayed as clueless about the social skills department. They are often shown watching science fiction, hoarding action figures, reading comic books, and wearing those iconic glasses. You see the college professor having a bad hair day, every day. These are mostly thought to be harmless, but some people can internalize the bias.

Belief in zodiac signs and the general practice is a taboo in some regions. In those regions, psychics and professional astrologers may find themselves facing exclusion of some sort. One may come up as a weird person who cannot be taken seriously. Anytime you are not taken seriously may mean reduced financial opportunities.

Sometimes it is possible to identify stigmatized jobs by the existing mitigation measures. People may try to rename or change the outward image of their work by adopting a socially correct term. You have heard of those nondescript titles that attempt to neutralize an occupation's stigma by concealing it.

Solutions facilitator
Gas transfer engineer
Preneed counselor
Media distribution officer
Product consultant
Sanitation officer

Asset protection specialist
Expired Patients technician
Gastronomical hygiene analyst

Occupational Inequality

Occupational segregation, the distribution of people based upon demographic characteristics, is a major concern. It can determine which group remains permanently low income. Occupational inequality keeps people stuck in a low-socioeconomic status because it reinforces other social exclusion factors like gender and race. If women, for instance, occupy only low-income occupations in a certain region, the gender economic gap will continue to grow.

Conglomeration of Exclusion Factors NUBC

Let's consider a young, racial-minority woman who lives in a bad neighborhood where only low paying jobs are available. Women are stereotyped as less likely to succeed in occupations related to science, technology, and mathematics. These are occupations that provide middle-class and upper-class wages in this region. Her NUBC concerns may look like this:

Occupation
Gender
Place
Social class
Age

Capsule of Talents

The first thing you have to do is to believe in yourself. Your unique conglomeration is just a bunch of risks classes that make up your raw data. These are concerns that may never materialize. Nuthology strategy is about optimization of your talents in a challenging backdrop. Always gather information and narrow your options based on the collected data instead of following other people's dreams.

Dare to be different if your talents and skill set call for it. Quality of life always trumps bank account. There will always be people who hold negative beliefs about some occupations they know nothing about. Societal perceptions can also change with circumstances. In areas contaminated with anti-cop debris, for example, a law enforcement occupation is viewed with a different lens than it would in an area that does not have that negative sentiment.

Be a good student of your backdrop. Develop a 360 view where you can see challenges as well as opportunities. If you are starting out, it is wise to examine your target occupation. Learn the pros and cons that come along with each. Internships, apprenticeships, and other methods mentioned in the mitigation chapter are good starting points. Every profession has its good and bad days. Keep an open mind. Be prepared for the lows and the highs.

Learning how occupation can be used to exclude you should be a part of your financial strategy. Do your own independent research. Catastrophizing and exacerbating will only limit your opportunities; try to see the big picture. One data point may not prove something. One swallow does not a summer make. Look for a pattern.

Addressing Gatekeepers Concerns

It is a delicate balance to live as authentically as possible without burdening your community. It your duty to identify and acquire transferable skills that make you marketable in a wide range of industries. You should research on both soft and hard skills.

Your career path should factor in the prevailing sentiment. Suppose you want to be a governor in a few years. You know that a stay-at-home parent can be viewed condescendingly when running for an elected office in your area. What should you do today?

TMI Tip

Occupation-related perception can hurt your grade. Can college professors unconsciously make assumptions about you based on your part-time job? Manage your information whenever necessary. You are the brand manager. What do you do for a living again?

Expand Your Networks

Seek information on resume and interview preparation. Past occupations or the lack of an occupation may work against you. Work on time gaps in your resume that may indicate the lack of an occupation. You may decide to highlight transferable skills if your new job is unrelated to the old one. Expand your networks beyond your current occupation or higher up the ladder.

Reducing Your Own Stereotype-Driven Aggression

Do not be a snob. Treat everybody with respect regardless of what they do for a living. Occupation does not define human worth. Do not be an inverted snob either. Avoid the petty overcompensation attitude that only hurts your growth and potential networks. Aspire to go a level higher in whatever occupation you are in. Most of the people in prestigious positions started way below that level. There is no reason to despise them because of their achievements.

Speak Up Regardless of Status

Become an advocate for horizontal coexistence where a person's worthiness is not determined by occupational prestige. Speak up against occupational inequality, which can be a placeholder for gender and race exclusions.

31

Parenthood, Childless, Caregiving

This is Pry City

It is Snoopee's twenty-ninth birthday for the fourth year in a row. It is a very sad day. It is the day her grace-period extension as a childless female in Pry City completely expires. It is not a written rule but one that everybody understands.

Snoopee will be expected to constantly answer a barrage of questions. They might as well ask a straight question. "Please provide an explanation for why you don't have children." These questions are apparently asked out of concern for her welfare, but they can be very annoying.

Why don't you have children yet?
When are you going to make us grandparents?
Who's going to take care of you when you're old?
What will you do with your time when you get old?
Who will remember you after you die?

Pry City people are naturally inquisitive. People are known to break after a few years of these questions. They comply with the societal demands and have kids. By then they are in their late thirties or early forties. This only invites more questions. "Why do you have kids at this age?"

Parenting questions are wide and varied. Women are discouraged from dating single dads. Men feel pressured not to date single moms. If you start dating a single parent, a question may come your way. "Why do you date somebody with kids?" There are questions for all kids of parenthood deviations. There are questions for those who have more or fewer kids than expected. "Why do you have so many kids?" "Are planning to give her a sister?" "Guess what, do you know they have a family planning clinic down the block?"

For a newly married couple, the questions will be different and sometimes very intrusive. You have a grace period of about six months after the wedding. Then the down pour of repackaged witty comments starts flowing:

So when are you guys going to get started?
Is your husband okay with you not wanting kids?
Why do you hate kids?
Are you unable to have kids or something?
Did the doctor say if it is you or him?
Do you have trouble with the engines?

For those on the receiving end, you have to keep fighting the urge to explode. You can develop headaches trying to contain the powder keg in your mouth.

Why is it your business?
Because God said so.
Why do you ask?
Was I supposed to?
I am sorry, next time I will do it.

But this is Pry City. Most of the questions are from close relatives and friends. You want to answer the questions without exacerbating the issue. Snoopee will have to go to a coping class before she turns into a mushroom cloud.

Manifestation of Parenthood, Childlessness, or Caregiving Social Exclusion

One of the assumptions of this strategy is that gatekeepers are part of the society we live in. An employer knows, for instance, that a working mom will be forced to juggle orthodontist appointments, soccer matches, and her work schedule. The question here is whether gatekeepers in your backdrop can use parenthood or lack of it against you. For those sandwiched between supporting aging parents and their own kids at the same time, this concern is very real.

There are stereotypes and common cultural assumptions even when the fact is that no one lifestyle is good for every person. Does a certain industry discriminate against candidates with kids? Does a certain industry discriminate against candidates without kids? Does a certain industry discriminate against candidates with too many kids? Does a certain industry discriminate against candidates with kids that are too young? Does the employer give more money, benefits, or other preference to people who have kids?

There are studies showing that mothers earn less than childless women. There are reported cases where employers ask female applicants and employees, but not male applicants and employees, about their childcare responsibilities. There are documented incidents where employers steered workers with caregiving responsibilities to less prestigious or lower-paying positions.

Workplace gatekeepers still disproportionately penalize female parents, so this exclusion is naturally not purely gender neutral. At the same time, this can work against any gender. We have seen cases where employers deny male workers', but not female workers', requests for leave related to caregiving responsibilities. Is it females only that can be caregivers? It is a gender role double bias. The men suffer because of female stereotyping. Lowering tides wreck all ships.

We have seen cases where employers are caught assuming that a worker's caretaking responsibilities will automatically interfere with his or her ability to perform. Employers might assume parents with young children or single parents may not be interested in positions that require significant travel. Employers might assume parents may not be interested in working unusual or long hours.

Some countries restrict questions about an applicant's or employee's children, plans to start a family, pregnancy, or other caregiving-related issues during interviews or performance reviews. "Are you sure you can do this as a single mom?"

There are situations where the whole society becomes one giant gatekeeper. Anybody who has ever run for office knows it is a business decision. Today voters feel entitled to know about your personal life. When was the last president elected unmarried or without a family? It doesn't matter how qualified you are, you may be judged by your marital and parenthood status. Your family becomes a resume item.

Conglomeration of Exclusion Factors NUBC

Consider a gatekeeper treating women of color who have caregiving responsibilities differently than other workers with caregiving responsibilities. Stereotyping welfare mothers as parasitic or lazy is something that happens in many cities. One factor is comingled with the others to form a perfect exclusion wall. This generates hurricane-grade convergence of:

Parenthood
Gender
Race
Marital status
Place
Social status

Capsule of Talents

The greatest danger of any exclusion is when you start seeing yourself as less deserving and less capable. That's when you transfer the divine power. You are perfectly fine. This realization empowers you tremendously. This is the only way you can design goals for yourself and not wait for others' approval. Learning how parenthood, childlessness, or caregiving can be used to exclude you should be a part of your financial intelligence. Can family responsibilities get you fired? How does the industry treat employees who miss work to care for a sick family member?

Addressing Gatekeepers' Concerns and Dilemmas

The distance between your values and those of the gatekeepers will determine the cultural fit; this time it pertains to your personal responsibilities. It is your duty to gather information about the industry and make informed decisions.

There will be cases where familial-status bias may exist legally. In some countries, for example, senior citizen housing arrangements can exclude you for have young children. Since this personal index is not concerned with legalities you will still count it as exclusion.

TMI Tip

We all love kids. But we also love common sense. Having little children brings about a variety of real or perceived inconveniences. It might work against you to bring it all up during the interview. The company is looking for help. Did you read the ad? "Help wanted" not "Who wants help." The take-away here is that the interview time may not be the best avenue for bragging about your twelve cute kids; five of whom have a perpetual stomach bug. Let's talk about the employer's problems and the solutions that you can provide to the company.

Reducing Your Own Stereotype-Driven Aggression

It is incredibly offensive for parents to assume that childfree people live like teenagers without priorities. One person's ideal happy life might be someone else's nightmare. "What do you do with your money? What do you do with your time?" Consider that some people may have physical health constraints that may affect their parental status before you open your mouth. Avoid looking down on people because of their parenthood status.

It is also offensive to assume that parents don't have a life when they are literally raising "lives." This happens with parents adjusting to their new lives after being childfree. They become embroiled in providing for their kids. Their priorities will differ and take a one-eighty turn. Their new priorities may crash with those of their still childless friends.

Not all questions about parenthood are a signs of aggression. You don't want to alienate people who are trying to be friendly by initiating small talk. Create a retaliatory maneuver based on the nonmaleficence principle. Do no harm to your networks and your purpose. Don't just blow up and lose a client or a job opportunity.

You should learn how to throw the topic back to questioner without sounding defensive or rude, unless the backdrop calls for it. After a while you will be able to tell the difference between polite interest and just plain nosy. Then you will pull out your best "change of subject' tool. While you should not entertain offensive and intrusive questions, it is your duty to create rejoinders, comebacks, and ripostes that makes you a light in a dark environment.

Speak Up Regardless of Status

Become an advocate for horizontal coexistence where no one is treated unfairly because of his or her parenthood, childless, or caregiving status. Donate your voice for better career "on-ramps" for parents returning after pregnancy or caring for children and sick or aging relatives.

32

Personality Traits

Silence Of The Empty Vessels

Henry has just created an app that utilizes a "special cough" to activate a dummy call. He has been working on this for months. This app is a lifesaver if you work with Mr. Chatterbox.

Mr. Chatterbox can talk life out of you for eight hours straight. The one direction conversationalist lost his mute button in a freak accident when he was three. He is known to constantly "butt in" in the middle of people's conversations. The hijacked conversation will always land miles away from the intended planet. God forbid you find yourself in his office; it becomes an hour-long hostage situation. You will leave there with ample knowledge, including how many times his cats used the potty the previous year.

Henry has been testing the Anti-talkaholic Device for months now, but he is afraid he might be using it too much. The app works as a distraction creator by making a dummy call to your phone. It is simple to use. You record your special cough or any other signal and save. Every time you cough your cell phone will ring and can also call your office phone. You will then give a contrived excuse hurriedly, and you are now Scott-free.

The last beta test was unplanned but out of this world. He successfully deployed the device last Sunday at the church outing when the parish TMI lady cornered him and initiated an instant interrogation. "Why aren't you married yet?" "Is it true what I heard?" He deployed the "cough" and excused himself without appearing rude. He enjoyed chatting away with "nobody" about a horse that was in labor somewhere. He even made it to his car and achieved four Gs in sixty seconds. People in this church deal with Mrs. TMI by avoiding her; it is an open secret.

The next project for Henry is more challenging. Mr. Still Waters, the back office worker, has a personality that is directly opposite that of Mr. Chatterbox's. He swallowed some mute buttons when he was three. He is one of those people who respond with one word answers even to open-ended questions.

"How does the new policy make you feel?" His answer will be "Yes." He then creates nuggets of silent periods in the conversation that makes you very uneasy. It is like he is buffering or something.

Henry plans to start his own company, Henry Conversational Dynamics, Inc. There has to be a better way. This tech company will deal with issues ranging from "verbal diarrhea" to the "talk challenged." This global epidemic has now met its match.

Manifestation of Personality Trait-Based Social Exclusion

There are many stereotypes about introverts, extroverts and other traits in just about every community. Apparently this is mainly due to the need to fit people into a box. Are all extroverts attention seekers and loud mouths? Are all soft-spoken, solitude-loving introverts eccentric and weird?

I understand there are more personality traits than introversion and extroversion. For most of us who are not experts in the field of psychology, extroversion and introversion are not on a single continuum. You are either one or the other. We know it is not true. It is possible to fall somewhere along the spectrum. There are also closeted introverts and closeted extroverts. People who enjoy both solitude and constructive conversations may be misidentified as introverts.

I am also aware that shyness is different from being introverted, but we are using these terms as loosely as folks on the streets. This book is not about definitions and splitting of hairs in an academic sense.

There are books out there that claim that extroverts are happier than introverts. There are books that claim the opposite. I am no expert on this topic, but I know happiness is relative. We all have a fundamental need to belong and connect with others. Who decides what degree of connectedness is optimum? Can you be excluded based on conversational paradigm status?

Introvert

You are so quiet and reserved. It appears you are not a people person. In some communities being loud is becoming the social norm. A quiet person comes off as mysterious. Social awkwardness and shyness are not associated with intellect deficiency. But it is not uncommon to find people confusing intelligence with self-confidence or even with delusional hubris. There are no studies that indicate that a big mouth equals intelligence.

The stereotype is that introverts are happiest when they are alone. Nothing is inherently wrong with that. Hey, time spent on your own is really valuable time. A man of action is a man of contemplation. The question here is if the introversion leads to social exclusion.

Are introverts passed over for leadership positions? There might be no correlation between the most talkative person in the conference room and the best ideas, but introverts are often underrepresented in middle level leadership positions. This is because an extrovert appears to have an upbeat personality and comes off as a people person. Most importantly, the extrovert is more readily seen as a team player than a perceived introvert.

Extroverts

Nothing is inherently wrong with being outgoing and talkative. However, some employers and employees may not like overwhelming extroverts. This can lead to exclusion too. When I was researching this topic, I came across all kinds of methods of dealing with a constant talker. The coping techniques range from changing the focus of the conversation, taking attention away from the patient, creating some distraction or faking a heart attack.

The stereotype is that extroverts crave constant interaction. That paints a negative picture of those who talk more than normal. Empty vessels make the most noise. You have one mouth and two ears for a reason.

Conglomeration of Exclusion Factors NUBC
You talk too much. Why are you always so quiet? These factors work with other factors and can be driven by perceptions.

National Origin and Place Factors
Foreigners with language or accent problems may be perceived as shy and introverted. Aloofness generated by culture shock and lack of language fluency can be confused with introversion. Some people may not want to attract attention. Many people in new job positions take time to understand the environment. It is too early to be all over the place. They may be classified as introverts. There are people who are very talkative at home and not at work. The opposite can be true.

Age, Gender, and Social Class Factors
You used to be very talkative when were young. You used to be very talkative when you had money. What happened to you? Some people are very vocal in specific situations. In some communities there are expectations about how much you should open your mouth based on age, gender, or social status.

Consider a naturally extroverted young woman from a small town who starts working with a mostly older, rich crowd on a complicated project in a big city. She is depending on them for transportation, housing, and living expenses. She comes off as shy and aloof because of this dependency situation. Her concerns can be summarized in a NUBC as:

Personality trait
Etiquette
Protocol
Place

Age
Social class
Transportation
Shelter

Capsule of Talents

Learning how your personality trait can be used to exclude you should be a part of your financial intelligence. Your personality trait is a natural gift. It is a part of your capsule of talents that you arrived here with. You should maintain that control and decide the optimum degree of connectedness that makes you happy. Living with other people is an art. It is a delicate balance to live as authentically as possible without burdening or disrespecting others.

Choosing a Career

Some experts believe personality traits predict job performance better than any other known evaluation methods. Whether this is true is not the question. If the overall market buys this argument then it will affect you.

Find an industry that matches your talents, purpose and priorities. Some industries may not fit you if you are a not very social. Is this a job where you are required to spend a good chunk of your day interacting with people? A customer-facing role, cashier or teller, is a good example of jobs that you may be required to whip out that elusive smile. The ability to laugh aloud when your boss tells lame jokes may count on your next performance review.

Addressing Gatekeepers' Concerns and Dilemmas

The Nuthology Index's microcosm assumption recognizes that gatekeepers will have preferences based on what they see in our society. The distance between your values and those of the gatekeepers will determine the cultural fit.

Do not keep all of your talents and ideas bottled up. Sometimes you may be so quiet that people seem to ignore you. Find ways to make yourself more approachable. In a world full of constant group work and rolling team meetings, for example, you may come off as ineffective.

For those with outgoing personality it is a good idea to pay attention to the talent. You may be considered an over-talker without knowing. You have to buy a leash for your runaway mouth. Remember your mom's advice. Or was it a rule? Listen, consider, and then respond. The gatekeeper may also be worried that you might release some valuable information when you are in insecure TMI mode.

Reduce Your Own Aggression Footprint

Do not disparage those who are on the other end of the continuum; it is not their fault. It is not even a fault. There are protocols and etiquette in every society that makes it easier for coexistence of difference personality traits to flourish. Promoting your personality trait as the perfect one is a counterproductive move even when you believe your group has been marginalized. Overcompensation and perpetuating blanket blame only limits your networks.

Speak Up Regardless of Status

Most personality trait related social exclusion incidents are based on stereotypes. This gives room to group attribution errors that end up costing members some quality opportunities. Dream of a world where no one is treated unfairly because of his or her degree of connectedness. Become an advocate for horizontal inter-personality coexistence that is based on respect.

33

Place

Port Rudderless

It is the most interesting place on earth, period. Most satellites can see the image of this locality, which lies two blocks from downtown Sin Timón. A blindfolded stranger can recognize Port Rudderless using sounds and smells alone. The groupthink magnetic field and the quick-sand-like poverty has trapped generations in Port Rudderless, creating a de facto residential segregation. I know you don't always go to new places. But when you do, you should go to Port Rudderless. How will you know you are there?

First look for strip malls with graffiti walls
Multiple check-cashing joints with steel-grilled doors
Coolness factor is defined by high-end grilles and rims
Kids with gold-grilled teeth being grilled by frowning drill sergeants
Poverty traps next to pawn shops that tout tax refunds
Rent-to-own joints that are next to day labor agencies
For the record, you didn't see anything. It is Port Rudderless
Abandoned homes and boarded up commercial buildings
Drug zombies on the curbsides, landings, and front porches
The smell of weed creates its own ozone layer
People with high levels of preventable disability on sidewalks

High financial and moral poverty visible through the windows
Homes contaminated with anti-education residue
For the record, you didn't see anything. It is Port Rudderless
Living rooms oozing high anti-middle-class vapor
Quick-buck appetites go through the roof
Kitchen walls full of smiling pictures of MIA guardians
Dining rooms oozing toxic anti-teacher sentiment
Schools full of post-traumatic pupils
Kids who abandoned their own talents at the school gate for mirages
For the record, you didn't see anything. It is Port Rudderless
Kids chasing quixotic projects in sports and entertainment
Kids with their own living kids to feed, clothe, and shelter
Streets contaminated with anti-cop preserved beef
Delinquent youth wearing pants half-mast
Open air pop-up pharmacies at every corner
Unorthodox medical suppliers in their high-end gear
For the record, you didn't see anything. It is Port Rudderless
Everyone sleeps on the edge: one eye perpetually open
Beef here is not cow meat; it just means we shouldn't meet
It means when I see you, get ready for ICU
That kid is hiding from mom, criminals, and police simultaneously
Used police yellow tapes and makeshift memorials adorn the front yards
Constantly moving emergency vehicles provide mobile Christmas lights
For the record, you didn't see anything. It is Port Rudderless
On the right it is the famous school-to-prison pipeline
The leadership vacuum is like the hurricane's eye
Residents who succeed in life never return here
State actors use threats of statutory force to gain respect
Non-state actors use the threat of street force to gain respect
The spiritual leaders use the threat of hell to gain respect
For the record, you didn't see anything. It is Port Rudderless

Manifestation of Place-Based Social Exclusion

As they say in real estate, place, place, place. It is the place, stupid. Okay, I made that up. Place is another basket that fits stereotypes and generalizations well. It is almost natural that every geographical area comes with its share of perceptions. This creates the perfect "us vs them" scenario without bringing up race and other sensitive exclusion labels. Both historical events and ignorance contribute to place-based negative stereotypes. One city is known for being uptight and rough around the edges. You know the area where folks are down-to-earth, laid-back, with very casual, very practical, and very honest people. If you see a customer from Scroogeville, don't expect a tip. They say you are what you eat. Apparently you are also where you come from or live.

Highland people
Lowland people
Ghetto dwellers
Trailer dwellers
Coastal people
People from the South
People from the North
People from south of the river
People from north of the river
The urban people
The mediaeval suburbanites
Inner-city people
Bible-belt inhabitants
Gated-community people
Midwestern people
People in the East
People in the West
Dwellers of the old continent
People from that region
People from that area
North and south of that line

People from there
The others

Economic silent treatment

Where place-induced political retribution games are involved, the ruling class's policies can lead to constant leakage of natural resources and the blockage of any meaningful investments. This negatively affects the economic development of the target place. Engineered and politically motivated place exclusion can take the form of:

Disinvestment in education
Choreographed traffic jams
Deindustrialization
Redlining
Gentrification
Last to get electrical grid repaired
Constant water, sewerage, and garbage system issues
The last street to get its snow plowed
Yawning museum-grade potholes
Slow disaster or emergency response
Targeted code and law enforcement
Inequitable urban redevelopment
Irresponsible zoning
Mischievous school redistricting
Suspect business zoning patterns
Delayed infrastructure projects
Engineered residency work or school requirements

In an economically disadvantaged area, you often have vulnerable people living in inherently vulnerable places. This is where financial illiteracy meets abject poverty. It becomes an endless supply of credulous gamblers; a charlatan's paradise. It becomes a place where predatory lenders prey on the vulnerable with impunity. This has the potential of creating other exclusion classes.

Poor health care and education inequalities
Low investment and diminished opportunities
Unjustified incarceration disparities
Unemployment-fueled crime and fragmented families
High incidences of violence, criminality, drug dependence, and squalor

People are products of their environment and tend to exhibit the same behaviors that they see acted out in their communities. Due to a lack of discretionary income, people in an area may adopt some ways that end up defining their character. You can tell a person who grew up in a certain neighborhood by the way they use certain products. For example, people in a certain location are known to reuse a household item several times or use it in a way a person from a different location may find interesting. The place-based behavior and language can block their mobility, especially if opportunities are in a different environment.

It may also cost more to live in a poor area. Many lower-income areas do not have supermarkets. That means the residents shop at convenient stores where product prices are almost double and the choices of healthy alternatives are almost nonexistent.

People from certain regions may be ignored or misrepresented in a national culture. You may often hear degrading and condescending stereotypes or negative newscasts about the region.

Conglomeration of Exclusion Factors NUBC

Imagine a kid who lives in a flight-or-fight, underserved area where public schools have a long history of subpar education. Young people in the area constantly deal with diminished safety, trauma, nutritional issues, emotional dysregulation, and behavioral issues. This kid has to learn to manage his adult life somehow. He has to comprehend his obligation to society, community, and family. He is expected to understand the value of being a good citizen. This includes attributes like good character, etiquette, and understanding of protocols. These are things that come naturally to kids in stable environments. This is not a stable environment.

A combination of factors may crop up and form a unique NUBC:

Place
Social class
Credit history
Social class
Disability
Age
Character
Etiquette and protocol

We are tempted to jump onto the causation and correlation wheel of misfortune. Remember, these are social exclusion factors that can stand on their own. Regardless of causation, they exist and they are causes of concern.

Nuthology Strategy and Capsule of Talents

Your location on this rock does not define who you are as a human being. Learning how place exclusion can be used to exclude you should be a part of your financial intelligence. Do not buy into negative stereotypes. The index counts all of the instances when you are excluded from some opportunity by a gatekeeper's commission or omission, whether legal or illegal, fair or unfair, conscious or unconscious. Not all discrimination is illegal. In most countries, employers can hire whomever they wish as long as they don't use the protected class in making that decision. Is "place" a protected class in your country?

Addressing Gatekeepers' Concerns and Dilemmas

Sometimes it is just logistics that blocks you from opportunities. The remoteness of a location can exclude you from opportunities. An example is where a hiring company is only interviewing local candidates.

You should learn to address the employer's location based concerns. This is more important if you want a job in a distant location.

"Why should I hire someone from three hundred miles away when I have a number of equally qualified candidates within a thirty-mile radius?"

One reason could be that you have a strong desire to move to the area because your family lives there. You have to show you are better than the other candidates. Who pays for interview travel expenses and relocation costs?

The distance between your values and those of the gatekeepers will determine the cultural fit; this time it is literally the distance. Government jobs are often restricted to people who live within its jurisdiction. It is quite normal for municipal employers to require that employees live within the municipality. States and nations can do the same.

Learn to read the line of questioning. "Do you live nearby?" A distance or transportation question can come out naturally. "How was your commute?"

Avoiding Petty Overcompensation

Both survival and success involve changing position literary or figuratively. Sometimes we cannot put our fingers on it, but the writing is on the wall. You have to change your environment to change your situation. It is something you have heard all your life.

Duck.
Move to clean fresh air.
Move to greener pastures.
Move your body for health.
Go to college.
Keep moving forward.
Fight for social mobility.
Position yourself for blessings.
Be in the right place at the right time.
Move from your mother's attic if you want this relationship to go anywhere.
Walk on this path.

Move to the Promised Land.
Move up the ladder
Move, move, move.

Kids need a stable environment in which to learn and flourish. Adults need a stable business environment in which to earn and grow rich. The definition of insanity is staying in the same place and expecting different landmarks. If you recently saw Egyptian pyramids or Mount Rushmore pass by your place, I want what you are smoking. You should be the one to decide if changing your position is good for you. Don't stay in a place to please others.

Movement between one or more layers of stratification is often correlated to physical movement. Show me one great leader who stayed where he was born. The gravitational pull of poverty is often tied to a geographical location. The solution must involve moving the mind, body or both.

Reducing Your Own Stereotype-Driven Aggression and Expand Your Networks

Are you regionally biased? Place chauvinism is something that comes naturally sometimes. Most place- related social exclusions are based on assumptions. It is easy to get caught up in delusional patriotism that can easily become unwarranted and petty parochialism. This may turn the love of ones location into xenophobia. The global economy and new technology require that you engage people from different regions with respect. Don't give people excuses for not meeting you. The modern business environment demands that you expand your networks beyond your provincial bubble.

Speak Up Regardless of Status

Become an advocate for horizontal coexistence where no one is treated unfairly because of his or her geographical status. Racism can easily be repackaged and laundered using unequal access to education, employment, transportation, and shelter to people in one place, especially when a gatekeeper can point to a few symbolic minority success stories in another location.

Lower-income area kids are likely to attend low-rated schools. In areas facing urban decay, the schools may not be well funded in the first place. Parents spend less time with their children because they are working two jobs or education is the least of their worries. This cycle must be broken somehow.

You cannot ignore the impact of where kids grow up. Place bias often has more impact than race and other factors. One can look at these from many angles, including life-expectancy data. Generally, the higher the number of jobless households per square mile, the higher the crime rate in the area. Place exclusion is a life member of the axis of poverty.

34

Pregnancy, Childbearing

Are You Planning to Have More?

Due to the adverse "economic climate," one employee had to be laid off. It just happened to be Sadza. Initially she understood the company's need to downsize. She was seven-months pregnant, so the timing was very bad. Two months later Sadza called one of her friends at the job to give her news about her new baby. That was how she learned that the company had filled her position within a month. Sadza knew that it took more than a month for things to improve in the industry, so she was suspicious. That was not the only fishy angle. They hired a mature male for the job. How convenient?

Sadza contacted a local labor attorney. This led to an attention-grabbing investigation that unearthed a major structural problem. It was both a company-wide and industry-wide problem. When the company lawyer cited "improvements in their revenues" in response to Sadza's case, even the presiding judge laughed. "You want me to buy the argument that economic conditions improved within thirty days?" The central government investigation discovered more dirt in every office. The problem was even worse in the company's other nine branches.

At the headquarters, an employee testified how she was grilled about baby plans based on her age and gender. When the twenty-two-year-old sensed that she was being considered a "pregnancy risk" she made it clear that she had no plans for starting a family. In an informal chat with the interviewer, she let her know that she not only hates children but also is incapable of having any. This employee had no doubt that the chat influenced the company's decision to hire her.

In the eastern office, a female employee was forced to quit her job because the management refused to excuse her from lifting heavy boxes during her pregnancy. At the same time, other workers recovering from back surgery were exempted from lifting heavy boxes.

In the southwest office, a supervisor started strictly enforcing the break time policy when two employees became visibly pregnant. The two were docked for time and disciplined for taking too many bathroom breaks, even though other workers with medical needs were not docked nor disciplined.

The conclusion was that the corporate culture there was toxic. There was case after case that pointed to age, pregnancy, gender, and parenthood bias. Single fathers were often portrayed as heroic, devoted, and selfless angels, while single mothers were painted as lazy or even promiscuous. It turned out that 80 percent of the female workers were either childless or unable to have children. A congressional review later in the year uncovered another little fact. The company had dozens of contracts with the central government.

Manifestation of Pregnancy-Based Social Exclusion

Nuthology is concerned with access to resources, opportunities, and rights from an individual perspective. Subtle pregnancy or childbearing discrimination is more common than overt aggression. You cannot pretend that this factor will not affect you at some point. Having a child does interfere with your career to some extent. There will be school runs, sick days, and medical visits. How do you have children and a career? Must it be an either or issue?

Social exclusion on the basis of pregnancy, childbirth, and related conditions can take many routes:

- Unfair hiring, firing, promotion, and demotions
- Frustration with employee after pregnancy-related leave
- Denial related to health insurance, bonuses
- Partial and targeted enforcement of company policies, standards, and production expectations during and after pregnancy
- Denial of opportunities based on future pregnancy expectations

Disability

Depending upon the individual and the job tasks, pregnancy certainly can affect your ability to work. On top of fatigue, there are also related medical conditions such as severe morning sickness, doctor-ordered bed rest and recovery from childbirth. For this reason, some countries have enacted laws where pregnancy is treated like a temporary disability. In these nations the employer is obligated to give pregnant employees the same treatment and benefits that it gives to employees with other temporary disabilities.

Even with laws in place, many people are still being discriminated against in work places or when applying for employment, because of pregnancy or childbearing potential. Some employers leave themselves enough deniability room making it harder to proof.

Dilemmas

Should a single pregnant woman work in a school that teaches abstinence? Some religious-based gatekeepers may have the right to prescribe pregnancy policies. In this case, a woman may be fired for being pregnant and unmarried. At the same time non-pregnant female employees and the males who violate the same morality rules are not be penalized. Modern medicine can make it more complicated. What about those women who gets pregnant through artificial insemination? Should they marry just to comply with policy? It becomes a battle between two rights. It is definitely something to think about when choosing a career.

Conglomeration of Exclusion Factors, NUBC

Change in appearance that occurs naturally during and after pregnancy may feed into other social exclusion classes like weight, attractiveness, and disability. This factor readily brings together several exclusions:

Pregnancy
Gender
Age
Parenthood status
Marital status
Weight
Attractiveness
Disability

Nuthology Strategy

These factors are just risks that may never materialize. Learning how the pregnancy factor can be used to exclude you should be a part of your financial strategy. This encourages you to look at situations and identify new ways to do things. Do companies in your target industry avoid hiring younger women to get around maternity leaves and pregnancy-related issues? The greatest danger of pregnancy exclusion the risk that you may start seeing yourself as less deserving and less capable. You may be tempted to set low career goals. The planning also means you get to develop snappy comebacks to stupid questions that you may encounter during a real or perceived pregnancy.

Cultural assumptions, pressures and influences drive the treatment of pregnant women in a society. There are places where pregnancy is sold as an "opting out" of the workforce step. The unconscious preconceptions and stereotypes can create structural obstacles to your career. Your success will therefore depend on how you manage both the capsule of talents and these concerns.

Mommy track is a term that is related to this topic. What is the mommy-track phenomenon? It is a career path that allows a mother flexible or reduced work hours but tends to slow or block advancement according to the dictionary. This can create a situation where women with family responsibilities are shunted to lower-paying jobs greatly contributing to the growing gender wage gap.

TMI Tip

Bringing up any personal issues during the interview can work against you. This includes pregnancy, divorce, or any other relationship issues. There will be time to discuss it. The company is looking for help at this stage.

Is a prospective employer allowed to ask if you plan to have children in the near future? The question is illegal in some countries. It is advisable to research for other tips that fit your backdrop from those who have been through this route or from legal professionals. Many issues related to parenthood and caregiving exclusion will also apply to pregnancy factor.

Index

Feel free to include any bias that is related to pregnancy in this category if it is not covered under another admitted class. Breastfeeding bias is a good example of such attributes.

Speak Up Regardless of Status

Become an advocate for horizontal coexistence where no one is treated unfairly based on pregnancy, childbearing age and related conditions. At the societal level, a lot of work needs to be done to address the perceived stigma of pregnancy and performance. There are also issues related to unwelcome jokes, comments and lines of questioning.

35

Race

Khutspe, the Plucky Underdog

Once upon a time there was a man with a funny name who had the loaded temerity to think he could occupy the highest office in the land against all odds. He had a few concerns behind the deceiving calmness.

Name

The funny name for sure was one of them. It was not a garden variety name, for sure. The name sounded foreign sponsored to start with.

Weight

He was too skinny and too new-age healthy looking. How could he relate with a nation dealing with obesity. He lacked the gravitas that comes from a few pounds of fat in the wrong places. He could have used a beer belly that showed power and influence.

National Origin

His dad was a foreign citizen. This fueled strong rumors that he was also born abroad. Popular rabble-rousers had a field day with that angle. The theory was that he was not a natural-born citizen and, consequently, was ineligible to be an office holder. Conspiracy theorists just needed to create enough reasonable doubt. It needn't to be true to be an effective obstacle.

Religion

His middle name left the aftertaste of a locally unpopular religion. In fact, he spent part of his childhood in a country where most people belong to that religion. He also had a second religious problem. He also dared to sit still in the pew as the pastor said something bad about his country. Who lets their pastor speak? This attracted intense media scrutiny but neutralized the foreign-religion angle.

Alma Mater

He was considered one of those educated elites for attending a prestigious school. The stereotype is that these folks tend to approach problems philosophically and intellectually. Elite is a five letter word: a political stigma associated with such schools' alumni. That means people who are too out of touch with the real needs of the citizens that they should not be given public office job applications, according to the new professional flamethrower's dictionary.

Affiliation

He was sold as one who lives to the extreme left of his left-wing party. He is so left that he uses his left hand to write. That can exclude you from half of the voting population.

Place

Liberal elite, as a political stigma, is also associated with actual geographical spaces. There were states that were considered liberal. That means he had little chance of winning non-liberal leaning states. Leaders from his local city were known for espousing corruption, tax hikes, government expansion, and suffering from patriotism deficiency according to a board certified polemist. He was too popular among the urban dwellers that he was perceived as out of touch with the country crowd.

Race

The candidate came from a racial group that is a small percentage of the population but whose past struggles for public office representation are well documented. No member of this race has ever garnered any significant percentage of votes, let alone come close to winning that position.

Colorism

There were some elements in his own racial group that thought he could have used an extra coat of paint or two. Apparently his skin was not a true representation of his race. Group membership based on darkness or lightness of his skin tone was a risk to be mitigated.

Age

The chutzpah-propelled candidate was relatively young compared to most former holders of the job. His hair was lacking enough gray wisdom highlights. His public office experience was an issue, even members of his own party complained that he should have waited for his turn.

Lifestyle

The young candidate struggled with a nicotine addiction and the public knew about. His past experience with substance abuse was well documented even in his own book, *Khutspe, The Plucky Underdog*.

Decision Time: A Risk Management Crash Course

The candidate was not naïve in his assessment of the odds. He saw himself as a plucky little David standing up to Goliath. He hired a guy named David who formed a goliath mitigating team.

The team came up with a list of his unique bias conglomeration:

Name
Weight
National origin
Religion
Alma mater

Affiliation
Place regional geographical
Race
Colorism
Age
Lifestyle

When it came to mitigating the potential social exclusions on the David vs Goliath campaign trail he approached each factor differently.

1. **Name Discrimination**: Make fun of the name. De-emphasize the middle name.
2. **National Origin Discrimination**: Produce a birth certificate. Poke fun at the birth controversy.
3. **Religion Discrimination**: Put emphasis on local religion and spirituality.
4. **Alma Mater Discrimination**: Put emphasis on education. Sell it as a plus.
5. **Affiliation Discrimination**: Moved to the middle. He became more pragmatic.
6. **Regional Geographical Discrimination**: Build youth networks in hostile zones.
7. **Racism**: Build up intense curiosity. Do you want to see a minority president in your lifetime?
8. **Colorism Discrimination**: Emphasis on roots. Parade the extended family around.
9. **Age Discrimination**: Downplay the experience part. Capitalize on youth.
10. **Lifestyle Discrimination**: Confess youthful sins outright. Humanize struggle.

Index Credits

The team also listed the credits. These are the things that worked for him. Besides the official job description, there were many unwritten rules. They looked at the patterns of data for the past job holders.

You have to be a relatively tall male. The average height of past office holders was 70.8 inches. At 73 inches, Plucky was taller than average. You have to be college educated. It had been seventy years since a president was elected without a college degree. Plucky had two degrees, just in case one was not enough.

You must have attended an Ivy League school. Nearly one-third of all past office holders attended Ivy League schools. In presidential elections, the Ivy League alumni had a leg up. No worries there.

One more thing: it was time to lawyer up. According to the learned friends, the office holder couldn't be a minority and peanut farmer. No, way. Would the country elect a racial minority haberdasher? Not this year. He had to be at least, a lawyer. Patterns of data? More than half of the past office holders started as lawyers. Plucky checked out again. The team was excited. They saw some hope on the horizon.

Plucky had political and intellectual talents that were above the ordinary. He had excellent communication skills, which included the ability to drive a crowd into a drunken euphoria. He had the ability to create networks that extended beyond his own race, thus benefiting from the multiplicity of cultures. Money was playing an ever-greater role in politics. He used his celebrity status to create a bullet proof war chest.

The man had the ability to read the signs of the times, make decisions without all the information, and display pragmatism. Plucky had a good dose of divine sprinkles of luck to seal the deal. When the dust settled, the man with a funny name won.

Manifestation of Race-Based Social Exclusion

Few factors epitomize social exclusion the way racism does. Most people agree that racism exists in one version or another. We don't have to pull tons of files full of dark legacies to explain race-based exclusion. We can also agree that, at least in most developed nations, racism is becoming more subtle in nature.

This book is mostly about the stealth type of racism that is impregnated and coated with enough deniability that it is hard to explicitly pinpoint. It is like abstract art. You know it is there. Racial discrimination can occur both without hostility and even without any intent to discriminate. In fact, most subtle discrimination today occurs as in-group favoritism. While passive coexistence that exists today in developed nations lacks the out-group derogation of the yesteryears, it still harbors enough power to prevent equal access to opportunities and equity in all aspects of life. As overt acts of discrimination continue to decline, it is easy for society to get the illusion of increased social equality.

Social Exclusion on the Basis of Race Takes Many Routes

Workplace and business opportunities:
This is the obvious one: unfair hiring, firing, promotions, demotions, and distribution of benefits. There is the targeted enforcement of company policies, standards, and production expectations. Racial discrimination in the workplace reduces a prospect's chances of earning a living and family sustaining wage. Denial of business opportunities and contracts is a common concern for racial minorities.

Unfair law enforcement and justice system:
You cannot ignore the impact of unfair law enforcement and an unfair justice system in race-based social exclusion. Looking at it through the economic lenses, this goes way beyond the initial loss of freedom. Criminal and other background checks disproportionately impact minorities in a deep way.

Exploitation:
There are occasions where some businesses seem to prefer specific minority workers because they are viewed as cheaper and complain less about unfair working conditions, wages and benefits.

Place and social exclusion:
This occurs when economic and political realities force one group to dwell in certain areas. Failure in both race and social class relations almost always go together.

Dominant but subjective:

In some countries racial classes are used when correcting historical inequalities. That means various forms of minority quotas have been established to correct past injustices. Consequently, it is the member of the dominant group that may count race as a factor since the government's action gives preference to the subjective groups based on race.

Working-class citizens who are nonracial minorities may face exclusion because they are regarded as the majority. Many people will argue that it is never fair to give preferential treatment to one race over another. At the societal level, this is an ongoing discussion.

The index is based on an individual perspective, so the policy is either for or against you. At the personal level, if you are perceived to be a member of a dominant group, this will work to your disadvantage. In cases where racial minorities are hired over other groups because the company needs more diversity and you happen to be a non-minority, this will be a racial exclusion in your index.

Conglomeration of Exclusion Factors NUBC

Consider the marginalized youth living in run-down urban center. If one happens to be a racial minority, then you have race, place, and social class exclusion factors working together. Is it possible that a youth will have geographical, race, social class, credit, unemployment, and, sometimes, shelter discrimination exclusion factors simultaneously? Is it possible to add gender, single parenthood, age, weight, colorism, affiliation, and sexual orientation concerns on this same individual's NUBC?

Race
Place
Social class
Credit
Unemployment
Shelter
Gender

Parenthood
Age
Marital status
Colorism
Affiliation
Sexual orientation

If my counting is good, these are thirteen bases of discrimination. Each one of these can function as a disfranchisement class by itself. We are assuming the individual has not been arrested, has good character, etiquette, and other factors in good order. So this list can grow. It is not lost on anybody that there are correlation and causation relationships among all these factors. We have deep outstanding legal, ethical, moral, and fairness questions. The take here is that addressing one exclusion factor may not help much.

What Can We Do to Mitigate Racial Bias?

For constantly marginalized individuals, the backdrop is constantly shifting, but the goal remains the same: maintain the right to be useful, respected, accepted, and an equal member of society. The economic importance of social stigmas cannot be ignored or wished away if we expect individuals to realize their full potential. Even when solutions are understandably elusive, the placebo effect of the analysis has a potential upside. At the very least, the individual realizes that his concern is being addressed.

Yes, there has been tremendous improvement in race relations in the last few decades. Yes, you can point out some racial minorities in some high places. It is hard to dream big when your achievement parameter is demarcated with a steel wall of race-based social exclusion. Rather than pretend racism doesn't exist, we can acknowledge the reality on the ground. This will free us to explore a personal strategy that is more color-conscious than color-blind. We can live decisively instead of floating and drifting in denial.

Nuthology Strategy

Should we fight racism or engage in personal development? There is enough of "you" to go around. Nuthology strongly encourages using individual obligation and responsibility to supplement society-based efforts. 3-PR means synchronizing public policy, and personal responsibly to effectively confront all aspects of social exclusion. It turns out you are wearing two hats. One is for the pursuit of personal achievement, and the other one for advocating for social justice in your small way.

At the individual level, you have bills to pay. You are competing with the other society members at the capitalist level. That means you have to find time to cater to your own well-being. When we all do that, we reduce the level of dependency in society. By removing the idea of a helpless bystander, that effectively reduces exclusion. Working on self-development, therefore, greatly enhances the efforts to eradicate racism. You make more impact with more wealth and experience.

Nuthology Strategy and Personal Approach

At the risk of sounding academic, the objective of any risk mitigation measure is to eliminate, mitigate, or design a coping strategy. Assuming that the elimination of the racism risk is not currently feasible, our discussion here will be primarily mitigating and coping with it. The theory and the index are interested in access to resources, opportunities, and rights from an individual perspective, as opposed to what we do as a group.

The strategy embraces and encourages a holistic approach to social exclusion that incorporates individual involvement in personal finance, obligations, opportunities, and lifestyle interventions. It does not replace professional help or any current societal level quest for equality. It is a personal tool, not an answer.

At the individual level, you have more choices than you think. Let's look at some options:

- Focusing your energies on things that matter to you alone
- Allocating most of your resources to your priorities in terms of time and energy
- Innovatively looking at situations and identifying new ways to do things
- Finding ways to effectively define your personal brand
- Reaching for tools and techniques that will enable you to discover your natural talents
- Learning how to build powerful networks in and out of your race
- Learning to gain more agreement and cooperation from people from all walks of life especially in today's global economy
- Taking ownership of your efforts and attitude

This approach is basically a risk management approach, not the magic panacea that we have all been waiting for. Even when you have a billion dollars you can still face racism. I am not telling you whether you will be discriminated against or not. I am also not promising snake oil miracle cures or extended energy fields. My message is straightforward. You must develop a wide view of the issue surrounding race exclusion.

Risk Convergence Zone

Compounding exclusion statuses will always produce a compound effect. This can only be mitigated using a compounding effort. The interplay between your statuses is something only you can totally visualize. Suppose you are an older, minority, homeless single mother living in a bad neighborhood and in need of transportation to look for a job. Strangers will see a minority, a single mother, a homeless person, or just a person in a bad place. Your compounding concerns might be:

1. Race
2. Gender
3. Marital status
4. Parenthood
5. Place
6. Shelter
7. Age
8. Unemployment stigma
9. Transportation

A remedy concentrating on one factor only will not help much. Long-term unemployment, place, and transportation may not even be classified as bona fide bias statuses in your community. Do we have businesses that avoid hiring people from specific places, who don't have cars, or who have not been employed for a long time? There are no complicated algorithms in this assessment.

If, for instance, society is fighting racism, there are other factors like gender, age, place, social class, credit status, and character that will prevent an individual from benefiting from its efforts. It is impossible for society to conceptualize, let alone take a multidimensional approach, because each of the members will have a unique combination of these factors. Only individual members have the flexibility to do this.

Choose the Parable of the Lawn

You spend a lot of time killing and uprooting weeds in your lawn. There are some spots that are good, and there are some spots where weeds keep shooting up. Don't wait until there are no weeds in the whole yard. There is a risk that the weeds will roll back your accomplishments. For those areas that are good, plant some more grass seeds. Water the seeds and apply adequate fertilizer. One day the healthy grass will overcome the weeds. The weeds will choke and wither away.

We all salute the efforts of current and past world human rights fighters. They make the human species look good. They are the salt, giving this mean world its flavor. Racism remains painfully real. Nuthology strategy implores everyone to occupy the "not enough" space that has already been created while pushing for more.

Failure to take advantage of the space will only encourage regression. Some areas that have seen progress may start reverting back. You will be honoring the sacrifices of the civil rights transformative figures by showing up at school, voting booths, and job sites. Choose to occupy the space. Choose to create a new lush lawn of healthy grass that chokes the nasty weeds of racism.

Choose to Leverage Your Unique Capsule of Talents

We don't receive divine talents in groups. Each of us is endowed with unique talents. All you need is to believe in yourself. I have no doubt you will succeed. You were made to succeed. The NUBC makes you more unique in a way. The biggest danger of real or perceived racism is a risk that that you may develop a lackadaisical attitude toward self-improvement efforts. That you may end up abandoning your divine provided talents to be a replica of other people. That is the risk that needs most of the attention.

The mere risk of internalizing the bias, even when its existence is unknown, can interfere with your ability to develop personal talents and potential. Believing in yourself can help you to develop high self-esteem and in turn unleash the creativity that you have been hoarding inside. This approach will only work if you claim individual control.

You can only discover the contents of your capsule of talents if you step away from groupthink for a moment. You can then unearth your very own idiosyncratic ideas, views, and responses to issues.

Becoming yourself includes not copying members of your own race. Copy the work ethics or methods, but do not try to be a replica. Our creative talents are very different. Nothing works against the advancement of marginalized racial minorities than groupthink.

Groupthink tends to give an illusion of comfort and invulnerability, and a placebo sense of belonging. This is often what blocks your individual innovation. Remember, in the context of capitalism you are also competing with members of your own racial sub-group.

There are no mysteries, complicated algorithms or snake oil ambiguities in this strategy. If you are dealing with race and gender exclusion concerns, for instance, having inadequate education, lack of transferable skills, poor etiquette, poor character, bad credit, and unplanned obligations will likely keep you glued to the poverty orbit. All this will only aggravate your initial risk status. Alternatively, a custom education regimen, custom transferable skills, and expanded networks are likely to propel you through some glass ceilings.

Choose to Develop Time and Energy Efficiencies

First you have to realize that society will tackle each social exclusion class as a single concept. Social exclusion factors are rarely alone. If you have bad character, bad credit, criminal, or long term unemployment issues, you should not ignore these factors at the personal level. These factors will almost always work with the racial exclusion factor to exclude you more. You should seek a comprehensive solution for all factors, not each separately like society does. This ensures you are not moving from one issue to another. You will save a lot of time and energy.

At the individual level, you will also have to decide what percent of your time will be spent waiting for a solution or arguing with deniers. There are people who believe in aliens, think vampires are real, and claim the moon landing was faked, but they don't accept racism exist. On the other side there will be people whose business models are based on the perpetual existence of the racism. How much of your time do you want to spend on them? Look for people who will not drain your energies.

Choose Careers Wisely and Deliberately

Because of your unique bias risks, your route to success will need minor custom adjustment. If you are a prospective college student, for example, with concerns that include race, gender, marital status, parenthood, place, shelter, age, unemployment, and transportation risks, your academic major selection criteria will need a tweak. Your GPA might be pointing to "chicken dancing" and "dinosaur milking degrees". The college counselor might even suggest them; it is the schools job to fill the classes. It doesn't matter if these are the easiest and everybody is taking them. You cannot afford take the oversubscribed degrees like the rest of the population.

Choose to Create a Preemptive Approach

Society approaches this factor in a reactive way most of the time. Anytime a bias-related event takes place, emotions run high and people understandably take to the streets. There is trading of blames. An investigation may follow, which may trigger legislation. Nuthology strategy is a peacetime and market-driven approach that is preemptive in nature. It does not replace the communal actions that are meant for overt and violent incidents, but it can reduce their occurrence.

Nuthology strategy works best as a predictive model. The user is able to visualize the effects of added exclusions before they manifest. Let us assume race excludes you from 50 percent of jobs in your country as an example. Suppose then that government statistics show a criminal record excludes you from 90 percent of jobs. If you factor in bad credit and character, your probability of getting a job with a livable wage will not be very promising. Each factor adds some weight.

Suppose you had a crystal ball and kept the exclusion at 50 percent because you cannot control the racial factor. Suppose you supersized your education, skills, and networks while keeping character, credit, criminal record, and protocol in check. You can bet that your chances of success will be several times better.

The index is a tool for you to gather relevant information and to collect market data.

It is by using the information that you can narrow your options and develop a 360 view where you can not only see obstacles but open doors and six-lane highways.

Choose to Embrace Academic Education, Financial Education, and Personal Branding

In a free market system, businesses give special attention to people that they think may add more value to their goals. People love to point out popular school dropouts to justify their bad decisions, ignoring talents, NUBC, and credits they might have. This entices marginalized kids to abandon their talents at the school gates. For the most part, millions of "stardom hungry dropouts" end up on the part of the street where the school-to-prison pipeline starts.

Most youth are unable to see any positive outcomes outside of sports and entertainment. Playing football without a helmet is not bravely. Dropping out of school without a safety net is a bad financial decision. Knowledge is needed to maneuver through most financial minefields.

Choose to Reengineer Your Personal and Business Goals

Start somewhere and move up the ladder. We all want to be millionaires, but middle-class life should not be sold as a negative. It is your duty to identify, acquire, and develop transferable skills that you can use in different industries.

Choose to Use Education and Skills to Become Part of the System

Education, reading, travel, and intellectual curiosity allow you to see the world in a different way. For decades, street protests have been the best way to address racial concerns. While this tactic is still used today after a tragic event, the new sustainable trend is fighting the system from inside. To be part of the policy-making body you will need education. It is very hard for anybody in most modern nations to get into an elected office without some post–high school credentials. It is even harder if you are a racial minority.

Choose to Create Wide and Meaningful Networks

Use modern technology to create networks that include people from all walks of life. Being pragmatic is not conforming. Compromise is not a derogatory term. Avoid groups that use factually incorrect material and gross overgeneralizations to create a situation where a whole race epitomizes all the evil in the world.

There will always be a good number of nonaggressive dominant group members who want to be a part of the solution and conversation. This should be taken as an asset. Categorically demonizing a whole group without carefully differentiating between persons of goodwill and those who consciously perpetuate racism only minimizes the scope of your network.

"I believe in the essential goodness of my fellow man, which leads me to believe that no problem of human relations is ever insoluble." Ralph Bunche

Blanket blame exacerbates the issue. This only limits your opportunities and ability to create a wider network. There are many working-class members of the dominant race who are in the same financial position as racial minorities or even worse. They may not like to be viewed as privileged, because they are not.

In real life, we have no community that can be all bad or, conversely, all good. Children do not choose the circumstances in which they come into the world. That also includes nonminority children.

"Darkness cannot drive out darkness; only light can do that. Hate cannot drive out hate; only love can do that." Martin Luther King Jr

Choose to Catch the Diversity Train

Racial lines still exist in modern society, but thank God they are becoming more blurred. Many companies have started to realize that businesses with more diverse workforce often get more customers. Increasing purchasing power of racial minorities helps the economy and reduces dependency drastically. It should be a no brainer. Compassion is not a zero-sum game where one group improves and the other is less well-off. Most countries have discovered the hard way that limiting the success of certain segments of a society diminishes the value of the whole nation in the long run.

Choose to Write Your Own Story

The days when people told your story without response are coming to an end. You are now able to start a social-media outreach from your phone and reach millions. It is good to note that while technology opens up the world for diversity, it is also a proverbial double-edged sword: it offers a means to propagate and reinforce every conceivable prejudice on this earth. You will have to play both offense and defense.

Choose to Always React Decisively

If the only thing that this strategy does to your life is to make you less antagonistic in conflict situations, that's a great step toward improving your life. What would you do if you found yourself in a contentious situation? What would you do after a subtle incident? There will be temptations to make a choice based on hurt, anger, or revenge.

You should always buy some time to create a response based on the nonmaleficence principle. Do no harm to your purpose. Most companies today have some mechanisms to handle bias incidents. You should always try that route first whenever possible. Speak to legal and spiritual experts if you have to. Take the high road in your response every step of the way. React decisively in a way that you come out as the winner. Make sure there is some response.

Choose to Avoid Anchoring and Catastrophizing

Every society has self-ordained activists whose programs are designed to discuss the world's status but never really to change it. The reconstruction of history and rewriting of facts is meant to be infinite. It is a business model by itself. Your independent research will help you avoid getting in this perpetual spin wheel in your own racial ecosystem.

Equality of outcome is not the goal of the free market system. Even when racism is absent, the risk of failure is always there. Lack of racism does not guarantee success. Be prepared to try and risk the failure. Our forefathers fought for opportunities. We need the equal chances to try and fail a million times. The key word here is equal opportunities.

While racism is a well-documented factor of social exclusion, it is not always the only factor in a situation. Sometimes it is not even a factor at all. If most people in your race, for example, have no problem getting opportunities, but you still find yourself blaming racism, there is a great possibility you are barking up the wrong tree.

We are talking about both the actual or perceived prejudice. It's a bad financial move to assume the risk of prejudice is perpetually there. It's also a bad financial move to assume a risk doesn't exist while the data shows otherwise.

Choose to Reduce Your Own Stereotype-Driven Aggression

Assuming a negative trait to be true for every member of a subjective or a dominant group is a self-defeating argument. Avoid making polarizing remarks concerning historical and institutional inequities at the workplace. There is a place for everything. Always maintain respect, strength, and honor. You should do this even with little or no guarantee of getting the same treatment in return.

Reduce your aggression against those who have achieved their goals. It is also worth noting that many capitalists in developed nations are first-generation, self-made millionaires. It might, therefore, be an insult to most of them to keep insisting that they inherited resources.

Avoid Petty Intragroup Conflicts

There is a risk that your pragmatic efforts and ability to compromise on issues will be sold as blasphemous capitulation by your own community. Just because you have been able to develop yourself to great heights, you are now officially a "sellout." Middle- and upper-class minorities often face unfair backlash from members of their sub-group. The fact that you risk being criticized or even attacked by your own community for doing well in school, obeying laws and polishing your talents is a depressing irony.

Nothing is gained when the lower-economic-class minorities blame the elite and middle-class minorities for their lack of upward mobility. Nothing is gained when elite and middle-class minorities blame lower-economic-class minorities for their societal predicament. Denigrating and condescending language that has been repackaged as advice by those who have overcome adversity only adds fuel to the fire.

Choose to Avoid Overcompensation

The idea that your cultural group is more exceptional than the others feeds into the same problem you are trying to mitigate. Racial equality should be a question of equitable access and equality as human beings, not a question of substituting the racial supremacy of others with yours.

"Do you know this famous person was my color?" Trying to prove your subjective group is better than the dominant group does not help your cause. It is claiming credit for unearned achievements based on the color of your skin; the very thing you have been condemning. Ethnic identity and pride should be portrayed as cultural richness. The loyalty should not be a source of toxic negative stereotypes and shameless self- promotion especially when collaborating with other groups.

Speak Up Regardless of Status

Speak against all forms social exclusion, not just the one that affects your mobility. It is often said that evil flourishes when good people do nothing. Laws can only go so far in stopping racism. There are no laws against believing in hateful stereotypes. Anger, fear, frustration and concerns on racism should not be dismissed with "work hard" comments.

There are no laws against thinking that certain kinds of hateful jokes are okay. There are no laws against thinking that hateful comments are funny. It is not even good to have too many laws. It will impede freedom and business productivity if every piece of common decency is legislated. Become an advocate for horizontal coexistence where no one is treated unfairly because of his or her race.

36

Religion, Sect, Spirituality

The Curious and the Believers

It started as a rainy day investigation of a ten-car pileup on Gawker Expressway a few blocks past Rubbernecks Junction. At first only one officer was dispatched to aid the tow trucks. After all, there were no injuries reported. Nobody was prepared for what happened next. Within a few hours the state would be forced to activate its military reserve.

It was not the rain that caused the pileup. A huge holy image had appeared on the rusty wet brick wall of an old abandoned brewery. Motorists had slowed down abruptly in order to see the surreal image, causing the accident.

The policeman called for backup. The eastbound lanes had also come to a standstill. Motorists started abandoning cars on the highway and forming prayer circles. Authorities were forced to partially close the expressway resulting in monumental traffic jams on both sides.

The image was fading quickly but had already attracted widespread social media attention. It has already developed a life of its own online. The mayor refused the governor's request to cover the twenty-foot image after consulting with religious leaders in the city. The image faded away when the wall dried but reappeared when it rained again. Local pastors started holding prayers and blessings near the wall.

Mr. Simulacra, a local investor, purchased the abandoned property from the city at a throwaway price. The news had attracted considerable interest among believers from faraway lands. One of the visitors who had driven four hundred miles was losing patience. He suggested using a water hose on the wall instead of waiting for rain. The visitor then proceeded to bless himself with the dripping water from the image.

Mr. Simulacra erected a wall blocking motorists' view from the road and installed a toll gate. Most visitors who came for the purpose of prayer or veneration didn't even know about the gate fees implementation. They had no option but to pay at the gate. It didn't take long before a "visitor" discovered another religious image on a felled tree on the same property. This was a rare phenomenon.

Within six months the once dead Rubbernecks Junction had exploded into such a huge shopping mall that it required highway redesign. The proliferation of retailers and the accompanying sprawl became a concern to the city. That would become the least of the problems the city would face.

Nobody saw it coming. Mr. Simulacra invited Mr. Daffy Gasket, the owner of a struggling small church in Gone Ballistic City, to form a partnership mega church. Haywire-Mental Church was moved from Banana Street to the old brewery. A sprinkler system was install to "activate" the breathtaking image for visitors.

The online footprint was now constantly generating curious guests. The two estimated one million visitors over the next two years alone. Mr. Simulacra expanded the enterprise by imprinting the image on T-shirts, mugs, and packaged water from the wall and selling the items in addition to the entrance fee.

The local churches and the authorities had never worried about Mr. Daffy Gasket and his little church before. Now that he had turned it around, increased regular attendance, and had growing membership they took notice. He quickly turned into a bigger problem.

Haywire-Mental Church members could only work three days a week. During the four months of "Lent", one could only work two days a week. Residents started converting en masse. Businesses went into panic mode. A lot of city employees had joined the congregation. It was illegal to discriminate based on religion in that country. Could businesses survive?

Manifestation of Religious-Based Social Exclusion

Does social exclusion based on religion exist? I guess a better question would be if there is a corner on this earth where it doesn't. In a rational world, the last place you would expect to find hatred would be in an institution that was created to fight it at the first place. Unfortunately, history is full of examples of religious-based social exclusion.

In most countries you won't need to look past the front page to find cases of persecution of either religious people or nonreligious people. Can we assume a guy who is ready to cause bodily harm to you based on your faith may not necessarily offer you a job or somewhere to sleep? I don't want to bore you with schematics here, but I need to point out that our subject here includes human rights of the non-believers.

Patterns of Data

Do we have cases where religion is being used to exclude people in our backdrops?

Religious or sectarian aggression
Limitations on religious practice or religious wear
Official and informal restrictions on faith
Attacks on nonbelievers
Official bans on certain religious aspects
Restrictions on dress, prayer times, fasting times, and religious symbols
Group attribution-based profiling
Negative stereotyping

Rankism

Some world religions are looked upon as primitive based on the members' ethnicity and location. The religion factor can also manifest as political power. Religion can dictate social class and rankism in the community. Social stigma can find legitimacy under the umbrella of a religion.

Exploitation of the Venerable

Some preachers prey on the desperate and emotionally vulnerable, especially in fragile regions where poverty is a factor. It is not uncommon for people to start a religion as a money-making enterprise. False preachers who pretend to "cure" serious conditions often target marginalized populations. People are encouraged to shun or delay modern medical procedures based on false hopes thus increasing exclusion factors. Then there is indoctrination and undue influence on the young that pushes them off the revenue-generation track. There are thousands of stories out there about cults and mind control. There are stories about people who left promising careers and headed for the hills. This creates both security and economic problems to the affected communities.

Conglomeration of Exclusion Factors NUBC

Consider a lady who wears a conspicuously religious dress. The ostensible dressing is associated with an unpopular country. She plans to work in an industry that dispenses medicine and offers clinical services, including counseling. Its common knowledge that her religion does not allow her to deal with gays. She may be required to fill birth control prescriptions, but her religion doesn't allow it. She cannot work some days of the week. Since men do not wear headdresses it is hard to tell their religious affiliation based on their attire. They may not face the same exclusions. Her NUBC will reflect all of the following concerns:

Religion
Affiliation
National origin
Gender
Appearance

Sexual orientation
Ethnicity

Nuthology Strategy

The strategy encourages you not to abandon your capsule of talents. You have to be in control of your purpose. Your purpose in this case includes earning a decent living. Learning how religion can be used to exclude you should be a part of your financial intelligence. Your success will depend on how you manage both your talents and your unique exclusion factors, which includes organized religion, spirituality, or lack thereof. It is your duty to ensure that your career is not out of sync with your religious beliefs. Some religions require that you abstain from certain tasks or actions. Matching a career and beliefs can be tough, but it can be done. It all depends on your unique backdrop concerns.

Research on Gatekeepers' Concerns and Dilemmas When Choosing Your Industry

Some countries have enacted laws to govern a potential employer's questions regarding religion or the religious holidays you must observe. One of the assumptions of the Nuthology Index is that gatekeepers are a microcosm of the society we live in. Consequently, the distance between your religious values and those of the gatekeepers' may determine if you are a cultural fit to the company.

Some businesses make decisions purely based on numbers, not necessarily on the emotional aspects of an issue. Does the expense or difficultly in meeting an employee's request for a religious accommodation exceed the cost and aggravation of defending a possible discrimination lawsuit?

In this case, it is not about whether a company agrees with or shares your religious beliefs or not. The question is if the employer can provide an accommodation without incurring an undue hardship. They may attempt to avoid you if they think you will push them in a corner. Don't worry about the legality, they will find other reasons to get rid of you.

There are many religious-related scenarios that society is still struggling with. You can only see them at your angle when planning a career path. What if your new faith prevents you from working certain days? What if your faith prevents doing some tasks during certain periods of the year, day, or month? What if your new faith requires long hair while the job requires short hair? What if your new faith requires headwear? Can a radio station require you to play a type of music that is against your faith?

There is no shortage of data on this subject. You may have heard about reports of pharmacies turning away women seeking to fill birth control prescriptions or others requiring employees to dispense drugs against their faith. Another case involved business owners refusing to provide insurance coverage for contraception claiming faith grounds. A social worker refusing to counsel people based on their sexual orientation is another health-related example. There are also wedding-based businesses closing their doors to same-sex couples planning their weddings. There is a story on religiously affiliated schools firing women because they became pregnant while not married.

When violent acts are committed under religious guise this creates a law enforcement dilemma. Should members of that religion come under the scrutiny? Is this a legitimate concern or an unreasonable suspicion?

TMI Tip

Religion is a slippery-slope subject. Most experts and company policies require that you do not discuss religion at work. Religion or lack of religion is essentially a personal thing. Follow your own path to spiritual enlightenment within your religion. Live a good life. Respect other people's spiritual paths.

"Which religion do you practice?" Although hiring managers and bosses still openly ask illegal questions, most of the religious bias is subtle in nature. Remember, perception of religion can be made based on symbols, dress, or some observable behavior. Every society, for example, has its own attitude toward cults, spirituality, atheism, devil worship, creationism, and anti-evolutionism. If one is viewed as nuts or crazy, chances are he may be judged and face some exclusion at some point. Even when questions are asked, it is not always intentional. The interviewer may be trying to figure out your work schedule. Which days or hours you are available. Which holidays you are not available.

Reducing Your Own Stereotype-Driven Aggression

Choose to avoid petty overcompensation. "My God can beat your God any day of the week and twice on Sunday." People should be treated fairly and equally under their right to believe or not to believe. Not judging does not constitute approval of other people's beliefs. Is freedom of belief for nonreligious groups as important as freedom of belief for the religious? Absolutely. If you are an observer of history you know that there obviously are nonbelievers with very good values and religious people with very bad values. The opposite is also true. You don't need the goal of heaven to be kind to other human beings. You don't need the threat of hell to be respectful.

Age, race, ethnicity, religion, place, national origin, social class, language, and tribalism can conglomerate naturally to produce a very destabilizing effect. Most of the world's major religions are made up of multiple sects or denominations. The need for differentiation is higher every time a new group branches off. Seek and join groups and religions that are moderate, compassionate, and tolerant. Seek to support compassionate and tolerant religion that respects human dignity.

Speak Up Regardless of Status

Most religious-based social exclusions are stereotypically, unfairly, and unconsciously implemented. Stigmas based on religion, ethnicity, national origin, and language often combine to form a group-attributed nefarious character trait, which becomes a formidable structural barrier to opportunities, rights, or both. Become an advocate for horizontal coexistence where no one is treated unfairly because of his or her religious beliefs.

37

Retaliatory

Silencing of the Tattletale

Patrick drove home so drunk that he, for a third time, mistakenly parked his car in Timothy's driveway thinking it was his home. This time he attempted to get into Timothy's house. That was the straw that broke the camel's back. Timothy had warned Patrick and even involved his wife during the previous incidents. Patrick, a respected local sheriff's deputy, was a great neighbor, well, at least when sober. Timothy was not afraid of years of unpleasantness that would obviously accompany the action he was about to take. He might get retaliatory traffic tickets. It was hard to turn in his neighbor. It didn't help that Timothy's own mother was killed by a drunk driver five years prior to this incident. With that in mind, Timothy called the cops on the cop.

Patrick and Timothy had worked together before especially against criminal neighbors. Now that Timothy had burned that bridge, he had no solid protection. Fuba City was going down. Like other economically challenged areas, its residents were increasingly depending on gangs, secret societies, crime syndicates, and self-appointed religious leaders to provide justice and security. The street justice system overseen by these non-state actors propagated a strong anti-informant culture. Detectives working to solve cases understood this chronic problem too well. "The snitch got the stitch" was the motto on the mean streets. It was not uncommon for witnesses to disappear or face violent attacks.

This made eye witnesses to violent crimes too afraid or simply unwilling to come forward. People blamed the trend on inadequate witness protection. But there sure were other factors and dilemmas. Even with an adequate protection program, separating witnesses from family or the general population seemed to be its own punishment. Timothy was a sitting duck.

Timothy's wife was also ready to leave Fuba City for good. She was a whistle-blogger. Her boss had discovered that she had been blogging about the company's low wages, poor benefits, and long work hours. The company did not like employees who wrote posts that were critical of working conditions. She had noticed unfair and targeted enforcement of company policies, standards, and production expectations against her. All of a sudden they had noticed that she had been late two and half minutes the year before.

Many people turned a blind eye at her job. The concept of self-preservation was not restricted to the streets. It was clearly reflected in other facets of society. In her workplace, most employees lived one paycheck away from homelessness and lacked other economic safety nets. They were inclined not to report bias and other issues. With a mortgage, two car loans, three kids in school, and a dog depending on the weekly paycheck, the temptations was there to keep the job at all cost. Even where whistle-blower and retaliatory laws were well established, "rocking the boat" and proving the case might be a concern. Factor in the fragile economy where jobs were scarce and you had yourself a full-blown conundrum. A month after the incident the couple left Fuba and headed south.

Manifestation of Retaliatory-Based Social Exclusion

A lot of law violations in many communities go unreported because people who know about them are afraid of some sort of retaliation. One of the assumptions of this strategy is that gatekeepers, who include employers, are part of our society. Marginalized people are likely to live in places where both the fear cops and that of criminals exist concurrently. People with social exclusion concerns are likely to find themselves complaining about the lack of respect, acceptance, and equality in their workplaces. Since this is a global-view book and not a legal guide, we will combine many issues relating to retaliatory actions after one has engaged in a protected or unprotected activity. Examples of activities may include but are not limited to:

Fielding complaints
Filing complaints or filing claims
Refusing to engage in illegal activity
Reporting corporate malfeasance
Refusing to participate in unethical or illegal behavior
Taking part in wage or work-condition strikes or protests
Whistle-blowing and whistle-blogging
Bringing proceedings under discrimination law
Making an allegation of discrimination
Publishing or expressing political views

Certain activities may be protected by law depending on where you live. It is also good to note that companies may use contrived excuses as cover for a disciplinary action. For this reason our discussion includes some actions that are subtle or can be packaged into smoke-screen-grade deniability. An employer may find ways to make the complaining employee's life at work very difficult. There are many ways that a vindictive gatekeeper can make working conditions intolerable. Don't use these at home, I mean at the office. Examples of retaliatory moves may include but are not limited to:

Transfers to the North Pole office
Increased disciplinary actions
Heightened production expectations
Evaporating promotion pathways
Breathing breaks may be reduced
Retaliatory investigations
Harassment
Intimidation

Demotion
Dismissal
Calculated micro-aggressions
Undercover blacklisting
Being criticized by colleagues
Salary reduction
Work hour reduction or increase
Job or shift reassignment
Surprise, negative performance review
Getting offered undesirable tasks
Loss or reduction of benefits
Excessive workload
Extremely abusive language
Silent treatment or shunning
Formally flexible work schedules become rigid

Conglomeration of Exclusion Factors NUBC
Consider a short and full-figured woman working in a male-dominated environment who has filed complaints about patterns of weight-related jokes. She is concerned that her schedule, workload, and performance review may change.

Retaliatory
Height
Weight
Attractiveness
Gender

Nuthology Strategy
Nuthology is meant to help identify areas of concerns involving access to resources, opportunities, and rights from an individual perspective. Potential retaliation should not discourage you from standing up for your rights. This subject is more important for marginalized populations who are still busy fighting for their rights to be useful, respected, accepted, and equal members of society.

Learning how retaliation can be used to exclude you should be a part of your financial intelligence. It is important that you learn to react decisively and on your own terms. This should happen preemptively long before you need to employ the knowledge. The person you want to be tomorrow will be determined by the research you do today.

There are many times that things will work better if you try to utilize the existing policies and procedures in your company. Before you publicly vent about workplace problems, try to solve them through the established channels.

The best way to start is to understand your rights and the company policy. Some countries have laws that can protect you. Consulting with an experienced legal professional is a good move. Seeking legal help will help you sift through laws about prohibitions on retaliation and other concerted activity protections. You may have to document patterns of antagonism and provide other related evidence.

It should be obvious that wrongdoers will not entertain being exposed. It takes a strong moral backbone to take on the wrongdoing in your society. The gatekeepers may attempt to discredit you from different angles. You may be required to summon your emotional wherewithal to withstand any backlash that may occur. This will enable you to stay calm and rational.

Be realistic and pragmatic in a manner that will enable you to think strategically. Consider the fact you may have to move, get a new job, or use some cash reserves. You don't want use your limited resources to fight the filings in court before you are ready to do so.

Expand your networks and gather information that will contribute to your purpose in the long run. This will help you to narrow your options and make the best action plan.

Speak Up

People should expect empathetic and sympathetic understanding of their grievances even when concrete solutions are elusive. Become an advocate for horizontal coexistence where no one is treated unfairly because of his or her whistle-blower status or their quest for a fair system.

38

Sexual Orientation

Masquerade For Convenience

Congee had many sleepless nights before this idea came to his mind. He had been playing the celibacy and chastity cards for the last six years. Both cards were now apparently expired. He had been able to get away with it because his family was very religious. With his twenty-third birthday approaching fast and some family members starting to run out of patience, he had to do something. His mom had been dropping subtle hints all over the compound. She wanted a daughter in law and the grandkid potential that comes with such an arrangement.

Congee was not ready to come out. It would trigger an avalanche. His dad was one of the community leaders calling for town-square shaming of all gays. His graduate school financing would be canceled within minutes. His dad would lose his church elder status. His mother didn't have the emotional capital to see her only son go that route. She would try to pray him "out" for months. It would be catastrophic.

The new solution was simple, and his partner, Funchi, was onboard. They would start a four-way dating arrangement that would involve a closeted lesbian couple. The couple had to swear to stay in the closet for at least two more years. The arrangement would enable the four of them to enjoy the love, acceptance, and privilege afforded to heterosexual human beings. At least until college was over.

Within a month both Congee and Funchi were able to launch their new "girlfriends." They made sure that the girls were seen as less religious so that their families would not rush into wedding mode. The fact that all four were still going through college helped. They even received the expected advice from Congee's mom, "Do not to rush the wedding bells."

It was Funchi who came up with an idea that would make them all rich. They started Clozeters Railroad a stigma-management website to help individuals who had the same dilemma. One of the main effects of heterosexism in the area was financial exclusion by parents. There were also cases of anti-LGBTQ related violence and abuse. Community members on the website would learn from each other how to masquerade as "straight" in order to enjoy the privileges afforded to the dominant group until one was ready and safe to come out. In a country where gay people married and had children because society pressured them into being straight, the plan was a big success.

Manifestation of Sexual Orientation-Based Social Exclusion

Nuthology is concerned with access to resources, opportunities, and rights from an individual perspective. This chapter addresses a system of attitudes, biases, and discrimination in favor of one type of sexual orientation that may force people to remain in the closet in an effort to pass for the preferred lifestyle. That is not breaking news to most people. There are antigay epithets in every nation. The "closet" metaphor in itself is an indication of stigma risk management. That means living a lifestyle unknown to colleagues, friends, and families.

Regardless of the politics surrounding this issue, an individual who is concerned about this obstacle will see it as an economic barrier. Unfair discrimination based on sexual orientation usually follows the gender stereotyping held by a society. Frustration of employees after disclosing their status and the denial of spousal benefits to legally married same-sex couples are common workplace complaints.

Negative Stereotypes

Being "gay" is not so easily defined in the societal context unless people are actively dating or married. For this reason being "gay" is often based on some stereotyped appearance and behavior. This is a very subjective and prejudiced method to begin with. You don't even have to be gay to be subjected to the prejudice.

There are numerous cases where heterosexual men who are perceived to exhibit effeminacy are treated as homosexuals. A man or a boy who displays traits, tastes, or habits traditionally considered feminine may encounter sexual orientation exclusion. A chubby kid who does not socialize with the opposite gender due to weight-related insecurities may be perceived as being gay and bullied if he lives in a backdrop where aggression against LGBTQ community exist.

Girls or women who appear to present a hyper-masculine image have been subjected to sexual orientation social exclusion. A girl who behaves like a boy or is viewed as not feminine enough may be at risk of this type of exclusion. At the end of the day, it is not even about the actual sexual orientation. It is about fitting people into pre-made boxes. This is also an indicator of how real LGBTQ members are treated in that community.

This factor covers the whole spectrum of sexual-orientation exclusion, which may include unconscious perceptions and stereotypes.

Too metrosexual
Gender presentation
Gender identity
Gender expression
Queer appearance
Feminine-looking males
Masculine-looking males
Gender nonconforming

Gender identity disorder
LGBTQ activism

Conglomeration of Exclusion Factors NUBC

Consider a poor racial minority woman who lives in a marginalized part of the city and has a history of LGBTQ activism and not actively dating. There is a risk of convergence of heavy factors of exclusion.

Sexual Orientation
Race
Gender
Place
Social class
Affiliation

Capsule of Talents

The realization that all humans are created equal and endowed with a unique capsule of talents should be central to your career planning strategy. This empowers you tremendously. You can live your life without being overly dependent on others' approval. Learning how sexual orientation can be used to exclude you should be a part of your financial strategy. Since most opportunities are controlled by the dominant group, it is your duty to research your own ecosystem and wherever possible find a more supportive environment to cultivate your talents.

Gatekeepers' Concerns and Dilemmas

Gatekeepers are part of society and have their own opinions on this issue. The distance between your values and those of the gatekeepers will determine the cultural fit. Look for ways to engage well-wishers in addressing concerns and conflicts related to this issue. You should note that there are cases where sexual-orientation rights may appear to be in conflict with people's religious rights. You should not dismiss other people's rights when fighting for yours.

Choose to Create Meaningful Networks

Seek to support a compassionate and tolerant approach that respects human dignity. Choose to avoid petty overcompensation. Work on reducing your own negative stereotypes toward the dominant group. Overcompensation and blanket blame can only reduce your networks. Making statements that your sexual orientation is better does not help your course. Selling heterosexual practice as a negative does not advance equal rights to all human beings. Promoting a theory that same-sex couples are "better parents" than opposite sex couples for example only helps in burning bridges.

Index

Feel free to include any bias that is based on actual or perceived lawful sexual activity in this category if it is not covered under another admitted class.

Speak Up Regardless of Status

Most data indicates that the shame and secrecy often associated with sexual orientation will slowly decline. Despite the cultural wars, most people start seeing the humanity component when a close relative comes out of the closet. They get an epiphany. I guess it is easier to discriminate against faceless strangers. They come out of the morality wall. They start to focus on mercy and compassion over morals.

Not judging does not constitute approval of other people's believes or lifestyle. Regardless of what side of the argument you are on concerning this issue, human rights should be the guiding principle. Discriminating against prospective employees based on sexual orientation or identity is against this principle. Everybody should have the freedom to work without discrimination

Despite significant progress in advancing civil rights and equality, it is still legal in many countries and states to fire or refuse employment to a person based on sexual orientation. Become an advocate for horizontal coexistence where no one is treated unfairly because of his or her sexual orientation...

39

Shelter Stigma

You Are Where You Dwell

Mr. Samp woke up early to start his weeklong praying routine at the corner of the cold, smelly cell. If any of the injured died, he was looking at life in prison. There was even talk of the death penalty. How had he transformed from the senior altar boy to a death-row candidate within such a short period?

For the millionth time that day, his mind went back to the fateful day a short week earlier. It was the most anticipated day of spring break. Boys from the middle-class suburb had nicknamed it Triple B Day, Beat the Bums Bowl. The sport involved attacking the makeshift homeless shelter in a war-like maneuver. The only rule was to have fun and possibly capture the most dramatic parts on video. The teens planned to shoot toy guns and hurl punches and rocks. Sending thirteen homeless individuals to the intensive care unit was never a part of the plan.

At first Samp's parents refused to believe it. Their denial was short-lived. When the videos surfaced online and the local police stormed in, reality hit home with a bang. The defense experts tried to diffuse the despicable actions. They blamed the trend on groupthink, peer pressure, and mob mentality. Naturally there had been pressure to supersede the previous year's performance. It was all about bragging rights. Samp just wanted the patients to stay alive.

Authorities and parents could not understand how attacking the homeless passed as amusement. Why would the teens videotape themselves committing a crime? Samp refused to talk to the other six teenagers involved. The national press was in town. The story was getting interesting every day.

Several unbelievable facts had emerged through press. Preliminary DNA tests exposed the fact that the man Samp was videotaped attacking was his actually his biological father. Samp was adopted as a child. He had spent a large part of his life wondering how his biological dad looked like and had longed to one day meet him. The man's children were also injured in the melee. Possible siblings in hospital? It was becoming a family story. The world seemed to collapse. "Please nobody dies". That day Samp the altar boy would pray twice as hard.

Samp perused the news pages for more developments in the never-ending nightmare. Newspapers were allowed in that jail. There was no television and definitely no electronic gadgets. It was on page six, but it was like a nail through his heart. It was not what he'd expected.

The Samp family's five-bedroom home was about to go. A financial storm had been brewing behind the scenes for the previous twelve months, but his parents had not told him. He knew the economy was hurting his father's business but was not aware that things were that grave. The modern suburban home was in the last stages of the foreclosure process per the news.

With the impending legal bills, thanks to him, Samp's parents would never be able to save the home. He was going to be the proverbial last straw that broke the camel's back. Having no home and shouldering hefty legal bills would mean the unfathomable. His family might easily end up on the streets. On the streets but not "homeless," he couldn't use that word for his family. Homeless shelter?

Samp started drafting a new version of the daily prayer. For a moment, the death penalty didn't seem so bad at all. Then somebody called out his name. It was heavily bandaged stranger. Samp collapsed.

Manifestation of Shelter-Based Social Exclusion

Nuthology strategy is about access to resources, opportunities, and rights from an individual perspective. Does your living arrangement dictate your value as a human being? Can a famous addresses make you special? If you live in a mansion or castle, do people see you in a different light? It is scary to think you are where you live. The 'stigma' of shelter.

Does shelter discrimination exist at the workplace? Between living under the bridge and the castle on the shinning hill there are millions of other living arrangements. There are people living on rooftops, in containers, in abandoned warehouses, in abandoned houses, in caves, in shanty houses, in cardboard boxes, in abandoned railcars, in moving cargo trains, at bus stops, on sidewalks, and in cars. One has to wonder where all these people fall on the shelter stigma spectrum.

Your case might be different from the examples in this section. I will confine my discussion to involuntary homelessness. Hundreds of millions of people worldwide are homeless. There are also lot of middle class families who live a paycheck away from being homeless. For most people even in the developed world, the biggest item by far in their family budget is housing. There are many things that can go wrong from sickness to layoffs that can throw off that budget.

Living arrangements-related stigma is a bias that is often taken for granted. Consider a forty-five-year-old who lives in his mother's basement with seven cats. Would you advise him to disclose this information on his first date? I didn't think so. People understand that cellar dwellers and basement people do not get dates easily. Who's to say that employers and gatekeepers will not have the same thinking?

Conglomeration of Exclusion Factors NUBC

For most people, having problems with shelter might be just one of their problems. They may not have a wage paying job, enough food, or adequate transportation. Consider a homeless woman who is finding it extremely hard to keep job interview appointments. She doesn't have bus fare and hasn't had a bath in a few months. She lost her job twelve months ago.

Shelter
Place
Transportation
Attractiveness
Unemployment
Social class
Character

Capsule of Talents

Your humanity and talents are not defined by your living arrangements. Having faith when the chips are down is critical in solving the problem at hand. Learning how your living arrangements can be used to exclude you should be a part of your financial strategy.

Gatekeepers' Concerns and Dilemmas

The index is interested in whether or not shelter discrimination is carried out by gatekeepers in society. It is your duty to evaluate your environment. The homeless can make some people uncomfortable and sometimes are seen as contributing to other societal problems. Property owners may be concerned that the homeless will bring values down and attract crime. They are considered "bad for business". Some cities have laws against feeding them.

While it is possible to find some odd jobs here and there, many employers do not appreciate the urban nomadic existence. You will have to decide how much shelter related information you disclose during the hiring process.

Research on Self-Development Strategies

Some of the tips that I found when researching this topic including getting a library card and buying a public gym membership. This assumes you have some income from panhandling. You need somewhere to research information about jobs. A public library is a good start. You buy a gym membership so that you have somewhere to shower and change clothes, especially before an interview. I am sure there are many other strategies of survival out there.

Create Meaningful Networks

It's good to remind yourself that not everybody hates you or is the cause of your predicament. Blanket blame only limits your network. Try to stay in your family's good graces. If you don't have family, then a least build a network of friends or acquaintances. The dangers of homelessness include exposure to elements and violence. Seek help though church, charitable organizations, and even law enforcement.

Reducing Your Own Stereotype-Driven Aggression

It is more comforting to think about homeless people as lazy and not wanting to work rather than think of them as people who hit a rough patch. We often concoct mental stories as to why they are out begging or sleeping outside. They must be drug abusers or something. I guess that makes us feel less guilty of culpability and less obligated to do something.

Deep down we know it is either a razor thin weekly paycheck or a simple twist of fate that separates us from the same predicament. The fact is that there are many people on the streets that are truly homeless due to events that were out of their control. Life can throw anybody a curve ball.

Of course there will be people that are homeless due to bad choices in lifestyle. Yes there are scammers. There is a possibility that you could be funding bad habits if you help. But not all of the homeless are that way. Each individual is different. To assume this is the situation of all of the homeless is very unfair.

Some will buy alcohol to see themselves through the night. You would probably do the same if you spent a few nights under a bridge in the winter. It is not like they are having a lovely wine-infused time.

Speak Up Regardless of Status

Become an advocate for horizontal coexistence where no one is treated unfairly because of living arrangements. If you are concerned about how the homeless will use funds, donate to a soup kitchen or church that caters to the dwelling challenged. We know homeless people are sometimes targeted by law enforcement. Advocate for a healthy balance between tolerance and law enforcement needs.

Where do kids learn to value people based on shelter? It is your duty to educate kids on this issue. We know there are many reasons people become homeless and nobody is immune to life's curve balls. A tornado, earthquake, flood, fire, domestic violence, job loss, illness, physical disability or an accident can happen to anybody. It is hard to imagine what living outside entails from the loss of personal dignity and extreme weather conditions to the risk of violence.

40

Social Class, Rankism

Do You Know Who I Am?

The older residents remember Tohts Gibeht when he was just a regular kid on the block. That was before fame and power went to his head, or so they thought. He was so humble, genuine, and adorable until he acquired his fiftieth donut shop. What did he do wrong? He became fifthly rich. Now he came across as the most obnoxious, corrupt, and narcissistic person on the planet.

In that city the wealthy tended to hang out with other wealthy people. Wealth meant being politically connected, being invited to the right parties, living in the right neighborhoods, driving the right cars, and sending your children to the right schools.

A culture of impunity was nothing new in the town where money was king. The wealthy or powerful were able to bribe and intimidate any justice department actor. They used their influence and money so that they were rarely held accountable for crimes. They hired people to write their chocolate-sprinkled hagiographies before they run for office. They were known to buy votes. All you had to do to be counted as one of them was to become rich.

Recently a rich guy wrote a book describing how poverty was a result of laziness. His intention was to help the poor, but the public outcry drowned any good intension. There was only one unwritten rule in political and advertising circles: you never talked ill of the poor. There was always tension between the rich and the poor. The popularity of that book greatly exacerbated the animosity between the classes.

With the best education, economies of scale, and corruption the rich were able to create barriers to entry against members of the lower classes. They were able to use their ranks to maintain positions of power long after it could be justified. Political term limits are only valid in theory. The way citizens were treated was based on their perceived rank in society. The lower the rank one was the higher the possibility for abuse. With money you could claim superior value as a human being.

Gibeht, an honest and hardworking businessman, had always found ways to give back to the community. He was not only the biggest employer in the city, but also the biggest tax payer. It was in the spirit of charity that he started the Midnight Donut Program to benefit the homeless and the very poor.

The federal health guidelines required that all fried dough confectionery be disposed of at the end of the day unless it is frozen. Gibeht found a way to help the community while abiding by those health regulations.

Then he encountered a big problem. Thousands of able-bodied people started flocking to his donut shops at night. People would buy beer, expensive wine, and cigarettes during the day then line up at midnight to get free donuts. Why should they buy donuts when they could get them for free? Donuts were the staple food in that country.

Within weeks some people even quit their jobs. Others found a way of getting those donuts for resale on the black market. One resident even sued the chain for making him fat. Apparently offering finger-licking confectionery was considered gross negligence involuntary fattening. No good deed goes unpunished. Donut sales dropped so dramatically that Gibeht was forced to reduce his staff for the first time. The city revenue went down because the sales tax declined. City employees were laid off and property taxes went up.

He had to cut the donut program cold turkey. Gibeht could never be obnoxious, corrupt, or narcissistic even if he tried. But the honest and genuine self-made millionaire would always be seen as part of the greedy group.

Manifestation of Social Class and Rank-Based Social Exclusion

This form of exclusion is as old as mankind. History is full of cases where human beings could be traded and owned as property. We also had voting laws that prevented those who did not own property from voting. Today the rich still get better breaks. Sometimes laws are bent to give them an advantage.

Nuthology PSER 400 Credits

Social class plays a very important part in the social exclusion discussion. In cases where the stereotype and group attribution are negative, high class members of that group appear to be better tolerated than the poor members. Racial and gender minorities who have wealth, education, and good connections, for example, do not encounter the same exclusion intensity as those in lower classes. This can also confirm the stereotype that the ones who are poor are just lazy.

Social status in the modern world is heavily influenced by social class. In most cases these are two sides of the same coin. The formally excluded in the upper class may contribute to exclusion of the lower classes. At some point when other variables like race, ethnicity, and gender become less dominant, social class readily occupies that space. Most policy-making bodies around the world today are full of the best money can buy. Social class is a bigger problem than most other forms of exclusion because material exclusion is the vehicle for most exclusion today.

Rankism

Abuse of power or position does not stop with wealth. This brings us to rankism. We all know places where people in authority specialize in strong-arm tactics and power-trips. Political authority, a badge, height, size, connections, schooling, beauty, gender, occupation or any other capricious value measurement can be used to claim unearned privilege.

These perceived social ranks are also the main reason people worship entertainers, sports figures, and politicians. In today's fame and status obsessed world the value of a human being may, sadly, be dictated by whether one is seen as "somebody".

Economic importance of rankism cannot be ignored. Most of gender inequality today, for instance, is related to rankism where one gender controls jobs, money, and property. You can say the same about race-based inequality. In some communities, rank is also based on age. The young may find themselves marginalized by the age-based superior value claims. What do you do for a living? Rankism can take many routes.

Fame and status can also get into your head to a point that you forget who you are. Those who work in law enforcement and the hospitality industry often encounter pompous Homo sapiens whose minds have been erased by acute self-inflation. "Do you know who I am?" They are known to condescendingly pounce on commoners without provocation especially when they get drunk. Police are sometimes forced to help these tantrum-prone citizens find themselves. A night in a county confinement center usually works wonders.

Do the Rich Face Social Exclusion?

While most of the class based exclusion goes against the lower class that is not always the case. It can go either way. We live in a world where financial success is seen as rewarding but can also make you the bad guy by default. People work hard and play the lottery to be rich one day. I am sure you have been praying for the day you get something you call yours. How would you feel if when your ship comes in it brings some unwanted catch in the form of haters?

Bashing the rich and celebrities is a national sport in some countries. This is a growing form of bullying. It is seen as a victimless crime. It's therapeutic for some people I guess. The rich are as diverse as poor people; each one is a different human being. They are not one homogeneous group of greedy capitalists. Because of their success and limited population, they form a minority group that is seen as deserving to be ostracized. Innovative capitalist who have made profits fairly become targets of group attributed negative stereotype. They are classified with those who have ill-begotten wealth. Does remaining poor make you a superior human being?

Conglomeration of Exclusion Factors NUBC

It is very common to find social class, racism, gender inequality, criminal record, bad credit, unemployment, and homelessness exclusion factors working together in concert. We can argue all day about what is an addition to what or what was caused by the other. The work of the index is to expose this galaxy of issues.

Consider a bus-riding politically talented minority who lives in a poor neighborhood. The street vendor is planning to run for congressional office to fight for job and housing issues.

NUBC
Social class
Transportation
Occupation
Place
Race

Now consider a wealthy and well-connected minority who lives in an upper-class neighborhood. The lawyer is planning to run for the same congressional office to fight for job and housing issues. In a two way match the candidates' race will become inconsequential. Social class and rank will become more important.

Nuthology Strategy

Your humanity is not determined by how well you are loaded, connected, uniformed, crowned, gowned, or furred. You have to believe in yourself. All the power will come from within. Giving away that power can lead to an irrational and negative belief about the situation, on top of that feeling of hopelessness. We live in a world where a person's value is often viewed through an economic stratification lens. Learning how social class can be used to exclude you should be a part of your financial strategy.

The best antipoverty measures should come from the individual. It is you and I who make up society and the government, right? You have the ability to combine activism with personal responsibility. Activism alone, while very important, creates a situation where you remain at the corner, perpetually alarmed and financially helpless.

Get over the "Guilt" of Making More Money

Living decently and helping others in the modern world requires that you have some money. Marginalized people can easily be sucked into developing negative attitudes toward money. Some people ironically profess about the evils of having money while waiting in line to buy a multimillion-dollar lottery ticket.

Is money evil? The market system is based on competition. At some point people will make more money than you. Does that automatically mean everybody with money must be an evil money-grabbing capitalist?

Your friend who burned the midnight oil and took the hardest major in college is now a well-compensated brain surgeon. You took the "underwater dancing" major and you are working at a dead end job. Capitalism rewards him with more money than you. Where is the evil in that arrangement?

Money is a liquid way of carrying food, shelter, and clothing for today's hunters and gatherers. It is easier than dragging a piece of cow around Europe. The house you are in is bought or rented using some money. Money is a standard measure of value, a medium of exchange, and a store of value. You can argue that love of material things is the root of evil. Money happens to be the most liquid of all assets so it gets the bad rap.

Money is like a legal weapon on the shelf: it is morally neutral. You can use it to protect or do harm. Like an uncharged atom, it derives its morality charge from the user.

Financial Education

Now that we have agreed that money is good, let's talk about making it. There are a lot of resources out there on how to budget, save, and protect assets, as well as other financial education concerns.

I want to touch a little bit on revenue generating activities that you should avoid as a conglomerate. Working on your capsule of talents involves designing a sustainable and self-respecting revenue plan. It also means staying away from various lotteries.

The regular regional or national lotteries that you play at a deli should not be part of your retirement plan. Buying a ticket and supporting your local education programs is a noble thing, planning for the nonexistent cash flow is not.

Litigation lotteries where you are looking to shakedown people and businesses through frivolous law suits should not be a part of your business model. Sports and entertainment lotteries where you peg your hopes on some nonexistent talent until you are eighty should not be a part of career plan. There is an age between sixteen and sixty that you should convince yourself that headhunters are not looking for you. Stay away from tabloid lotteries where you lay in wait to sell somebody's pictures or story after invading their privacy. Dependence on these lotteries can make you abandon your capsule of talents and regret it when it is too late. Stay away from get rich quick pyramids and other groupthink schemes. You will thank me later.

Budgeting and Saving

The desire for social class inclusion is a landmine for people who are trying to get out of poverty. There is a risk that people already in a hole may start digging themselves deeper. They are tempted to buy big ticket items to show the world they made it or to fit into a perceived upper class. This could be shiny houses, cars, clothes, boats, and other toys. This only creates another exclusion class: credit history exclusion.

One proven saving strategy is to live like the class below you. Avoid temptations to act a class higher than you. Simple math will show you that net worth is usually a product of living a class below you.

Asset Protection

What about the desire not to be seen as a bad person? Some people who grew up poor and hit it big often find themselves in this trap. They become targets of reverse psychology. There are dozens of examples of people who have lost wealth trying to prove to family members and the community that they are not rich monsters. "Look at me; money and fame have not changed me at all." The audience then lets you demonstrate that fact with a spending spree.

Money can buy the illusion of love and tolerance, but it cannot buy genuine acceptance. Not everybody will like you when you get a lot of money. The golden rule states that it is always good to empathize but don't subsidize.

When you get into serious money, become famous, or both, you quickly discover you have an uncle named Source who has kids with names like Unnamed Source, Anonymous Source, Reliable Source, Close Sources, and even Former Personal Rep. By some strange coincidence, they know you better than you know yourself and have chosen themselves to represent you.

It is in this spirit that the kind "relatives" who barely know you will sell your story. It won't be the story you like. You spend years building a productive business model only to become somebody's business model. Your life can be packed into a juicy tabloid takedown piece. You may then be forced to spend money and energy to defend your brand in the public court of opinion.

There is another way to look at it. If you are a self-made capitalist who came from adversity, there are always some vultures waiting to lick your bones dry. If there is a prevailing negative stereotype about how your group handles money, you may slide directly into it.

It is important to understand the fundamentals of finance, especially asset protection, in this context. Even when you can afford to pay asset managers, it is critical that to be within the knowledge territory. Some of your managers may have the ability and the intent to take you to the cleaners.

Net-worth hemorrhage can be in the form of unpaid taxes, mooching, pilfering, fraud, mismanagement, frivolous lawsuits, identity theft, or sale of your privacy. You do not have to have a lot of money to require this financial knowledge. It applies to everybody.

Expand Your Networks

When saving money you want to live like the class below you. When creating self-improvement networks it is a good idea to seek a mentor from a higher class than yours. Network up class, spend down class.

If you are homeless, for example, look for people with permanent shelter. If you are lower class, look for middle-class or upper-class mentors. If you want to start a business, seek people with experience.

Avoid asking for handouts and other vertical relationships wherever possible. You are not there to beg and dispose of your dignity. Look for job referrals, mentorships, internships, apprenticeships, or advice instead of cash.

Avoid groups that promote aggression toward the rich just because of their economic status. Poverty is a by-product of many factors. Resentment only creates more hate.

Don't forget horizontal relationships in the process. You also want to go beyond your comfort zone in terms of other variables like place, race, ethnicity, age, political affiliation, and gender. Limiting your networks because of some stereotype only hurts your bottom line.

Reducing Your Own Stereotype-Driven Aggression Print

Monitor your own exclusionary practices or remarks against those whose ship has arrived before yours.

Most poor folks have been stuck in the same gear for generations. Blaming the rich as a group for problems that have multiple causes creates social exclusion against hardworking achievers we all aspire to be. There is an assumption that there should be zero sympathy or empathy towards the rich. Many rich people are the formerly poor who started way below their current social class.

There are people out there who made genuine money and are helping other people. Since today's gatherer cannot give nuts to the poor, he gives them coins. There are things that are more important than money, but sometimes you need money to get them. It is the rich people who are better placed to provide medicine, food, and education to poor parts of the world.

Avoid groups that believe in taking property by force or creative excessive taxation just to get even with the rich. Some poor folks are quick to point out unethical and criminal behavior by rich people they don't know enough about. It is possible to condemn unethical and criminal behavior without creating class warfare. Use the upper class as your inspiration instead seeing them as the enemy

In a capitalistic economy that works on demand and supply, why should one's earning be limited? How is it anyone else's business to dictate how someone else should spend their money? What is too much money anyway? We don't have a number.

The assumption that the growing number of rich citizens must be causing the immobility of the poor is a popular political platform in many countries. While this may hold some truth, it also provides a perfect hedge for any ineffective policy decisions the politicians expect to make. It gives the politician a solid cover

Should we condemn those kids who were born into prosperity? This one is a new low. The key word here is that they were born. Meaning they had as much choice as those kids who were born in the slums.

On the other hand, we all know that fame, money, and power can corrupt people. This reminds me of Abraham Lincoln's quote **"Nearly all men can stand adversity, but if you want to test a man's character, give him power."**

The vitriol from those that do have money can be as scathing as that from those who do not. Let's us look at the other side of aggression that comes from some of those who have it. Some rich folks are quick to point out that it is the unethical and criminal behavior by poor people that keeps these folks poor. Just because you made money does not mean every poor person in this world is lazy and freeloading. There are many people who are in their early self-growth stage. Their ships have not arrived because yours was on the dock. It is possible to give money advice with empathy and without condescending scorn.

The "work harder" mantra should not be used as an insult to those seeking equal opportunity. There are poor people working multiple jobs to make ends meet. Working hard is not the reason they are poor.

Noblesse oblige

Earn respect by practicing human respect. Treat people with respect despite their perceived status in society's food chain. This goes to those that have the privilege of being in authority. Does a badge, uniform, or some little authority all of a sudden make you the wind god, Aeolus?

"Two things define your personality, the way you manage things when you have nothing, and the way you behave when you have everything." Unknown

Speak Up Regardless of Status

Social class exclusion is a major human rights problem since insufficient access to social rights throughout history is always accompanied by some form of material deprivation. Become an advocate for horizontal coexistence where humanity is not determined by the depth of one's pocket. Promote capitalism that abides by basic human rights and is not fueled by reckless greed.

41

Speech, Sound, Tone

The Yelling Ghost

The kids are now finding their way home. It looks like a scene from a scary movie, but the kids are used to it. They have gone through this dance a thousand times. They have developed their own coping mechanisms. The path they take has a textbook precision. The whole process looks routine and rehearsed. But this maneuver is as natural as breathing.

That morning was not an exception. The kids had broken the TV remote for the fourth time this summer. These have been turbulent times on the farm since Grandpa lost his job. As he walked into the living room with a bowl of weapon-grade Carolina Reaper soup, the kids took cover and sheltered in place. He froze at the site of the damaged remote. There was a half a minute delay as Grandpa sucked in every ounce of oxygen on-site. Then he let out the most thunderous and deafening scream. He threw imaginary stuff around. He broke imaginary things. He sweated profusely. Golf-size beads of sweat escaped his brow. He yelled and screamed. By just looking at his melodramatic movements, you could imagine him lifting a car-size boulder and smashing it into a glass wall.

The million glass pieces filled the air, turning his voice from brassy to hoarse as the kids ran through the back door to escape the pollution. The kids could hear the now screechy, piercing voice turn into strained croaky groans. They stopped at the one-mile mark and waited for the decibel particles to subside. They played with pebbles as they waited out the storm. Then the signal came: a deep bass yelling from damaged vocal chords that promised clear skies. It was time to cautiously head back to the house.

The kids are now finding their way home two hours after the episode. Grandpa is still breaking imaginary things. He is still sweating profusely. He is still yelling. But his voice is now soft and breathy. He is less animated. He is taking short soup and smoking breaks. Yes, the corrosive battery-grade soup and the thick home-made cigarette are playing a big part. They can hear the damaged throat fibers cracking, peeling, and shredding. Then there is a grand finale as the kids approach the homestead: a loud silence.

The kids can see him through the window. He is now embedded in a solid cloud of tobacco smoke like an ancient ghost. There are visible intermittent fireworks as the ghost takes lungsful of puffs. Grandpa is still breaking imaginary things. He is still sweating profusely. He is still yelling and screaming. But there is no sound. He has blown his vocal cords again. He is now as mute as a dancing maggot. His animation is now like slow motion replay. The pine tree's branches had also stopped quivering.

Soon he will calm down and sleep. But his voice will take two days to come back. There will be calm in this house. Grandpa will be communicating using homemade sign language. The kids have this figured to a phonation science. This is not their first vocal folds rodeo.

Manifestation of Speech Sound Tone Social Exclusion

Every community has its unwritten standards when it comes to voice pitch, clarity, speed, and general timbre. Any deviation from normal can lead to social exclusion. What is a normal voice anyway? Who gets to decide the completely normal manner of speaking that falls within all parameters? This judgment will also depend on the context. The voice expected from a husky five-star general will be different from that of a tiny preschool teacher. These expectations are often unconsciously created as society tries to match faces and voices.

How do you sound to others?

Authoritative
Brassy
Calming
Childish
Creepy
Croaky
Deep
Feminine
Forceful
Froggy
Hoarse
Husky
Masculine
Nauseating
Old
Persuasive
Piercing
Pitchy
Raspy
Screechy
Sexy
Soft and breathy
Soothing
Squeaky
Strained
Too high
Too low
Trustworthy
Unpleasant

Velvety
Weird

Can you use voice to project success? Voters may favor a political candidate with a deeper voice, especially when such is viewed as part of a confident and commanding physical presence. There is research out there showing that men with a deeper voice earn more on average than a men with a higher pitch.

Various cultures have their definition of a sexy voice as opposed to a scratchy, annoying voice. This can be a deal breaker in various employment circumstances when voice is important. Females with male voices may be perceived as abnormal. Males with female voices may be perceived as abnormal.

An unusual voice can lead to low self-esteem, shame, embarrassment, and public speaking fears. Some people are unable to present themselves clearly in an interview or a dating environment.

Lack of Sound and Other Speech Impediments

There are many disorders that affect the human voice. There are many people dealing with speech impediments. Growths and lesions on the vocal cords can affect anybody. The voice can also be affected by a head injury, tumor, stroke, drug use or any other event. While this can happen to anybody, speech impediment discrimination is a major issue in many communities.

This factor also covers lack of sound. While muteness describes people who can hear but cannot talk, we know it is often associated with deafness. This is probably because people who have been unable to hear from birth may not be able to articulate words correctly. A person can also become mute later in life due to injury or disease.

Lack of sound and other speech impediments greatly affects life at home and at work, as well as family and personal relationships.

Conglomeration of Exclusion Factors NUBC

This factor becomes more potent when combined with other classes. Women who stutter, for instance, may have a social exclusion factor within another. It is not hard for a bias conglomeration to form. Even when talking is not a major part of the job, if you add pitch to other exclusion yardsticks such as gender, age, size, weight, height, and attractiveness, the NUBC takes a new dimension.

Speech
Gender
Attractiveness
Disability
Disease stigma
Age
Size
Weight
Height

Capsule of Talents

You are endowed with unique talents regardless of your voice. You are not just another human being. That unique position divinely provides you with power that you should not abandon. Nuthology recognizes that speech, sound, and tone can be used to deny access to resources, opportunities, and rights. It is your duty to gather information, narrow your options, and make decisions that are realistic.

Career Planning

Learning how speech can be used to exclude you should be a part of your financial strategy, especially when it comes to career planning. There are occasions where your voice may be a disqualifier rather than a bias, especially where extensive talking is required. Some client-facing jobs, TV, radio, and other entertainment careers may be looking for a specific voice quality. Then again, there are jobs looking for your kind of voice or lack thereof. Build networks that are meaningful and include people of all walks of life.

Voice should be protected as a natural resource. It is important to note that some habits like constant yelling, screaming, smoking, and consuming spicy foods, have been known to damage voice. Your damaged voice may become your employer's concern. Consult qualified professionals and voice therapists if you have issues with your voice. This is important, especially if your paycheck depends on your voice or tone.

Reducing Your Own Stereotype-Driven Aggression

Those with a speech disorder may be targets of bullying. This can easily result in decreased self-esteem.

This is a situation that nobody chooses to be in. Looking down on people with speech problems is despicable. There are people who are nonverbal or partially verbal due to disease complications.

Speak Up Regardless of Status

Become an advocate for horizontal coexistence where no one is treated unfairly because of the timbre of his or her voice. Promote increased opportunities, empowerment, leadership, and acceptance for people facing voice-related social exclusion.

42

Transportation

Reliable Transportation Required

A medium sedan pulled into the parking lot fifteen minutes before the interview. Miss Hirer had an ultimatum to hire five people before Friday or lose her job. The last group of qualified candidates did not pass "internal" background checks. This is the hardest part of being an in-house recruiter: the unwritten company rules. Mr. Mojo Drainer can see the candidates arrive from his second-floor office.

Miss Hirer had everything figured out. The threat to her job had her thinking about the last group of candidates. She remembered some advice she was given when she started. "You can tell a person's character by the car he or she drives."

Deep inside Miss Hirer understood that a means of transportation does not mean much. A ride can be borrowed or rented. All the candidates were vetted beforehand anyway. But she had to keep her job. It was how the candidates were perceived to fit Mojo Drainer's values that mattered not her opinion. She went through the front area surveillance video, talking to herself, trying to think like Mojo Drainer. She looked at the tapes paying special attention to each candidate's transportation choices.

Tape A: Mr. Archive Arriving in museum-worthy old cracker that has seen all its better days. It is hard to tell what the original make or color of the car was. That rusty bucket will not look well to clients.

He had the nerve to ask for a jump start after the interview. The camera shows Mojo Drainer passing by looking curious about the vehicles hoods being up.

Tape B: Mr. Goat E is flying down Testosterone Avenue in a noisy chopper on a rainy, windy day waking up all the neighborhood babies. His leather jacket with a giant logo at the back made him fit into a biker's stigma; a sign of rebellion and chronic non-juvenile delinquency. The bad-outlaw-biker stereotype is still ripe in this city. That was the deal breaker.

Tape C: Mr. One Upper arrived in a shiny Cadillac with forty-three-inch alloy rims and airplane grills. Is he trying to outshine Mojo Drainer? For Mojo Drainer, a car is a status symbol. Park in his spot or try to outshine him in the automobile department and you won't know what hit you. This is a ten-dollar an hour job. Where does the guy get all the money? Is he into something "hot" and wants to use this job as a front? Will he start asking for a raise before orientation ends? Then again, it could be his wife's car. The doubt ended when he pulled into a "VP reserved" parking spot. That was a deal breaker.

Tape D: Mr. Handicap Placard Duper arrived in a decent garden variety sedan. But it had handicap plates. That means nothing, the car was probably borrowed from a relative. But that was enough to give Mojo Drainer acute diarrhea. The thought that accessibility modifications and special accommodations may be required was probably the deal breaker.

Tape E: Mr. Donkare, the rebel without etiquette, arrived in style. Political, offensive, and obscene bumper stickers, affiliation decals, and flags that could be considered borderline insane covered most of his car's exterior. This one was a no brainer. Mojo Drainer had already fired people for offensive bumper stickers and was not ready to hire another offender. He had found unrelated silly reasons to get rid of them to avoid law suits. He was known to confront employees with a campaign stickers. "Go work for that presidential candidate."

Tape F: Mr. Antics was doing tricks and playing loud music in a bouncy car in the parking lot. Most employees thought it was funny except the big boss. Never mind the interview. He was escorted off the property before he stepped out of the car.

Tape G: Mr. Walker had no chance. He came in a decent ride, not too showy, not too abnormal. He was the perfect candidate, until he opened his mouth. "Does number nine come this way?" It turned out he had borrowed the car. No Car, No Job. That was the unwritten rule. No one has ever been hired here without a car.

Presently, the medium sedan pulled out of the parking lot, took a sharp right turn, and carried all of Miss Hirer hopes with it as it headed for the highway. Damn it!

Then a miracle happened. Two and a half minutes before the interview, the sedan approached the parking lot for landing. Miss Hirer was already holding the front door open and waving. Her paycheck depended on the sedan and its occupant. She could see Mojo Drainer at his window. For the first time this in months he was smiling. As far as the boss was concerned, you are what you drive.

Manifestation of Transportation-Based Social Exclusion

What was your first car? What kind of car do you drive? How does the car you drive affect your self-image? Do you hide it from your date? Is that crappy car in the parking lot that's bringing the property value down yours?

Means of transportation may mean different things in our daily lives. Sometimes it is nothing serious. So what if Mr. Hyper Machismo refuses to drive the pink small car to save his life? There are many stereotypes and assumptions concerning cars and those who drive them. Certain types of cars are associated with certain types of people in terms of gender, age, nationality, ethnicity, sexual orientation, political affiliation, place, activism and other variables.

No Car, No Job, No House?

There is a new definition to "cultural fit." We live in a world where you need a job to get a car, but actually you need a car to get the job. When the means of transportation is used as a filtering mechanism against minorities and people from poor backgrounds it becomes a way to work around bias laws. Gatekeepers are aware that nobody is about to claim that lack of money to buy a car is an immutable characteristic. Asking about reliable transportation becomes a politically correct way to weed out low-class or unwanted populations.

Sometimes minorities are socially stigmatized for having no cars or having cars that are too good. Consider recent cases where hard-working minorities have been targeted for driving a cars that are deemed too expensive for their group-attributed class.

There are also many questions that need to be answered at the policy-making level that have nothing to do with racial minorities. Is it reasonable for an employer to ask you to be a car owner in order to secure a job? If yes, whose car is it then? There are also people who can't drive because of a medical condition but are qualified to perform their jobs and have the means to get there. Why should they be written off? Also related to this exclusion is the situation where a physically disabled job candidate is seen as an expense risk. A disabled person may require amenities like wheelchair ramps and elevators.

Lack of affordable transportation is barrier by itself to begin with. You may not have access jobs, education, health care, and even other important opportunities.

Conglomeration of Exclusion Factors NUBC

Consider a minority young man trying to crawl his way out of poverty. He has no car, he is homeless, he has bad credit, and he has a canyon of gaps in his employment history.

Transportation
Race
Age
Shelter
Place
Credit history

Unemployment
Social class

Capsule of Talents

Your worth as a human being is not determined by what you drive or your lack of transportation. You are who you are today. The person you want to be tomorrow will be determined by the choices you make today. Start seeing yourself as deserving and capable of doing your best. You must polish your unique talents and work towards your purpose one inch at a time. This requires showing up on time for appointments and at the job site. Be ready to roll, crawl, and walk to make that happen.

Nuthology is concerned with access to resources, opportunities and rights from an individual perspective. Learning how transportation can be used to exclude you should be a part of your financial strategy

Addressing Gatekeepers' Concerns and Dilemmas

Transportation-based exclusion does not have to be rooted in aggression. The gatekeeper may have legitimate questions. Depending on where you live, it can be hard to get a job without a reliable means of transportation. If most of the jobs are located in the surrounding regions and there is no public transportation to get there, this is a factor to consider. The employer may want to know how you will get to work each day. He may want to make sure you won't constantly call in sick or that you will not always be late because you couldn't get a ride.

In major cities public transportation is easy to access and normal. In that case a car will not be an issue. Trains and buses are known to run late. They may also have rigid schedules that don't go well with the work schedule. A bus rider may be seen as unreliable when the bus is not a common means of transportation or shifts may alternate. There are jobs that require you to work at night or stay late. The employer may also be concerned that the length of your commute will affect your job performance.

Watch out for industries where transportation may be a requirement. Most messenger or delivery businesses for example expect you to have a car. It is your duty to research your unique backdrop. Does the job involve fieldwork, site visits, and product delivery? Is this a job where you need to perform errands periodically or get around to clients' locations?

Look for patterns of data in job advertisements:

Must have own car
Must have valid driver's license
Reliable transportation required
Buses do not come this way

Look for patterns of data in interviews:
Do you have your own car? How was your commute?

Narrowing Your Options and Making Selections
Navigating transportation exclusion may require a little work and creativity. How do you get or keep a job without a car?

- Consider moving in with Aunt Becky in the city
- Get a cheap apartment near the job
- Ensure public transportation is available near the job site
- Walk if possible, save on gym and healthcare expenses
- Carpool with friends. Pay for the gas. No mooching
- Purchase a scooter or a bicycle if living in rural areas

TMI Tip
Some employers may not even ask about transportation arrangements. They may just observe as you struggle to read the bus schedule after the interview. Being overly concerned about transportation arrangements may make the hiring manager uncomfortable. Do the research outside of the company. Emphasize your strengths and values not means of getting to work during the interview

Unless you want to be conveniently naïve, there is bound to be some power play in the workplace that does not show up on the official policy. You may come across as attempting to outshine those who sign your checks even without necessarily intending to. You may come across as rebel just based on your means of transportation. Offensive bumper stickers may turn people off. They may never tell you. That should be part of your financial intelligence.

Reducing Your Own Aggression

There are many negative stereotypes associated with this exclusion. Who drives the minivan or the station wagon in your community? Who carries twenty-six people in a small sedan? It's all fun, right? Apparently your ride can tell a lot about your environmental activism, ethnicity, sexual orientation, aging-anxiety, gender, hygiene, insecurity, social status and political affiliation. Some people claim they can tell the age, gender or ethnicity of a driver by observing driving skills only. These assumptions are often used by gatekeepers to exclude individuals from opportunities or rights.

Speak Up Regardless of Status

Become an advocate for horizontal coexistence where no one is treated unfairly because of his or her ride or lack thereof. Speak up against employers' who sidestep discrimination laws by using transportation as a filtering mechanism against the marginalized populations.

43

Tribal, Clan, Family

Ethnic Pride Cover

Mr. Harapash is from the Fubanian tribe. He has been working as a nurse in the diaspora for the last ten years. He never thought he would ever encounter tribe-based exclusion in foreign lands. There was an incident where he was ill-treated by a Bakrdanian hiring manager during an interview. That was last year. At that time he did not think of the issue in terms of tribalism. Mr. Harapash's wife was Bakrdanian by tribe. Not a big deal.

Early this year, a social group was formed by city Motherlandians to help with medical and funeral expenses, which are a big concern for this community. The group founders turned out to be from the Bakrdanian tribe. When Mr. Harapash's wife showed up to register, she was turned down because she was married to a Fubanian. When Mr. Harapash heard about it, he remembered the mistreatment he had received from the Bakrdanian hiring manager. It was a rude awakening.

Many Motherlandians had found new dwellings in developed countries in their quest for greener grass like their ancestors had for centuries. They often became targets of race-based social exclusion due to their skin color. As despicable as racism is, given the historical context, it was not necessarily breaking news to the immigrants.

The big surprise was how some immigrants discriminated against other immigrants based on tribe and clans thousands of miles from home. The fact that you can encounter tribalism in the far-flung corners of the world. Racism and tribalism are close cousins. They are the same disease but different virus strains. They are both delusional claims of privilege by descent. They are both based on immutable characteristics.

"The fact that tribalism has been able to be imported that intact is a testament to the strength of this disease. Most of the inequality in our motherland is caused by tribalism. You can safely conclude that it is because of tribalism that we are here in the first place. It is depressingly ironic and sad. I get a headache just thinking about it," said Mr. Harapash in a recent blog piece.

Manifestation of Tribal and Family Clan Social Exclusion

Due to weak national institutions, tribalism in some countries is a stronger determinant of who gets an opportunity than racism is in the developed nations. We have some countries where every citizen is perceived to have an affiliation and loyalty to a tribe, clan, or family and depends on it in many ways. Almost every aspect of life takes on an ethnic dimension.

Failure in both tribal and social class relations almost always go together. That tendency of members to unite against an outside tribe creates some form of de facto residential segregation, even in urban areas, and a permanent "warrior mode" status everywhere. It also generates a high-risk investor climate. Without businesses and investors, poverty moves in like a desert storm weakening institutions further.

Nobody is disputing the fact that extended family, the clan, and tribal affiliations do play vital roles in society. The native tribal identity and pride should be portrayed as cultural richness. It is a natural source of strength. That is not what happens. For some gatekeepers the same tribal loyalty is a source of toxic negative stereotypes, out-group attribution bias, and shameless in-group favoritism. It becomes a perfect front for cronyism, nepotism, and corruption that drags on for years.

Social Exclusion on the Basis of Tribe, Family, or Clan Can Take Many Routes

- Unfair hiring, firing, promotion, and demotions
- Denial of benefits to members of rival tribes
- Partial and targeted enforcement of law, company policies, standards, and production expectations
- Denial of business opportunities
- Uneven distribution of social and economic amenities

In some countries you don't need to look far to find examples of petty tribal vendetta including orchestrated road closings, office closings, water shortages, lost files, food shortages, missing bridges, missing journalists, missing activists, and retaliatory layoffs. We also know that candidates with family political legacies will often have an advantage on the campaign trail even in advanced democracies.

What is the Difference between a Tribe and an Ethnic Group?

We live in a world that is so biased that there is a bias in definitions themselves. In most books the word "tribe" has connotations of being primitive, so it usually associated with people who are perceived to be primitive. The word "ethnic" does not give primitive vibes so it used to describe more advanced human species, right? These terms are also used interchangeable in some cases. "Ethnicity" and "tribalism" are highly charged words in some parts of the word. We shall not go into split-hair definitions here.

Nuthology Strategy

One of the assumptions of this strategy is the free market economy environment. There is no country with a pure free market economy, so there is bound to be an element of capitalism force in your environment. Nuthology mitigation strategy greatly depends on the forces of scarcity, demand, and supply. That means it will be least effective in situations where markets are not allowed to prosper. It will not work if there is a risk that your safety may be compromised. This could be in fragile states, bad neighborhoods, or any situation where personal security is a concern. It is a personal strategy for peaceful times. The Nuthology Index and NUBC will still be applicable.

Conglomeration of Exclusion Factors NUBC

Consider a foreign-educated, fifty-year-old nurse looking for a job in the diaspora where she is concerned about alma mater, tribalism, racism, gender, age, national origin, accent, and social class based exclusion factors all at the same time. Her NUBC:

Tribalism
Racism
Colorism
Gender
Age
National origin
Language accent
Social class
Alma mater

Capsule of Talents

We are all endowed with unique gifts. Every child is a divine issue. Tribal identity does not define your status as a human being. Your tribe is an immutable characteristic that is perfect by design. You should never feel pressured to move from who you are in order to develop. The greatest risk of tribal- based exclusion is that you will start seeing yourself as less deserving and less capable based on some stereotypes. As long you do not negatively judge yourself based on some negative group attribution, you are in total control. It is all in your hands. Yes, you belong to that group, but you just came to this world recently. Nobody can claim to really comprehend your capabilities or purpose.

Your biography is a historical record not a rail line to your destiny. You are who you are today. The person you want to be tomorrow will be determined by the strategy you design today. Learning how tribe, family or clan status can be used to exclude you should be a part of your financial strategy.

Expand Your Networks

In today's age, your network should include people from all walks of life. Categorically demonizing a whole tribe without carefully differentiating between persons of goodwill and those who consciously perpetuate tribalism only minimizes the scope of your network.

Addressing Gatekeepers' Concerns and Dilemmas

Develop a 360 view of your situation. That is the only way you will be able to see beyond superficial obstacles. Combine all your concerns so that you develop a comprehensive strategy.

Gather enough information. Collect enough quality data. This will ensure that you are not competing for jobs with everybody. There are careers that will always have jobs regardless of your tribe. With this in mind, you can narrow your options and make selections from a point of strength.

Language, accent, and articulation issues can be a problem when interviewing for a job in a new environment. What are the other cultural differences? Look for shared values. It is important to distinguish discrimination from business concerns. You should not view every rejection or setback as tribe-based aggression.

Learn to identify patterns of aggression in local language. Every tribe has some epithets that are used to disparage members of other tribes.

Tell Your Story

With the advancement of new technology and specifically the Internet, you should be able to tell your story better than strangers. The era of breaking news is over. If your culture has been sold as backward, violent, and immoral, the best you can do is not to reinforce that stereotype. Take it a step farther, and you are selling the culture as a source of strength and pride.

Reducing Your Own Stereotype-Driven Aggression

Not everyone who loves their family, language, and culture hates yours. This third rock from the sun has more than six billion humans who share many similarities and differences, which are the basis for social groups. Some of these differences could be physical, language, customs, or beliefs. Every one of these six billion is a member of some group, even if they don't always realize it. We have differing preferences, hopes, dreams, fears, and feelings of every kind imaginable.

Avoid groups that use factually incorrect material and gross overgeneralizations to create a situation where a whole tribe epitomizes all the evil in the world. Avoid groups that promote pitting one tribe against others.

Avoid Overcompensation

Tribal equality should be a question of equitable access and equality as human beings, not a question of substituting the tribal supremacy of others with yours. Strong loyalty to your own tribe should not cloud your judgment when it comes to creating sustainable networks and treating others with respect. Trying to prove your tribe, family, or clan is better than the dominant arrangement does not help your cause. It is claiming credit for unearned achievements based on acts of nature.

Speak Up Regardless of Status

One of the obstacles to democracy and equality in the world is the hereditary transmission of political influence, social status, and opportunities within one tribe, clan, or family. Loyalties that are based on tribe, clan and family are perfect incubators of corruption and inefficiency in many countries. Become an ambassador for horizontal coexistence where no one is treated unfairly because of his or her descent.

44

Unemployment Stigma

LITO Work from Home Project

It was seen as the most groundbreaking thing the company had ever done toward promoting employee work-life balance. That is how the LITO work from home program was sold to the five-thousand-strong occupants of this sprawling campus. Even the often skeptical press was sucked into the celebration. The customer service experts were excited. For the first time ever they would get to work in their pajamas. They would get to be home when their kids left for school and when they came home.

When Mr. Kachamak, the new CEO, announced that the work from home system was ready in a town hall meeting, he received a solid two minute standing ovation. Employees were hugging each other in joy. There was clapping and impromptu songs. “LITO! LITO! LITO!” The hall exploded in praise. The CEO was quick to deliver. Within six months, every employee would be able to work from home at least three days a week.

Then Mr. Kachamak went in for the kill. His calculations were simple. If an employee can work online from 10 miles away with considerable efficiency, can another employee work from 10,000 miles away for a tenth of the cost? You bet he can. And he did. The work from home system implementation had been one giant test. The code name, LITO, stood for “Layoffs in the Offing.” The company’s concern for a flexible employee work arrangement was one evil charade.

Within nine months, only one hundred employees were working for the company in this country. Most duties included oversight of hundreds of low-paid part timers in overcrowded overseas call centers. Meanwhile the company stock doubled and so did the CEO's salary. The books never looked better. Mr. Kachamak had delivered without increasing a single dime in revenue. This time he had even made employees applaud for their own impending mass layoffs. He was that good at being bad. To him, corporations were people and people were numbers that occupied them.

Hupfu was one of the employees whose job was outsourced in that operation. He was working from home when the cold e-mail came. "Log off and shelter in place." He was not able to retrieve his electronic paystubs and other documents that would help in a job search. That was two years ago, but it seemed like an eternity. Now, four hundred applications and three interviews later, the forty-eight-year-old father of three high school kids is still unemployed. The once respected little league coach felt small and cheated.

Who can blame him? In those short years he has used up all his retirement funds, seen his home get into foreclosure and his family squeezed into a tiny subsidized apartment a block away from the homeless shelter. Hupfu rarely ventures into public. He no longer volunteers for little league coaching.

Manifestation of Unemployment Social Exclusion and Stigma

It is no secret that it is easier to get a job when you have one. It is also common knowledge that the longer you are out of work, the harder it is to find work. There is often open preference for hiring the already employed candidate. I guess it is harder for us mere mortals to get this genius gatekeeper's logic. "We won't give you a job because you could not find a job in the last six months."

Long-term unemployment is one of those neglected stigmas that receive little attention but packs a big punch. It is not considered a bias status at the societal level. At the individual level it is not just status. It can give birth to many other statuses. Losing employment leads to the loss of homes and cars. You may have to dip into savings including your nest egg. That is lost savings and increased debt simultaneously.

Social Exclusion on the Basis of Unemployment Can Take Many Routes

There is a perception that people who have been out of work have lost their energy level and their skills have diminished. For those who are getting into the system, employers can make you walk through the biggest catch-22 cloud ever invented. You need experience to get a job but you can't get experience without job. You are looking for a job to pay bills, but because you can't pay bills you get bad credit, and you can't get some jobs with bad credit. It is a conundrum inside a quandary. Do you want flies with that?

Mental Health

Work is related to individuals' identities and feelings of self-worth. Lack of work takes these away. Long-term unemployment can be degrading, humiliating, and demoralizing. You don't need to be an expert to understand the damaging effects of prolonged lack of a decent job. Studies indicate that long-term unemployment has been linked to various forms of mental illnesses.

Age

There is a significant diminishing prospect of getting a job for older unemployed candidates. These are people who already have a record of holding down employment and have positively contributed to society. But they get the greatest share of unemployment exclusion and stigma.

Conglomeration of Exclusion Factors NUBC

Let us talk about the multidimensionality of exclusion related to long-term unemployment. Consider an older former employee who has depleted savings, maxed out credit cards, and accumulated other debts in order to stay alive. He has lost his home, cars, and marriage. He is now depressed and drinking too much. We are no longer talking about unemployment stigma alone. His NUBC now include:

Unemployment stigma
Age
Shelter
Credit history
Social class
Transportation
Marital status
Character
Disease stigma

Capsule of Talents

Enough of the bad news already. Understanding the situation is the first step in solving the problem. At the individual level, what do you do? Learning how long-term unemployment can be used to exclude you should be a part of your financial strategy.

The first thing you have to do, as hard as this might be, is keep your spirits up. You will need your conscious in this process. Work is not just about money. It feeds into many different aspects of our lives including self-esteem. Seek support from health agencies, nonprofit groups, and relatives. Even without clinical issues, just watching your skills depreciate can be very stressing. The thought of commuting longer distances, learning new skills, transitioning to a new area, field, or industry does not help your sanity.

Addressing Gatekeepers' Concerns and Dilemmas

Some employers assume skills do deteriorate without use. You may need to explain what you have been doing with your time since you have been out of work. There are some things that you can do to improve you situation depending on your backdrop. Here are just a few:

- Seek internships, apprenticeships, and other "ships"
- Start a small business and put it on your resume to fill the gaps

- Seek free education and training
- Keep your knowledge current. Keep up with your profession through journals and organizations
- Volunteer your time and put it on your resume
- Avoid appearing antiquated or embarking on anti-new-media campaigns. This will make you fit into some age-related stereotypes
- Watch your physical health during this time.

Expand Your Networks

You can't afford to wait for someone to contact you. You will need to be proactive. Take that extra step and make it happen. You are in charge of your own destiny.

Reducing Your Own Stereotype-Driven Aggression

There is a lot of finger-pointing when it comes to long-term unemployment. There are people who will have jobs that you may think should be yours. This can make you more antagonistic in nature. The belief that society owes you a job only creates anger and reduces your networking capabilities.

Speak Up

Become an advocate for horizontal coexistence where no one is treated unfairly because of his or her employment status. Speak up against the unfair stigma against those who have been long-term unemployed for no vault of their own.

45

Weight, Size

Insufficiently Corpulent

Mary's story reads like a work of fiction, unless you have been to her home country. Grasa-Land is an island nation three hundred miles west of Tierra Flaco with a long history of droughts and famines. According to a recent world health study, Grasa-Land has the highest case of obesity in the world despite being caught in a deadly cycle of droughts and famines for the last ten decades.

It is one of a few countries in the world where being fat is not only considered attractive but a sign of material prosperity. The ideal female figure is literary a well-rounded one, size circle. Like many girls growing up in this hell on earth, Mary remembers being force-fed daily to increase her chances of marrying into a wealthy family or even getting married at all. She was one of the "lucky" kids because she was genetically predisposed to be fat and had a medical condition that kept her in the perfect well-rounded form. It was like finding a conundrum in a box of green dilemmas.

In Grasa-Land, heaviness means happiness and wealth. The slim people are portrayed as stingy and socially subversive. In a country ravaged by AIDS, obesity becomes not only a sign of prosperity but also a clear sign of health. Ironically, it is the people who are neither sick nor poor that often face constant negative implications and anti-social connotations.

Traditional strength competitions are national events that show the essence of real men. Men are motivated to pile on weight to qualify for the sport. For these men, being huge is a double reward: it creates a perception of higher socioeconomic status and a chance to showcase your muscles.

Those who have 'high-net-worth' diseases like gout and diabetes can be seen flaunting their swollen toes like prize-winning dairy cattle. Those who are healthy but poor are known to fake the ailments using canes to simulate the rich man's walk, hoping to impress the women one pound at a time. They make sure rumors about "the illness" spreads around like wild fire.

Mary was happily married at an early age. Pursuit of obesity in Grasa-Land does not stop at the altar. A fat wife is a symbol of wealth and a hardworking husband. The problem started when her medical condition improved. She was a poor eater. She started shedding weight like crazy.

Losing a few pounds will get frowned upon, especially if you are married into a respectable family. Being insufficiently corpulent was not easy to hide. To save her life, she was smuggled out of the country by a family friend who lives in Tierra Flaco.

When Mary migrated to Tierra Flaco, she could not believe how public perception could change from one area to another. Obesity became a new animal altogether. She was considered very obese, again. In this new town one needed an entirely new "waist" management game plan. It was considered rude to tell people they were fat in the new country. "Did you gain some pounds?" That was not a complement. In the new world, thinness symbolized discipline, hard work, ambition, and will power. You had to be a size negative to avoid being regarded as fat.

Manifestation of Weight and Size-Based Social Exclusion

Weight-related bias is not protected in many countries. Weight is usually a centerpiece of late night jokes, comedy routines and tabloid pieces. Is weight the new acceptable prejudice? Fat people in some countries are often stereotyped as gluttonous and lazy. They are blamed for failing to take personal responsibility for their own health. They are often depicted in media binging on unhealthy food and large-size sugary drinks.

On the other hand, being fat means you are successful in some countries. Consequently, thin people in that part of the world are often blamed for being lazy and for failing to take personal responsibility for their own financial situations. This is an exclusion that can go either way.

Those who work in front of a camera or in some client-facing positions can certainly relate to this topic. You will know when weight gain becomes problematic. There will be a writing somewhere on proverbial wall. Sometimes the wall is actually is a pink slip.

Group attribution character related to weight may seem subtle and inconsequential but it is often a threat to individual achievement. There are real patterns of data out there that you can analyze. On average, skinny political candidates get more votes than overweight ones. Recent studies show that on average obese people have skinnier paychecks than those who aren't as heavy. You just need to look at patterns of data in your country. Is it a coincidence that almost none of the Fortune 500 CEOs are obese? A heavy executive may be judged as less capable or having diminished self-discipline if they were to be obese.

Male jurors may show prejudice against plus-size female defendants while the slender and conventionally beautiful may get a break. Heavier and bigger men are seen as the aggressor in court. Consider a tall male who is 450 pounds in a domestic violence situation. He may experience a hard time trying to convince the judge that a four feet tall, 125 pound old lady assaulted him even when that was the case. It is a David and Goliath scenario. He will be viewed as the Goliath even when he was not the aggressor.

Racism

Size discrimination may combine with other forms and present unique challenges to the affected individual. For a young big minority man for example racism may be intensified by size, weight, gender, height, place, age and social class forms of discrimination. A smaller minority man may not face the same level of aggression.

Gender
Society puts an incredible amount of pressure on women to look perfect. Weight and size bias are usually related to physical appearance. Weight is considered part of that attractiveness package. Since attractiveness bias weighs heavily on the female gender, weightism will also tend to do the same.

Social Class
Patterns of data on this subject point to a troubling common denominator: both starvation and obesity are closely linked with poverty. Children take what they can get. Their choices of diet and physical activity habits are influenced by their surrounding environment. Weight is a major issue in low-income neighborhoods.

Conglomeration of Exclusion Factors NUBC
An older, short, and poor plus-size minority woman from a neglected neighborhood looking for a client-facing position may be concerned with converging multiple exclusions risks. It is possible to have a combination of factors depending on the backdrop.

Weight
Gender
Attractiveness
Social class
Height
Age
Race
Place

Nuthology Strategy
The greatest danger of weight exclusion is that you may start seeing yourself as less deserving or less capable of blasting through your

dreams. We know that judgmental assessments are simplistic but, to the extent they affect individual achievement, they need to be addressed. You are endowed with a unique capsule of talents. Your weight does not define your worth as a human being. Research or work with a healthcare professional on insecurity issues. Learning what your rights are can also be empowering.

I know I emphasized obesity, but weight stigma depends on your backdrop. You don't have to be clinically obese. If you are perceived as too thin or too thick then this factor should be counted in your planning. Remember, strategic planning does not mean abandoning your dreams. It means you might be more efficient with your time and energy in order to achieve those dreams. It is possible to fight against size-related bullying and promote a healthy lifestyle. Both are positive financial moves.

Addressing Gatekeepers' Concerns and Dilemmas

The gatekeepers' concerns depend on your society. Some employers may have concern about the effect excess weight can have on health insurance rates. Corporate sales image, impairment, obesity as disability, and obesity as disease are also a part of that mix. Most of these are driven by the anti-fat sentiment or anti-thin sentiment. First of all, you have to maintain a good degree of confidence in yourself. Do not be constrained by weight related exclusion. Research your industry thoroughly. Start with the basics. How do others in the same situation successfully dispel a potential employer's concerns?

Avoiding Petty Overcompensation

How do you handle body insecurity and the pressure to be thin? Should you stay obese just to prove a point even when you know reducing your weight can improve both your health and wealth? "Oh, I will show them." While we are fighting discrimination against overweight people, we cannot ignore the personal financial angle. Remember, this is a personal-driven strategy, so feel free to have a 360 view.

Apart from the health aspect it is a great financial strategy to stay active and eat a healthy diet whenever possible. Imagine the money pits associated with obesity from medical expenses to diminished revenue generating opportunities. Think of doctors' visits, medicine, missed work days, weight loss surgeries, weight-related diseases, complications, and disability.

For those that do not have medical issues staying active helps the economy. Overweight and obesity are linked to more deaths worldwide than underweight. Hospitals have to upgrade to accommodate the obese from larger beds, wheelchairs, MRI machines, stronger toilets, bigger scales, doors, and other areas.

Workplace accommodation costs related to weight add up to billions of dollars. Modes of transportation like buses, airplanes, ambulances, and trains have to be modified. Government and business costs will eventually find their way to taxpayers' and consumers' pockets.

Reducing Your Own Stereotype-Driven Aggression

Do people who are obese eat a lot? What if they do? Is appearance of the person the deciding factor in whether the person should be respected or not? Recognize that some people are genetically predisposed to being fat or have a medical condition that contributes to having large body sizes. It is never okay to judge people based on size. Medication side effects can cause obesity too. Diseases like thyroid complications can cause weight-related issues. Pregnancy and parenthood can also cause the appearance of weight gain.

There are people who are naturally very skinny or have a harder time gaining weight. Most exclusion issues are not about fat being healthy or unhealthy but fat being attractive or unattractive as portrayed by media. Weight-related bullying leads to self-esteem issues in our schools. Stories of the chubby being bullied are not uncommon. The very thin are also burdened. For young adults it can affect work and interpersonal relationships.

Speak Up Regardless of Status

Speak up against the causes of obesity. Speak up against size-based stigma. Both are wrong. In a nutshell, you will become a double advocate for the population-based and the culturally relevant approach to fighting both obesity and size-based stigma. Both pose a threat to individual achievement. Weight discrimination increases the risk of obesity instead of motivating individuals to lose weight. Size-based stigma is wrong but unhealthy weight may be dangerous and not something to promote as a "good thing," even in the name of "just being you."

46

Nuthology Zones

Nuthology Index and Personal Finance

While financial independence cannot buy acceptance, it is a great down payment. It is tied to the hip with basic freedoms. Money and education are not the most important things in the world, but for a conglomerate they are up there with fresh water. Since money holds the food, clothing, shelter, health, justice, and pursuit of happiness, for this modern hunter it is a lifeline.

Lack of adequate financial literacy is one of the biggest obstacles affecting the fight for equality. Many personal decisions, including handling cash, debt, saving, and investing, require some financial knowledge. You don't need to be a financial major. It is hard to find an entity where business decisions are not given importance. It is no wonder the greatest percentage of inequality discussion has to do with money.

Finance and accounting seem to be all about dry and complex numbers. It is true these subjects can be sleep-inducing. There is a reason there are no TV shows called *Dancing with the Mutual Funds*, *Compound Interest Idol*, or *Desperate Assets of Wall Street.* This education can be a boring necessity. In most countries elementary school systems are not armed to teach money management skills.

So What Has Social Exclusion Index to Do with Financial Literacy?

For bias conglomerates, financial literacy means too much to be optional. Financial ignorance is especially more disastrous for those with limited means. It is not uncommon to see scores of millionaire disciples and predatory lenders roaming the economically challenged neighborhoods because this is the congruent of financial illiteracy and social exclusion-induced desperation.

Regardless of the desired occupation or career, you must develop some financial curiosity. Even in cases where you are able to hire a money expert, you will want to give him or her clear guidelines. Poor financial management and discipline can offset even a good income, real quickly.

Start Somewhere

If you were jobless and homeless, for example, would read about credit swap derivatives, deferred taxes, and other pain-inducing financial topics? Absolutely, not. You would look for information that can help your situation in the short run. Buying a public gym membership would be good financial move. You can take showers and change clothes before an interview. It would be remiss of me if I did not share some pointers on personal finance given that material exclusion is the most effective and obvious manifestation of bias today.

Revenue

Nothing erodes your dignity, independence, and self-respect more than a vertical relationship created by perpetual unearned income dependency. Very few achievements are more liberating than being able to afford one's own basic human needs. There is no greater therapy than being the one lending a helping hand.

How do you bring in some income? You could always come up with that zillion-dollar contract or idea. For most of us mortals, working for somebody else opens our doors. We start with a job. We clean toilets and deliver newspapers for the existing entrepreneurships if we have to.

There is no doubt that entrepreneurship is the golden route to making millions. My point here is that getting a wage-paying job should not be sold as a negative to the youth. Don't be fooled by drive-by, instant-millionaire disciples. Most self-employed people start with a job and then move to self-employment. For the most part, entrepreneurship involves selling, failing, and handling rejection. You should not think of it as the "easy route."

These routes are not mutually exclusive anyway. There are many entrepreneurs holding day jobs. It is your obligation to see the big picture, analyze opportunities and risks. You just need to come up with a plan that brings in some earned income.

Whether employed or in business for yourself, the fact is that you will earn a living by meeting the needs and wants of others. It is a rewarding experience. No matter what route you choose, being self-sufficient should be your goal.

Earning money is also how we grow a civilized society and love our neighbors. Let us see how your revenue-generation activity or lack of it affects your neighbor. Maybe you never looked at it this way.

Where Does the Government Get Money?

In most modern economies, the government gets its money mainly from tax revenue, which is paid by the citizens and businesses of that country. The money is then budgeted for different uses. One of the categories is benefits. Sometimes the government will raise the taxes to meet the demand of these programs. That simply means taxes go up and the taxpayer's take-home pay, consequently, goes down. For the business, the taxpayer's employer, the income goes down as this tax expense goes up.

The taxpayers are then forced to work long hours or multiple jobs to make up for the lost revenue in their home budgets. It is your neighbor's take-home paycheck that goes down not some abstract entity. Yes, that "stupid" neighbor who works eighty hours a week and misses all the fun at your block party. Maybe you never looked at it that way.

I mentioned above that tax increase is a business expense going up and income taking the hit. Now something has to give. Business actions often include reduction of employees as a result of expense increase. Now your poor neighbor is out of a job, thank you very much. Then again, maybe you never looked at it that way.

The take-away here is that mooching is not a financial strategy except in cases involving the elderly, disabled, or anybody looking for a job after an understandable rough patch. *Mooching* includes living rent free and conveniently forgetting your wallet every time you go to a restaurant with friends.

How Do You Start Learning and Earning?

The basics of financial independence literacy are not that complicated. There are three options: increase revenue, cut costs, and, my best, do both. Then you protect your assets and share some with the inhabitants of this rock. That's all what personal finance is about.

If you have to learn only three financial concepts related to personal finance I would suggest selling, budgeting, and compounding any day. These will get you in the mood for making money, keeping it, and making it work for you.

Selling

If you have to learn only one skill related to personal finance and just about any facet of your life, I would suggest selling. This should be a mandatory class in high school.

Whether you want to work for somebody or become self-employed, there will be a need to sell yourself, sell your ideas, sell a service, or sell a product. When self-employed you have to persuade that client or customer that you have the best product since sliced bread. When looking for a job, your customer is the potential employer. You sell yourself to the employer then sell the company's products, services, or image. Interviews, public speaking, and personal branding are forms of selling in one version or another.

Selling is one skill you will need even when you are begging on the streets. You have to persuade strangers to donate and others not to detonate a can of space worms. This is a skill that will get you the first date after that 150-year dry spell. This is the skill you need if you are running for office or past a speed-radar-wielding officer while driving as if on the autobahn. The most influential political, community, business, or religious leaders you know are good at selling.

I can write a book on this. What about managing an advertisement campaign, writing a convincing marketing copy, moderating a cease-fire in the middle of something, and negotiating a hostage situation? There is an element of selling in all these.

You even need to learn selling to protect yourself from sellers. Selling is why we end up with mediocre leaders and unwanted stuff in our garages year after year. Selling is the art that casts a spell. How else did you end up with that leaking and squeaking lemon in your driveway? The fact that you still call the flood-damaged, salvaged thing "a collectible" makes my point. In all seriousness though, you will need to demonstrate integrity and a high level of ethics if you want to be a credible person. It is very important to learn the art of persuasion and practice it. Try it.

Persuade that fellow church member to give you a job referral

Convince the neighbor to get you an apprenticeship

Persuade that gatekeeper to offer you a job for what you can do for him

Persuade the gatekeepers that a raise will keep you around without saying it outright

Persuade the nauseous customer that it is not your product that is stinking

Navigate office culture without a helmet, just using negotiating acumen

Butter up those thorny-shelled investors with bare persuasion

Wheedle your way onto the golden castle court and head straight to the honey fountain

Handle that rejection and constructive criticism without turning into a mushroom cloud

Permit yourself to fail repeatedly without collapsing into your own self-pity cocoon

I dare you to show me anything else that combines rapport building, objection handling, presentation, questioning, persistence, persuasion, and a ton of organizational skills into one small capsule. No matter what your occupation is, you will need selling skills.

You will find yourself learning what your mom has been warning you against all your life as a kid: striking up conversations with strangers. Selling is a skill for daily life and a revenue generating machine.

Congratulations, you have a check on the way. Let us plan for it. I know it is not enough. It is a limited resource. That is even a better reason to plan for it.

Budgeting

This is another subject that should be mandatory in high school but it is mostly ignored. Management of personal credit, debt, and savings all rely on a simple budget. How do you make a budget? List all of your income. List all of your expenses. Where is your money coming from? How much? Where is your money going? Do you have a deficit, a surplus, or breaking even?

Making a budget is the easy part. Problems arise in sticking to it. Following a tight budget is not about being cheap; it is about setting financial priorities. Do the things that will force you to stay within that budget. Where can you cut your expenses? Live below your means.

There are tons of resources to learn about cutting costs if you want to. The ideas are simple. Wait before you buy a new item. Compare prices before you buy anything. There are tons of resources to learn about how to save. Save money automatically. Start with that small amount you can afford.

Borrow wisely if you must. Establish credit, use it wisely, and monitor your credit profile constantly. Avoid anything that will hurt your credit score. Avoid cosigning any debt; if your BFF doesn't pay, it becomes your loan. Why is your credit so bad? The answer is BFF, which now stands for "borrowed for friends".

Credit card money is a loan not a gift. That plastic has a lot of preloaded curse particles. That explains that devilish feeling you get every time the credit limit goes up. Yes, the feeling that you deserve nice things and you have nothing to lose. That is the only way one can explain the overwhelming allure to join the debt-fueled grandstanding marathon in cyberspace.

Be the Best Version of Yourself

The brag level in the social media can be nauseating. Unlike you, your friends have permanent smiling and constantly vacationing families. Look at their recent post. They just bought stuff that matches other stuff in the full closet. When are you going to get out there and show them? You have two options. First option, plastic fast draw. The duel is on. You whip out that shinny platinum plastic and you borrow to the hilt. Nobody lives twice, right? Just read the yawning ads. They proclaim in big monumental tablets:

You deserve it. If you miss this 70 percent sale, something bad will happen. You will regret it. That's all I know. It is a one day annual sale, as in this happens once a year. I take that back. In fact, it ends at noon.

But deep down you know it is wrong. You cannot lie to other people without lying to yourself. That is the way the numbers work since he wrote them. When the dust settles, your gut tells you the chickens will come home to roost. They will lay some eggs in your mailbox. Not the good kind of eggs, the egging kind.

Option two, you do something that is rare these days: you think independently. You decide to become the best version of yourself instead of a cheap copy of the proverbial Joneses. You develop your own skeptical meter about sales promotions. You discover the smorgasbord of possibilities inside that divine capsule of talents. You are divine issue that requires no validation or some superficial online grandstanding.

Learn to delay obligations, especially long-term ones like babies and mortgages. Wait before you buy into a longtime obligation like a car loan, a house, or even raising a family. Most of the time a home is an expense and not an investment.

Is it possible to delay having kids until you are financially stable? The cost of raising kids keeps growing. Plan how all this will fit into your future budgets. It is your life. You are the chief financial officer of your life.

Watch for "enabler's trap" potholes. You don't want to delay your wants only to pick up other people's messes. What is the difference between helping and enabling? It is always good to help people in need any way you can, but that is not an excuse to let able-bodied people pull you back. Always remember that while growing old is inevitable, acting one's age is optional. Dependent friends and relatives can break both your budget and growth momentum simultaneously. The theory of lazy relatives' inertia states that the able body perpetually at rest on your couch will remain at rest unless an outside force from your foot acts on its behind or your fridge is empty, whichever comes first. Not a true theory? It is now. You get my point.

Compounding

If you have to learn one more financial concept in your entire life, I would suggest the laws of compounding. People spend their entire lives in debt because of compounding. Wars have been fought over it. On the other hand, people spend their entire lives on assets created by compounding. In the market economy, compounding can be your best friend or your worst enemy. Forget the general theory of relativity for a moment.

"Compound interest is the eighth wonder of the world." Albert Einstein.

This quote has also been attributed to other great thinkers for good reason: it is an amazing investment concept. Compound interest is the concept of adding accumulated interest to principal so that the interest is earned from the new principal from that moment on.

10 percent on $100 is $10 = $110
New principal $110 earns $11 = $121
New principal $121 earns $12.10 = $133.10
New principal $133.10 earns $13.31 = $146.41

Your homework today is to continue this tree. It is the only time you will find money growing on a tree. The interest gets bigger as the principal increases. Use online calculators to see how this amazing concept works.

Young people have the greatest advantage when it comes to compounding: time. Do everything to understand the impact of compounding from a saving and borrowing perspective. You are either earning interest or paying it. Think of it this way: everything you spend is money that will not compound for you. Everything you invest is money that will compound for you.

How come your credit card balance keeps going up? The power of compound interest is working against you big time. I have not even started factoring in late fees, overbalance fees, and other penalties yet. Think of it this way: any money you borrow is compounding for the other guy.

This is another subject that should be mandatory in high school. We live in a world where the rich stay rich by saving and investing. On the other hand, the poor stay poor by spending and borrowing.

Nuthology Financial Independence Zones

In modern societies, stratification is broadly organized into three main layers: upper class, middle class, and lower class. This method is basically classification of people into groups based on shared socioeconomic conditions, which is kind of confusing from an individual perspective. We all know people who live debt-induced upper-class or middle-class lifestyles. Sometimes we are those people. I have come up with a simple table that you can use to position your movements without these class structure labels.

This table is simple: you start your life from somewhere and then target a point where your assets are earning enough money to sustain your lifestyle, preferably before the usual retirement age. Then you sit back. Let the money work hard and smart for you. The specific dollar amounts will still depend on your area's living standards.

First, let us look at financial independence zones.

At the personal zone you are surviving, thriving, or prospering economically.

Nuthology Financial Independence Zones				
Zones		EMPLOYMENT/DEPENDENT		SELF EMPLOYMENT/INDEPENDENT
SURVIVING	F 3	Low Income/Low Net Worth	E3	Low Cash Flow Income-Producing Investments/ Low Net Worth
THRIVING	D 2	Average Income /Average Net Worth	C2	Average Cash flow Income-producing Investments/Average Net Worth
PROSPERING	B 1	High Income/High Net Worth	A1	High Cash flow Income-Producing Investments/ High Net Worth

Letters A, B, C, D, E, and F represent income (not grades)
Numbers 1, 2, 3 represent Net worth
Example One: A3 means High Cash Flow Income Producing Investments, Low Net worth
Example Two: B3 means High Income, Low net worth
Example Three: BC2 means High Income (from employment), Average Cash Flow (from investments), and Average Net Worth
The actual amounts depend on your area's living standards. The goal is to move near and possibly get to A1 before retirement.

Measuring Progress Using Net Worth

Determine your net worth by subtracting all your liabilities from all your assets. You are simply totaling up what you own and subtracting what you owe. It will either be positive or negative net worth. If you are a high net worth individual with assets that produce sustainable cash flow we can say you are prospering financially. Who are we kidding? It's not where you'd like it to be. It's probably on the negative territory. Believe me, you are not alone. But you a looking at it for once. It's a work in progress.

Become a Better Advocate for Equality

Understanding finance will make you a better advocate for the disfranchised. Financial literacy will help you understand how the systems work. For example, the growing gap between the rich and the poor is not that complicated to visualize.

Investments generally grow faster than wages. Who is likely to buy better-performing investments? Investments are likely to be taxed less than wages. Who is likely to depend on wages and who is likely to depend on investments as a means of income?

Debt is very expensive. Who is likely to depend on debts to survive? Who is likely to pay more interest on loans? The government makes decisions on fair lending and banking practices. Who is likely to be in the government? Who is likely to influence politicians and government? How many empirical studies do we need to see that the deck is clearly stacked against the little guy? In your own unique way, join the defenders of freedom, equality, respect, justice and basic human rights.

Final Thought

For practical and political reasons, discrimination is a very touchy subject full of emotional eggshells. It requires a lot of tact. Only leaders with superb political adroitness are able to discuss it and come out unscathed. Amazingly, most people are aware that the issue is out there. Most people won't touch it with a ten-foot pole. Family, friends, and community leaders in your backdrop may avoid talking about bias unless there is tragic event. By then the pressure is too high that the opposing sides can only see things through an emotional prism. For a bias conglomerate employing thoughtfulness and strategy to increase the odds of success should be as important as other career and personal finance strategies. I hope the arguments made in this book come out in a way that opens rather than closes discussion and thought..

Your forefathers had a village in which to find a profitable niche and compete. You have the entire globe to do the same. This technology-induced phenomenon can be your best blessing. The Nuthology Index is here to help you move past the analysis paralysis of career choice and narrow down your options faster. I hope you will use data and analytics to gain a competitive edge, as well as adapt to any environment without conforming to bias or promoting it. You can teach yourself how to study patterns of data, not just for what they reveal but most importantly for how they affect your financial independence.

Like I said many times in this book, Nuthology strategy is based on your unique capsule of talents. This puts you in the driver's seat. The goal is to reach a point where you don't let any stigmas create self-doubt or shame. By taking personal responsibility you design a goal that lets you live as authentically as possible without burdening the society.

You don't stop there when it comes to capitalism. You discover something else. That you can choose careers and business ventures that you feel ethically aligned with. You don't have to choose between meaning and money, you can have both. Here is the best part: you can compete with compassion, have fun, and respect human dignity all at the same time. Show me anything more spiritually satisfying.

Nobody is suggesting that you can walk on water. Everyone has strengths and weaknesses, no matter who they are. Everyone has advantages and limitations, no matter who they are. We're all unique. Situational awareness does not mean self-absorption and entitlement. Be aware correlation and causation pitfalls as you plan your future. Don't get caught up in the blame game. Even without bias, life constantly dishes disappointments and challenges.

You must demand the best from yourself given whatever circumstances you find yourself in today. Slower than you want, but faster than you think, you will succeed in your goals. I hope you make tons of money in a capitalist atmosphere that values competition, empathy, compassion, and kindness. Namaste.

www.ingramcontent.com/pod-product-compliance
Lightning Source LLC
LaVergne TN
LVHW052221200926
848481LV00001B/173